THE POETICS
OF IMPERIALISM

THE POETICS
—— OF ——
IMPERIALISM

Translation and
Colonization from
The Tempest to *Tarzan*

EXPANDED EDITION

ERIC CHEYFITZ

UNIVERSITY OF PENNSYLVANIA PRESS

Philadelphia

First published 1991 by Oxford University Press
Copyright © 1991 Oxford University Press, Inc.

Expanded Edition copyright © 1997 University of Pennsylvania Press
All rights reserved
Printed in the United States of America on acid-free paper

10 9 8 7 6 5 4 3 2 1

Published by
University of Pennsylvania Press
Philadelphia, Pennsylvania 19104-6097

Library of Congress Cataloging-in-Publication Data

Cheyfitz, Eric.
  The poetics of imperialism : translation and colonization from
The tempest to Tarzan / Eric Cheyfitz. — Expanded ed., 1st pbk. ed.
    p. cm.
  Includes bibliographical references and index.
  ISBN 0-8122-1609-1 (pbk. : alk. paper)
    1. American literature—History and criticism—Theory, etc.
2. English literature—History and criticism—Theory, etc.
3. American literature—European influences.   4. Translating
and interpreting—History.   5. Imperialism in literature.
6. Minorities in literature.   7. Colonies in literature.   I. Title.
PS169.I45C4   1997
325′.32′091821—dc21   96-45596
                                                          CIP

In memory of Edward and Joseph Cheyfitz,
Faye Stevenson, and Isadore Pollock,
the strong sources of my social vision

Acknowledgments

THE RESEARCH for this book was supported by a yearlong NEH fellowship at the Newberry Library in 1984–1985. I am grateful for the support, for the generous help and hospitality of the administrators and staff at the Library, and for the opportunity to share my work with other scholars working in my own and related fields. My project benefited in invaluable ways from the interdisciplinary community at the Newberry. Georgetown University supported this project as well with summer research grants.

Over the years this project has gained productive exposure in various forums in addition to the Newberry. Early in its conception, when it was going to be a book on the figure of translation in Cooper's Leatherstocking Tales, David Marshall and Margaret Ferguson invited me to present part of it at a colloquium at Yale University. My essay on translation in *The Pioneers* was subsequently published in an anthology of criticism on Cooper, edited by Robert Clark. Although my work on Cooper receives only brief mention in this book, the theory of translation that informs the book was first articulated in the Cooper material and in the forums that welcomed it. I first presented what would become the chapter on *Tarzan* at a panel organized by Amy Kaplan for the American Studies Association's annual convention; and the chapter first appeared in *American Literary History*, whose editor, Gordon Hutner, has been generously supportive of my work. Parts of this book also received valuable criticism from colloquia at the University of Chicago, where I was a visiting professor of English in the fall of 1989, and at Southern Methodist University. My students at Chicago and Georgetown have engaged this material in ways that allowed me to read it anew as the project was proceeding. I am thankful for the energy of this engagement, which constantly helped to renew my own.

Peter Hulme saw an early prospectus for this project and generously sent me some of his own work on the discourse of colonialism, which was subsequently published in his book *Colonial Encounters*. I engage this book in my own, and I can only make explicit what is implicit in this engagement: that I have learned a lot from it. My footnotes articulate other intellectual debts, though these notes by no means contain all these debts. For example, Richard Drinnon's *Facing West,* which I make no mention of, has strongly influenced my vision of the historical context of U.S. foreign policy toward the Third World.

Along the way, colleagues in various parts of the country have been supportive in ways for which I am grateful. Neil Saccamano sent me Roland Barthes' essay on metaphor, which was instrumental in provoking my thoughts on the subject. David Miller supplied me with useful bibliographies on the American Indians. Mary Beth Rose helped situate me in the Renaissance and talked with me about my project throughout my year at the Newberry. Robert Ferguson has given me the constant benefit of both his intellectual insight and his encouragement. Over the past six years, Dan Moshenberg and I have carried on a conversation about matters of literacy and power that informs this book. And I have learned much as well from Michael Ragussis, who has always taken the time to respond to my work. Eric Sundquist, Sacvan Bercovitch, William Brown, Chris Looby, Laura Tracy, John Carlos Rowe, Richard Brodhead, Donald Kartiganer, Catherine Ingraham, Walter Benn Michaels, and John Irwin have all helped out when help was needed. Bill Sisler at Oxford University Press has facilitated the realization of this project as a book in ways that have made working with him over the years the best of experiences.

Finally and first, there are those who are closest to me and have helped sustain this project at the place where love and criticism come together: my mother and my brother, my daughters (Rachel, Cara, and Ilana), my friend Jennifer Evans, and Darlene Evans, whose critical response to sections of this book proved crucial, and who has taught me much about persistence and devotion.

Contents

Preface to the Expanded Edition

IN ITS BROADEST TERMS *The Poetics of Imperialism: Translation and Colonization from* The Tempest *to* Tarzan is about the central function of translation in foreign policy. More specifically, it is about the central function of translation in the history of Anglo-American imperial foreign policy, which the book traces from its classical origins in Aristotle's theory of metaphor to the classical and Renaissance rhetorics that in significant part sprang from this theory. *The Poetics of Imperialism* reads the settlement at Jamestown in 1607, where Anglo-American imperialism founded its first permanent colony and Shakespeare's *The Tempest* found its inspiration, through the prism of these rhetorics. And it reads in them, as well, the imperial figure of Tarzan of the Apes, a displaced English nobleman, the apotheosis of Prospero and John Smith, created by an American, a rejected applicant to the Rough Riders, Edgar Rice Burroughs. From the traditional perspective of certain disciplines, history and political science, for example, this conception of foreign policy may seem entirely, even frivolously, figurative. I hope, however, that for readers who assume this perspective, *The Poetics of Imperialism* will demonstrate how this figure of foreign policy is grounded in the literal or in what Renaissance rhetorics typically term the *proper*.

Every foreign policy, of course, implies a domestic policy, just as the very term *translation* is defined by the relationship between a notion of the *foreign* and a notion of the *domestic*. The relationship between the domestic and the foreign is at once literal and figurative, that is to say, material and ideological. To remark, in addition, that the material and the ideological are always already figures of one another is to remark that they are always already translations of one another. This, in turn, is to note not only the intertwined etymological history of *metaphor* and *translation,* but also that this history is a political history. As its title insists, *The Poetics of Imperialism* reads this political history of figuration as the history of Anglo-American imperialism. This history begins with, and is still driven by, a theory of metaphor grounded in the desire of what names itself the *domestic* to dominate what it simultaneously distinguishes as the *foreign*—in the desire of what imagines itself as the *literal* or, crucially, the *proper,* to bring what it formulates as the *figurative* under control. In this history, the proper, resistant to notions of cultural relativity, rarely (Montaigne is the significant exception here) imagines itself as anything but absolute: the proper rarely imagines its own figurative status.

Within the sphere of the Americas, this theory of metaphor is first put into practice in 1492 with the European desire to dominate Native America, which was, for Europe, the very figure of the figurative, the very heart of speech itself, with all its danger and possibility in need of cultivation. Europeans imagined that this domination would take place through the persuasive powers of eloquence, which would translate Native Americans fluidly in European terms. But persuasion necessarily failed from the beginning. For the kind of translation Europeans imagined was never a possibility, except through force and fraud. From the beginning to the present, fictions of translation have rationalized this force and fraud through the figures of eloquent orators like Prospero and Tarzan and Ronald Reagan, the "great communicator," whose central task in these fictions is always to "civilize" the "savages," to cultivate or make them proper, in whatever form they take.

From the beginning, as well, Native American communities have resisted this force and fraud not only with counterforce but, crucially, by refusing, in their own oral and textual traditions, the figurative position that Europeans have assigned them in these fictions of translation, which include a range of interrelated texts from what Europeans term "imaginative literature" to the law in its various forms: edict, statute, and treaty. The central work that *The Poetics of Imperialism* undertakes is the political work of analyzing these fictions of translation, with the polemical intent of exposing the rhetorical technologies that rationalize an ongoing Anglo-American imperialism in the Americas.

In the United States this imperialism since 1823 has taken the form of an internal colonialism, in which, through the institutional structure of the Bureau of Indian Affairs, first established in 1824, the federal government has assumed ultimate "title" to Indian lands. In 1823 the Supreme Court's decision in the case of *Johnson and Graham's Lessee v. M'Intosh,* through the authorship of Chief Justice John Marshall, effectively translated all Indian lands into *property,* so that the title of this property, in the first and last instance, could be "legally" transferred to the United States Government.[1] It is this act of translating communal lands, which could not be alienated under Native traditions, into property that constitutes the heart of darkness of the fictions of translation that *The Poetics of Imperialism* analyzes.

Within the Marshall Court's fiction of translation, sovereign Indian communities, defined by the Court for the first time as "domestic dependent nations," found themselves translated in that oxymoronic phrase (for how can a nation be the domestic dependent of another nation and still be a nation itself?) into a political space *between* the domestic and the foreign, where they were neither one nor the other. The *imposition* of citizenship on all Native Americans in 1924 did not resolve this contradiction, but only heightened it.[2] For the Native American political agenda continued (and continues) to be, even with the conflicts within Indian communities generated by this colonial structure, one of sovereignty, not one of integration with the dominant U.S. social structure. This structure was and remains driven by the acquisitive individualism of capitalism, an ideology utterly foreign to the traditional values of Native American communalism. And here we must understand *tradition* as dynamic forms of historically motivated resistance, all focused on issues of *land/property* in the Americas, such as the Pueblo Revolt of 1680 against the Spanish *encomiendas;* or the ongoing struggle of the Mayan communities in Guatemala, which has reached a tentative peace that will ultimately depend for its continuation on the return of Indian communal lands usurped by a Eurohispanic elite with the aid of the United States government; or the continuing battle of the Lakota people for the return of their sacred Black Hills, which were attached by the U.S. government in 1877 in violation of the 1868 Treaty of Fort Laramie but, ironically, in perfect keeping with the legal force of *Johnson and Graham's Lessee v. M'Intosh.* Within the context of Lakota resistance to the force and fraud of this confiscation, it should be emphasized that in the twentieth century this resistance has taken the form of refusing cash payment for the Black Hills—of refusing, that is, the commodification of the land.[3]

For Native American identity is inseparable from historic communal relations with the land. To alienate the land, then, in cash or other forms of property, is to alienate that identity.

Johnson and Graham's Lessee v. M'Intosh, which in its prescriptions for U.S. relations with Indian communities blurs the frontier between foreign and domestic policy, grounds itself, going back to the European invasion of the Americas beginning in 1492, in the so-called "doctrine of discovery." This doctrine, even before the fact of actual possession, translated Native lands into European property through the patents granted by the rulers of European nation-states to the leaders of the invasions. Thus, from the beginning, *in theory,* the foreign country of America was simultaneously a continuation of the domestic space of Europe. *The Poetics of Imperialism* explores, then, in the ways I have suggested, how foreign and domestic policy are translations of one another. Within its history, Anglo-American imperialism has alienated the world outside the West in the form of the other, so that it could dream the other's redemption in the form of the self. In this dynamic of domination all the nuances of translation are lost, so the imperialist finds himself lost in the figurative, which he necessarily mistakes for the literal. This is destructive in massive ways. But *between* the domestic and the foreign, in translations of its own making, the literal resists this destruction.

The Poetics of Imperialism is, perhaps, more focused on processes of figuration than on literal resistance, but resistance is certainly strongly implied in its polemical tone and explored in the crucial figures of Douglass, Fanon, Montaigne's Tupi Indians, Basso's Cibecue Apaches, and Silko, among others. For the expanded edition of *The Poetics of Imperialism* I have written a new chapter on the Roanoke voyages of 1584–1590, which comes at the end of the book as an Afterword. In this new material I explore both how, in the European narratives of "discovery" and early settlement, we might read the signs of Native American resistance to an incipient European hegemony, and how the twentieth-century historiography of this Euramerican–Native American contact repeats, in the Freudian sense of the term, the fictions of translation that these narratives fabricated and that the Indians resisted. In the Afterword, then, I search for signs of literal resistance within complex processes of figuration.

Since publishing the cloth edition of *The Poetics of Imperialism* in 1991, I have moved from Southern Methodist University to the University of Pennsylvania, where I have found a most supportive and challenging intellectual community of students and faculty, within my own department, English, and extending to other departments as well. The new material in this book is enriched by the formal and informal conversations I have had since coming to Penn in 1993. In particular I appreciate the community extended to me by the Center for the Study of Black Literature and Culture and its director, Houston Baker, Jr., with whom I have developed an increasingly energizing dialogue in friendship. Fred Hoxie and Kendall Johnson took their valuable time to collect and mail me material that was indispensable in the research of the Afterword. My editor at the University of Pennsylvania Press, Jerome Singerman, in addition to his much appreciated enthusiasm for the project of reprinting *The Poetics of Imperialism,* offered crucial suggestions on cover art as well as the new written material, affording me the space to expand the original in its new form. Mindy Brown, the project editor, helped me bring the new sections to their final, formal shape. The Afterword was written in the course of a year's leave, afforded me by a National Endowment for the Humanities Fellowship to pursue research and writing, for which I am most grateful. Finally, I would like to thank my wife, Darlene Evans, for all I have learned from her about Native America, for her acute critical eye in matters of style and content, and for her love, which is sustaining.

Notes

1. For a discussion of the *Johnson* decision, see Eric Cheyfitz, "Savage Law: The Plot Against American Indians in *Johnson and Graham's Lessee v. M'Intosh* and *The Pioneers,*" in *The Cultures of United States Imperialism,* ed. Amy Kaplan and Donald E. Pease (Durham, N.C.: Duke University Press, 1993), 109–28. In his book *Struggle for the Land: Indigenous Resistance to Genocide, Ecocide and Expropriation in Contemporary North America* (Monroe, Maine: Common Courage Press, 1993), Ward Churchill has a cogent discussion of *Johnson* and its enduring effects in the colonization of Native America (see the essay "Perversions of Justice: Examining the Doctrine of U.S. Rights to Occupancy in North America," 33–83). However, Churchill's reading of the "doctrine of discovery" —that "the legal posture of early European colonization . . . recognize[d] that indigenous peoples constituted bona fide nations holding essentially the same rights to land and sovereignty as any other" (37)—is contradicted by both Marshall's interpretation of the doctrine and, for example, the patents of 1584 granted

to Walter Raleigh by Queen Elizabeth, which effectively gave him title to all the land in America his venture might "discover," that is, all the land not already held by a Christian nation. From the beginning, Native rights to sovereignty/land were always already compromised in European law. I discuss this issue at the end of the Preface and throughout this book.

2. I follow Churchill's language here (51), recognizing that others will not see the granting of citizenship as an imposition.

3. See Churchill, "The Black Hills Are Not for Sale: The Lakota Struggle for the 1868 Treaty Territory," in *Struggle for the Land,* 113–41.

Introduction

Academic evidence is a euphemism for linguistic colonization of oral traditions and popular memories.

GERALD VIZENOR

I never heard of the mind/body split until I entered a Christian church.

A MENOMINEE INDIAN MAN AT A
NEWBERRY LIBRARY SEMINAR
(I quote this from my own oral tradition)

I embrace the world. I am the world. The white man has never understood this magic substitution. The white man wants the world; he wants it for himself alone. . . . He enslaves it. An acquisitive relation is established between the world and him. But there exist other values that fit only my forms.

* * *

Uprooted, pursued, baffled, doomed to watch the dissolution of the truths that he has worked out for himself one after another, he has to give up projecting onto the world an antimony that coexists with him.

FRANTZ FANON

But the fifth world had become entangled with European names . . . all of creation suddenly had two names: an Indian name and a white name. Christianity separated the people from themselves; it tried to crush the single clan name, encouraging each person to stand alone, because Jesus Christ would save only the individual soul; Jesus Christ was not like the Mother who loved and cared for them as her children, as her family. . . . But now the feelings were twisted, tangled roots, and all the names for the source of this growth were buried under English words, out of reach.

* * *

Everywhere he looked, he saw a world made of stories.

*   *   *

[W]e invented white people; it was Indian witchery that made white people in the first place.

LESLIE MARMON SILKO

WHEN I WAS TWENTY, I went out for a while with a black woman, who lived with her mother and sisters in a housing project in Washington, D.C. One night, after I had been seeing her for a while, her mother asked me if I was Jewish. I said, simply, that I was. Her mother replied: I knew you weren't white.

In Fanon's *Black Skin, White Masks,* a book that I have been returning to continually for the past twenty-five years, the paradigm for black alienation under colonialism is the historic situation of the Jews.[1] In the mythology of European New-World "discovery" of the sixteenth and seventeenth century, the Indians were conceptualized, among other fantasies that Europeans fashioned of them, as the lost tribes of Israel. And in Shakespeare's *The Tempest,* which is important to the colonial history I write in what follows, Caliban—inescapably, as I will argue, Shakespeare's version of Native Americans—wears "garberdine"[2] a garment associated in the Renaissance Christian mind with Jews. Analyzing the appearance of ethnic stereotypes in American war movies of the 1950s, Vine Deloria noticed that "[t]he Jewish intellectual and the Indian formed some kind of attachment and were curiously the last ones killed." In his diagram of American society in the 1960s, Deloria provides another suggestive juxtaposition: "American society has always been divided into the mainstream white and black Americans who shared integrationist philosophies and the Indians, Mexicans, Jews, and ethnic concentrations who stubbornly held traditions and customs brought over from the old country. These are the OTHERS so casually mentioned when social problems are discussed." And for Deloria, who is particularly interested in the associations he reads between Jews and Indians, these others are communal peoples: "Moses took a loose confederation of tribal people, stuck in industrialized urban Egypt, and brought them out of Egypt after totally destroying the country. He then formed a much broader conception of religion based upon their experiences in that urban society, and reconstituted the tribal structure with

In focusing this study on patriarchal forms of imperial violence, I have necessarily had to stand in another place to critique these forms. Because my central historical concern is with Anglo-American and Native American conflict, though my range in this book takes in slavery in the United States as well as colonization in the Caribbean, the other place that I have chosen to stand, the place from which I launch my critique of the patriarchy, is the kinship economy that informed Native North American cultures at the time of contact and continues to inform them, a communal economy that Leslie Marmon Silko, among others, identifies with female forces. Given the difficult politics of identification that I want to negotiate in this work, my stand in this economy must be ironic. I hope, though, that this necessary irony has something in common with the liberating irony that I read (in Chapter 7) as the driving force of Montaigne's essay "Of the Caniballes." As I understand it, the central concern of Montaigne's essay *is* the difficult politics of identification; and so my reading of his essay, among other things, is an articulation of my own place in writing this book.

This place is the place of translation. Like Montaigne, I know no Indian languages. This should present no methodological difficulties. For, like Montaigne, I am not writing to understand Native American cultures but to critique the violence of my own culture, specifically the violence of my own language. Yet, as mentioned, to activate such a critique, I, like Montaigne, must place myself in the cultures, in the languages, against which this violence has been and continues to be practiced. This problem of placement presents methodological difficulties. Like Montaigne, I can only deal with these difficulties through translators, all of whom, though, it must be emphasized, must deal with the problem of translation to varying degrees. The early voyagers, for example, on whom I, like Montaigne, must depend, knew virtually nothing of the native languages of the Americas, even as they freely translated them. I have made it a central part of my inquiry to ask what "translation" means under such circumstances. To take another example, I am dependent for my placement in Native American cultures on Keith Basso's *Portraits of "The Whiteman": Linguistic Play and Cultural Symbols Among the Western Apache.*[4] While Basso is conversant with the language of the Cibecue Apaches whom he studies, his study is so acutely aware of the politics of intercultural communication that we realize that even the *expert* translator requires a translator in order to speak, that immediacy is a fiction of power, not an actual possibility.

Basso's place in relation to Cibecue culture is clearly not that of the voyagers to Native American cultures, not only because of his linguistic expertise, but for political and historical reasons as well. Yet Basso's place, like the voyagers, is just as clearly not the place of the Indian culture he translates.

A final example. I also depend in my study on the writing of contemporary Native Americans, some of whom, articulating the specific dynamics of Native American cultures in relation to Anglo-American culture, do not speak their native languages. These people, like Scott Momaday and Leslie Marmon Silko, have access to their cultures primarily through English.[5] Yet because of their kinship in these cultures, the undoubted power of their writing takes on an immediacy that Basso's, for example, does not have. Still, we recognize that problems of translation exist here as well, perhaps most acutely here, where the place of the person in the culture is also the place of the person between cultures. Here problems of intercultural and intracultural communication intersect.

We must be in translation between cultures and between groups within our own culture if we are to understand the dynamics of our imperialism. For our imperialism historically has functioned (and continues to function) by substituting for the difficult politics of translation another politics of translation that represses these difficulties. It is the purpose of *The Poetics of Imperialism* to articulate the interplay between these two opposing politics of translation.

This book had two previous working titles, the first of which I have retained in a modified form as a subtitle. At the beginning of this project, I titled it *The Frontier of Translation: Language and Colonization from "The Tempest" to "Tarzan,"* which was intended to indicate the centrality of translation in defining the American frontier specifically (and any frontier for that matter). I have retained "translation" in the present subtitle to emphasize this centrality. Writing in the late 1970s about contact between settlers and Indians in the colonial South, Richard Beale Davis commented:

> Communication between red man and white came primarily through the interpreter as intermediary; the oratory of representatives of both races in parleys, dialogues, and conferences; and the treaties, which employed both interpreter and orator and were art forms as well as historical documents. . . . The present writer has found no book or essay which is concerned with the special role . . . of the work of this familiar figure.[6]

I also have found no book or essay that deals with the central role of the translator in these negotiations. Nor have I found a book or essay that deals with the theoretical/historical problem of translation as it structures the Anglo-American/Native American frontier. *The Poetics of Imperialism* is the second kind of book. I hope it provides a conceptual framework for the first kind of study, if anyone should undertake it. It needs to be done.

Work has been done, of course, on problems of language and colonization, in which translation is an implicit problem. I find Basso's *Portraits of "The Whiteman"* and passages in Silko's *Ceremony* and Frederick Douglass's 1845 *Narrative* indispensable in this regard, as I do the first chapter of Frantz Fanon's *Black Skin, White Masks*, "The Negro and Language." I address these works within the figure of the frontier of translation in Chapter 6. (A significant part of Chapter 2 is also devoted to Douglass.) In Chapter 6 I address Stephen Greenblatt's and Tzvetan Todorov's work on language and colonization as well.[7] In a brief essay on Shakespeare's *The Tempest,* Greenblatt broaches some crucial figures of the linguistic colonization of the Americas that I delve into in this book. Among them is the figure of figures, metaphor, which I see functioning in a radically different way in Anglo-American colonial thinking than does Greenblatt. It is the historic relationship between translation and metaphor, the relationship articulated by the classical figure of *translatio,* that is the driving force of *The Poetics of Imperialism,* a relationship that has not been considered in the work on language and colonization.

In considering the function of metaphor in a poetics of imperialism, I am particularly interested in the way European invaders mapped the "New World" according to the opposition between the *metaphoric* and the *proper,* or *literal.* In the classical tradition of rhetoric from which this opposition is taken, the opposed terms are typically those of the *metaphoric* and the *proper,* the *literal* being a particular species of the *proper,* referring to a particular kind of textual interpretation. In the sixteenth-century English rhetorics that interest me here, then, as in the classical rhetorics of which they are virtually translations, the opposition is between the *metaphoric* and *proper.* It is only after the sixteenth century that the term *proper* as the antonym for metaphoric begins to become obsolete in English, until it is finally displaced by the term *literal,* which in the process tends to lose its specialized, or proper, meaning: pertaining to the letter. In the course of this book, I have occasion to use both forms of this opposition (metaphoric/literal; metaphoric/proper), because both linguistic forms entail political forms that are crucial to an understanding of Anglo-American imperialism in the Americas. The notion of the *proper,* I argue, must be understood in relation to European notions of property and identity. As for the *literal,* it no doubt entails an ideology that privileges writing over the oral tradition of kinship cultures, while its figurative use for the notion of the *proper* has historically taken on a meta-physical force that naturalizes writing, concealing it as a technology—that is, as a form of politics.

While Todorov seems to recognize that writing is a cultural force, he nevertheless naturalizes it by placing it in an evolutionary scheme where it is an advance over the oral tradition. For him—and this is typical of much of the writing on European/Native American contact, even some of the most sensitive writing—there is nothing objectionable in the way the following statement figures the question of technology in general: "Societies that employ writing are more advanced than societies without writing" (252). By not querying what the word "advanced" means, Todorov universalizes and thus naturalizes a culturally specific form of technology. And while Todorov, who is wary of his evolutionary model even as he can't resist using it, tells us that the notion of *advance* "does not involve a superiority on the level of moral and social values" (252), I would suggest that the model he uses to represent Native American life in *The Conquest of America* does imply such a superiority in European culture. This model is Aztec culture. And an extremely partial model it is. It lasted barely a moment in the historical scheme of things, and it is not at all representative of the vast majority of cultures in the Americas that were contemporaneous with it and whose representatives survive today. These are the egalitarian, or, perhaps more precisely, consensual, cultures based on the communal economy of kinship, of which Todorov seems oblivious. But his historical amnesia has an ideological point. For this Eastern European emigré in France wants to valorize Western European political/linguistic forms. Within the context of this desire, *The Conquest of America* is an allegory for capitalist democracy's superiority to Communism, with the European conquerors and the Aztecs functioning respectively as protofigures of the former and latter. Within this allegory, individualism and egalitarianism become rigidly linked, as do communalism, or "sociality," and hierarchy, which inevitably evolve into totalitarianism (252). For these identities to operate, Todorov must undertake the massive work of repressing the presence of kinship economies in the Americas. These economies, as Eric Wolf has argued cogently in a work that I read in part in Chapter 3 of this book,[8] are egalitarian and communal, as opposed to capitalism's hierarchical forms, based on a class system, in which it could be argued that authentic individualism, which would end the worker's alienation from the productive forces of their labor, is suppressed along the lines of race and gender, as well as class.

While my immediate differences with Todorov have to do with his understanding of the initial contact between Columbus and the Arawaks (a kinship culture) and the model of intercultural communication that he derives from this encounter (a model to which Greenblatt also subscribes and which I analyze in Chapter 6), I have taken the time to note our radically different theoretical/historical views of the New World, because they produce radically different models of intercultural communication informed by divergent political agendas. It may be that I am no less of an allegorist than Todorov. It may be that anthropology can only be an allegory of Western culture.[9] Yet the models of intercultural communication that anthropology produces (and as allegory these intercultural models are intracultural) influence the actual contact between cultures, which is only to acknowledge that the models are political productions that produce politics. The politics of these models is, therefore, crucial and cannot be separated from the necessity of recognizing them as models, as figures of the other, not fact. Only the other has the right to decide if these figures touch his or her facts. If we are practicing the difficult politics of translation, rather than the politics of translation that represses this difficult politics, then such touch, however tentative, should occur. Todorov believes that the "representatives of Western civilization" (249) are now practicing the difficult politics of translation. As Chapter 1 makes clear, I believe that these representatives continue to practice the politics of translation that repress translation as dialogue in order to constitute it, under the guise of dialogue, as monologue.

My discussion of *Tarzan of the Apes* (1912)[10] places it at the end of a historical trajectory that commences with *The Tempest* (1611). In the initial conception of this work, I planned to work chronologically from *The Tempest* to *Tarzan*, exploring how the American frontier of translation articulated itself in a number of historical periods and literary texts. In the original title of this book, I juxtaposed *The Tempest* with *Tarzan* both to indicate the chronological scheme and to suggest the blurring of boundaries that ideology compels between "high" and "popular" culture. The retention of this juxtaposition in the subtitle now only *suggests* a chronological scheme. For in *The Poetics of Imperialism*, I have substituted a dramatic structure for the original chronological scheme. After my reading of *Tarzan* in Chapter 1, I interpret a range of texts in various genres that span the late fifteenth to the twentieth centuries, while weaving in and out of a reading of *The Tempest*.

When I substituted the present structure for the chronological scheme, I changed my working title to *Crowning Powhatan: Translation and Empire in the Founding of Anglo-America*, indicating the concentrated historical focus that I had decided would be more efficient in many ways, from the intellectual to the economic, in dealing with the problems of translation. In addition it gave me a commanding figure, the English crowning of Powhatan at Werowocomoco in 1608, for the monologic politics of translation, and it foregrounded the crucial relation between translation and empire that my first title had not articulated. In brief, the present book articulates the historical relationship in the New World between translation, *translatio,* and the *translatio imperii et studii,* between, that is, a theory of communication, a theory of figurative language, and a theory of the transmission of power. These three forms of translation, I argue, find their most powerful and persistent expression, in both theoretical and historical terms, in a central or primal scene from classical rhetoric: the scene in which an orator through the power of eloquence "civilizes" "savage" humanity. And this scene, I also argue, is the driving force of Anglo-American imperialism in the New World from *The Tempest* to *Tarzan*.

Given the dramatic structure of this book and my intent to articulate the structure of a dramatic scene at the heart of our imperialism, it seemed to me as I brought this project to a close that, following the model of Aristotle's *Poetics,* however informally, I was writing a poetics of imperialism rather than composing a historical narrative. Hence, the present primary title. But if I seem to oppose history and theory in this conclusion, let me note that my present primary title, *The Poetics of Imperialism,* juxtaposes them, in its conjunction of poetics and imperialism. I have tried in what follows, then, to put history and theory into play; for in actuality they are in play. This is what constitutes politics. And there is no way out of that.

THE POETICS
OF IMPERIALISM

To rob a man of his language in the very name of language: this is the first step in all legal murders.

ROLAND BARTHES

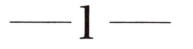

1

Tarzan of the Apes: U.S. Foreign Policy in the Twentieth Century

> I have come across the ages out of the dim and distant past from the lair of the primeval man to claim you—for your sake I have become a civilized man—for your sake I have crossed oceans and continents—for your sake I will be whatever you will me to be.
>
> EDGAR RICE BURROUGHS

WE COULD UNDERSTAND these words, which I have taken out of context for the moment, from Edgar Rice Burroughs's exceptionally popular 1912 romance *Tarzan of the Apes,* as articulating the deepest desires of U.S. foreign policy toward the Third World in the twentieth century (243). From Teddy Roosevelt, its first clear voice, to Ronald Reagan and George Bush, its most recent (and we can consider Bush as no more than an echo of Reagan), this policy craves, in its deepest, most rapturous dreams, this response: the "barbarian" or "savage," or the "communist" or "terrorist," coming to claim the United States, not in the barbarian's terms, of course, nor in our own language struggling to translate itself, realizing the difficulty of translation, into the realities of those terms, but purely in America's terms, the savage in loving submission to our will, willingly speaking proper English, the language of "civilization," or, to translate this curious word "civilization," of capitalist democracy. When Reagan sends a cake and Bible as a sign to putative moderates in Iran, it seems to be this hallucinatory response that he seeks.

Written by a Chicagoan (son of the white, Protestant, upper middle class; sometime cowboy and gold miner; Indian fighter *manqué;* failed businessman, until he turned writer; superpatriot; and rejected applicant to the Rough Riders), *Tarzan of the Apes* appeared at a time when the second great wave of immigration to the United States, begun in the 1820s, was at its crest. And, as John Higham remarks, "[w]hereas the First Immigration had been entirely white and predominantly English-speaking [and Protestant], the second brought a Babel of tongues and an array of complexions" that threatened the Protestant vision of a homogenous America and provoked a resurgence of the Anglo-Saxon myth of race that "summoned Anglo-Saxon America to protect herself at home [from these foreigners] and to demonstrate her mastery [of them] abroad."[1] In such a climate, when those perceived as foreigners— appearing in a range of figures from the colonial subject to the immigrant worker to the black citizen—threaten to become America itself, it is not surprising, however ironic, that a new American superhero, heir to the frontier individualism of Natty Bumppo, should be an English nobleman, epitome of the Anglo-Saxon race, John Clayton the second, Lord Greystoke, alias Tarzan of the Apes. Nor is it surprising that in an age when the United States was beginning to seek new frontiers in expansionist adventures abroad that the scene of action for this Anglo-Saxon hero would be an American wilderness displaced to a fantasized European colonial Africa. In this way Americans could savor, in the act of denying, their own imperial ventures.

> "The object lesson" of expansion is, [Teddy Roosevelt] declared, "that peace must be brought about in the world's waste spaces. . . . Peace cannot be had until the civilized nations have expanded in some shape over the barbarous nations." . . . "It is our duty toward the people living in barbarism to see that they are freed from their chains," he told Minnesotans a fortnight before he became President [in 1901], "and we can free them only by destroying barbarism itself. . . . Exactly as it is the duty of a civilized power scrupulously to repect the rights of weaker civilized powers . . . so it is its duty to put down savagery and barbarism."[2]

We can translate "civilized" in Roosevelt's parlance as Anglo-Saxon, or white, and "savagery and barbarism" as the state of every people beyond that pale. For Roosevelt subscribed to that version of the myth of Anglo-Saxon superiority that saw the American people as the apotheosis of this race of races. The imperialist foreign policy that this myth buttressed began, in the twentieth century, with the war with Spain; its formative beginnings, however, were in that expansion across the continent that commenced officially with the establishment of the Jamestown colony in 1607, then steadily and violently displaced the Indians westward, momentarily culminating in the massacre at Wounded Knee in 1890, before extending in fact and vision beyond the geographical limits of the United States. A strain of American thought throughout the nineteenth century, this myth of racial superiority, particularly under the influence first of Darwinism and then, at the turn of the century, of the new science of genetics, "became," as John Higham notes, "permeated with race feelings. Increasingly, Anglo-Saxon culture seemed to depend on the persistence of a physical type. Nationalism was naturalized; and 'race' in every sense came to imply a biological determinism" (46). Howard K. Beale writes that lecturing at Oxford in 1910, Roosevelt "defined 'the so-called white races' as 'the group of peoples living in Europe, who undoubtedly have a certain kinship of blood, who profess the Christian religion, and trace back their culture to Greece and Rome'" (27). "Yet," Beale argues, "he was unlike many racists in that he laid these differences of 'race' to acquired characteristics and to the effect of geographic environment" (29). Roosevelt's invocation of "blood" as a determinant of racial difference must ironize Beale's apologia, particularly given an intellectual climate in which, since the beginning of the nineteenth century and the naturalization—or, more particularly, the *biologization*—of race, such an invocation could only signal the petrifaction of racial hierarchy, the resistance of racial "types" to assimilation or homogenization. Nevertheless, we must recognize a progressive strain in this imperial foreign policy, one that apparently welcomes homogenization, but—and here homogeneity harmonizes itself with hierarchy—only in the terms of the policy maker, who writes a script in which the other, in order to be heard, must say: "for your sake I have become a civilized man . . . for your sake I will be whatever you will me to be."

This script is neither a uniquely twentieth-century one nor uniquely American. Scrutinizing the history of the script, which is the project of this book, allows us to represent the United States not as an unprecedented phenomenon, which is the way American ideology typically represents it, but as the apotheosis of its Western European past, its projection or shadow. From its ideological inception or, if you will, its "discovery," America was Western Europe's dream of immediate or absolute power. Shakespeare's *The Tempest,* with its imperial vision of Prospero acting magically to bring political order to the frontier between the Old and the New World manifests even as it ironizes the dream; for in order to realize itself, Prospero's immediate, or magical, power must be mediated by the figures that are its object: Caliban, Ariel, and Miranda. And the United States that emerges from America is Europe's alibi for this dream, even as Western Europe in this (what do we call it?) postcolonial or neocolonial world appears to have given up this dream, like Prospero promising to renounce his magic, while gesturing toward a home we never see him return to at the end of the drama.

In his *Discourse of Western Planting* (1584), which marks the moment of, by supplying the rationale for, a full-scale English commitment to colonizing North America, the younger Richard Hakluyt gave us an instrumental version of this script of foreign policy when he informed his royal reader, Queen Elizabeth, that, according to the authoritative reports of certain European voyagers, Native Americans "are very easie to be perswaded, and doo all that they sawe the Christians doo in their devine service with like imitation and devotion, and were very desirous to become Christians." All it would take to realize this desire, Hakluyt went on to say, would be for the English to "plant[. . .] one or twoo Colonies of our nation uppon that fyrme . . . and firste learne the language of the people nere adjoyninge (the gifte of tongues beinge nowe taken awaye), and by little and little acquainte themselves with their manner, and so with discrecion and myldenes distill into their purged myndes the swete and lively liquor of the gospell. . . ."[3] Twenty-five years later, in 1609, with the memory of the failure of Roanoke still quite alive and Jamestown on the brink of failure, *Instructions* from the London Council of the Virginia Company (in which Hakluyt was a principal stockholder) ordered Sir Thomas Gates, prospective interim governor of the colony, to institute a plan, using force if necessary, for educating the children of *weroances* (Algonquian leaders) "in [the English] language, and manners"; for "if you intreate well and educate those which are younge and to succeede in the government in your Manners and Religion, their people will easily obey you and become in time Civill and Christian."[4]

Between the *Discourse* of 1584 and the *Instructions* of 1609 experience has intervened. (The Indians, apparently, are not so desirous of becoming Christians; in fact they are resistant; moreover, at this stage the

English find themselves dependent on the Indians' technological expertise for survival, a blow to English fantasies of immediate power.) And this intervention, as we can read, is marked by a shift in the strategy of translation, a strategy that, as I want to suggest, is at the heart of Anglo-America's expansionist foreign policy from its inception to the present. In the *Discourse,* it is the colonists who will learn the "language of the people" (in actuality, the languages of the peoples; already a certain homogenous image of the other is in place), while in the *Instructions,* it is the Indians who must learn English.

We might consider this shift moot, because in both cases the object is to convert the Indians into English men and women, that is, to Protestant Christians (and in this case national and religious identity are identical). But, it seems to me, the shift is crucial. For it shows us that in the years intervening between the *Discourse* and the *Instructions* the English have rewritten the script of this foreign policy so that only those who speak English, and "standard" English at that, will have a voice, or a place, in this script (in Chapter 5 I define the parameters of "standard" English in the sixteenth century). The problem of translation, the complex interactions between cultures and histories, is at once announced and annulled. This rewriting has significant repercussions in the conflict between oral and written cultures under consideration here. And we can read these repercussions in the European travel narratives, where what were necessarily the difficulties, discords, indeed, absences of translation, are displaced into fictive accords of communication, composed, except for a scattering of transliterated native terms, wholly in European tongues. Such an accord, for example, constitutes the reasoning of the important and well-known propaganda pamphlet, *A True Declaration of the Estate of the Colonie in Virginia* (1610), issued by the London Council of the Virginia Company. "There is no other, moderate, and mixt course, to bring [the Virginia Algonquians] to conuersion," the pamphlet announces, "but by dailie conuersation, where they may see the life, and learne the language each of other."[5] It is not simply the phrase "to bring them to conuersion" that annuls the announcement of intercultural communication ("and learne the language each of other"); it is that throughout this discourse, which is an argument for, by way of a narrative of, English colonization in Virginia, the Indians speak unquestionably in English political and economic terms. Thus *A True Declaration* tells us that the English are lawfully in Virginia "chieflie because *Paspehay,* one of their Kings, sold vnto vs for copper, land to inherit and inhabite.

Powhatan, their chiefe King, receiued voluntarilie a crown and a sceptre, with a full acknowledgment of dutie and submission." In dressing up its savages in royal array, this discourse never asks what the problems in translation might be in rendering *king, sceptre,* and *crown* into the Algonquian languages, nor does it register the impossibility of translating the English notion of "selling land" into these languages, which did not contain the concept of land as *property,* that is, as an alienable commodity. And yet, as we know, even at this relatively early moment of contact, the colonists, through the intermediacy of translators from both European and Native American cultures, were at least beginning to be aware of crucial cultural differences in the economic and political realms. One of the first accounts that we have from Virginia, for example, remarks in an idiom that typifies early European perceptions of kinship-based American cultures that "the inhabitantes have . . . no comerce with any nation, no respect of profitt, neither is there scarce that we call meum et tuum among them save only the kinges know their owne territoryes, & the people their severall gardens . . ." (Barbour, 1, 101). While we must read this protoanthropology as at least in part a projection of European "golden age" mythology on what Europeans understood, ideologically, as the tabula rasa of the New World, we must also acknowledge that this anthropology began to translate, however ethnocentrically, *the* crucial difference between what Eric Wolf, following Marx, has termed the kin-ordered mode of production and modes of production he refers to as tributary (of which a mercantilist feudalism would be the prime Western form) and capitalist (73–100).[6] The difference (which I will discuss at some length in Chapter 3) is that the latter two modes are characterized by the alienation of labor from the means of production (in this case, centrally, the land).[7] And this alienation produces a particular version of *meum et tuum* (what *"we* call meum et tuum"), which is significantly different from what *they* (kin-ordered societies) appear to translate *meum et tuum* as in their languages. Invoking the violence of the General Allotment Act of 1887, which sought to shift Indian landholdings from a communal to a private basis, Jimmie Durham, a Cherokee, comments on this significant difference: "The mere concept of parcels of owned land is an insult to Cherokees. . . . Talking about it is impossible; in our own language the possessive pronouns can only be used for things that you can physically give to another person, such as, 'my woodcarving,' 'my basket.'"[8]

In the political realm as well, the early English colonists seem to have been aware of significant cultural differences, even as they translated these differences into their terms. So, in the matter of *"Powhatan, their chiefe King, receiu[ing] voluntarilie a crown,"* a ceremony that took place in the fall of 1608 in Powhatan's village of Werowocomoco, John Smith, who in his own writing routinely translates Algonquian political relationships into English terms, remarks in *A Map of Virginia* (1612) "what a fowle trouble there was to make him kneele to receaue his crowne, he neither knowing the maiestie, nor meaning of a Crowne" (Barbour, 2, 414). There were, as we know, translators from both cultures who could have explained to Powhatan the meaning of a crown, if he didn't already know its meaning all too well after more than a year of dealing with the English in Virginia. But that, I take it, is not the point. That is, we are not to read Smith's statement, with its ambiguous sarcasm (is he mocking what he takes to be English or Indian ignorance?) entirely literally. It is, rather, a sign, however incipient, of the difficulty of translating the Algonquian *weroance,* because of its inseparability from a kin-ordered mode of production, into the English *king* or *emperor* (another frequent designation of Powhatan), because of the inseparability of these terms from tributary or emergent capitalist modes.[9]

Unless we are attentive to the repressed problem of translation, narratives of the type that *A True Declaration* represents will continue to teach us what they have taught us: to froget the other side of the story. Indeed, what we have today, growing out of and perpetuating the dynamics of these narratives, is a foreign policy of forgetfulness. We can read the contemporary form of these dynamics in a foreign-policy message delivered to Congress on March 14, 1986. Employing a certain contemporary liberal rhetoric that apparently recognizes the integrity of postcolonial polities, Ronald Reagan gives a passing nod to "the diversity of regional conflicts and of the conditions in which they arise. Most of the world's turbulence has indigenous causes," he goes on to say, "and not every regional conflict should be viewed as part of the East-West conflict." Yet the rest of his message betrays this apparent commitment to recognizing the integrity of cultural and historical diversity, for it reduces all conflicts to a figure of this "East-West conflict." In the world at large, as it is figured in this rhetoric, everyone is ultimately either a citizen of the Soviet Union (inevitably "an evil empire") or of the United States (the home of true civilization). While Reagan tells Congress that "[t]he drive for national freedom and popular rule takes different forms in different countries, for each nation is the authentic product of a unique history and culture," he is simultaneously (and apparently unconsciously) translating all the "forms" of "national freedom and popular rule" into one form, that of capitalist democracy. And, as we know, in the often fantastic language of U.S. domestic and foreign policy, *democracy* and *capitalism,* whatever their actual contradictions, are synonymous. Thus while Reagan nods to a world of cultural and historical pluralism—the world that is actually out there in all its complexity, beyond his superficial evocation of it—he projects, and implicitly threatens to realize, a world of steadily increasing homogeneity, inhabited by "the growing ranks of those who share our interests and values."[10]

What the English and Europeans could not achieve in actuality they achieved textually in these early narratives: the translation of the Indians into proper English. But as the balance of power shifted from Indians to Europeans—and in America this shift was rapid and massive after the Revolution had shattered the Iroquois's power—these narratives became models of actuality, models for legal decisions in which the Indians were literally forced to speak proper English, to speak, that is, whether they could speak English or not, in the letter of a law that recognized only the terms of *property*. The Indians "were admitted to be the rightful occupants of the soil, with a legal as well as just claim to retain possession of it, and to use it according to their own discretion," Chief Justice John Marshall wrote in 1823, in the course of articulating the Supreme Court's opinion in *Johnson and Graham's Lessee v. M'Intosh*, a case, explicitly grounded in the early narratives I have been reviewing, that upheld a lower court decision invalidating Indians' rights to sell land to individuals; "but," Marshall continued, "their rights to complete sovereignty, as independent nations, were necessarily diminished, and their power to dispose of the soil at their own will, to whomsoever they pleased, was denied by the original fundamental principle that discovery gave exclusive title to those who made it." The letter of the law violently blurs the frontier between foreign and domestic policy, as it articulates *the* crucial western distinction between *possession* and *title*. The Indians comprise foreign nations that, nevertheless, because they are not entirely foreign—that is, sovereign—must speak in domestic terms, terms that ironically allow the Indians "to be the rightful occupants of the soil, with a legal as well as just claim to retain possession of it," so that they can be legally dispossessed of it; "the original fundamental principle" of European "discovery" grants *title* to the occupying Western powers, as if the

Indians' prior arrival in America did not itself constitute a "discovery." Because of their "savagery," the Indians, the Marshall Court claimed in 1823, could neither be assimilated to Western culture nor governed "as a distinct people."[11] They were, as Marshall made explicit in an 1831 decision, "domestic dependent nations."[12] Neither foreign nor domestic (neither themselves nor us) in the legal documents that translated them inescapably into English, the Indians were compelled by these documents to speak this English, but without the crucial legal rights to property that this English conveyed to its European speakers.

This notion of "domestic dependent nations," which, as Vine Deloria, Jr., and Clifford Lytle suggest, still haunts U.S.–Indian relations (2–4), even after the Indian Citizenship Act of 1924, appears also to haunt, to be the implicit vision of, U.S. foreign policy in the twentieth century, as this policy has conjured and continues to conjure the Hispanics, Asians, and Arabs of the Middle East whom it addresses. For no matter how delusory this vision may appear in a postcolonial world, U.S. foreign policy still seems unable to deal with these peoples as integral, different entities, speaking their own languages. Rather, they remain in our official documents and in the media strange hybrids, neither themselves nor us, translated into an English that rinsed of its complexities offers these apparitions only two postures of the same language, the speech of the savage ("I will devour you entire") or the speech of the convert: "I have come across the ages out of the dim and distant past from the lair of the primeval man to claim you—for your sake I have become a civilized man—for your sake I have crossed oceans and continents—for your sake I will be whatever you will me to be."

These are the words of Tarzan's marriage proposal to Jane Porter, the Baltimore woman who with her "delicate . . . snowy skin" (140) holds the most powerful sway over Tarzan, representing for him, like Miranda for that archetypal imperialist Prospero, everything in "civilization" that must be protected from the apes and black Africans, latter-day Calibans, who, in addition to two gangs of mutinous sailors (defined by their speech as conspicuously lower class), are the villains of the novel. Indeed, these "ignorant, half-brute" (12) sailors, representative of the working class in the novel, along with Jane's black maid, Esmeralda, who is also portrayed, though for comic relief, as an ignorant half-brute, are relegated to the realm of the foreign inhabited by the apes and the Africans, when in characterizing "a crude message printed almost illegibly [by the mutineers], and with many evidences of an unaccustomed task,'' Burroughs tells us that it must be ''[t]ranslated'' (10) by Tarzan's upper-class parents, for whom it is intended as a warning not to interfere in the mutiny that sets the action of the novel going. In this imperial romance the lower class is as much a foreign country to the upper class as Africa is to Europe.

The irony of Tarzan's proposal is that to ''become a civilized man'' he already has to be one, the son of Lord and Lady Greystoke, who, sailing to Africa in 1888 to pursue Lord Greystoke's work for the British Colonial Office, are abandoned on an island off the African coast by the mutinous sailors (led by a fleeting character named, appropriately enough, given the way the romance blends its racist and class politics, Black Michael). It is here that the young Lord Greystoke is born. His mother soon dies of the prolonged trauma induced by what we can fairly call, given the miscegenist fantasies of the book, an attempted rape (Lady Greystoke in a swoon shoots the perpetrator) by one of the male apes of the primal horde of Kerchak; he subsequently kills Tarzan's father, leaving the infant nobleman, ignorant of his identity, an orphan to be raised by his parents' killers. Twenty-one years later, in 1909 (the last year of Teddy Roosevelt's administration), Tarzan meets Jane, who, like his parents, has been abandoned on the island by mutineers, along with her father (Professor Archimedes Q. Porter) and a small group of others, including her suitor, Tarzan's cousin, William Cecil Clayton, who, ignorant of the existence of the rightful Lord Greystoke, has assumed the title himself. After a series of adventures, one of which recalls the attempted rape of Tarzan's mother (Tarzan rescues Jane from the clutches of the ape Terkoz, son of Tublat, Tarzan's foster-father, whom Tarzan has killed earlier in the novel in a barely veiled Oedipal scene), Tarzan follows Jane to America, and, after saving her from a forest fire in Wisconsin and thwarting the designs of an unwanted suitor (the American Robert Canler), makes his proposal of marriage.

But Jane must refuse the proposal, even though she wants to accept it. Plagued by doubts about Tarzan's identity (none of the characters know who he actually is, and Tarzan himself lacks one crucial piece of evidence to complete the puzzle) and seeing in his cousin William Clayton ''a man trained in the same school of environment in which she had been trained—a man with social position and culture such as she had been taught to consider as the prime essentials to congenial association'' (242), Jane has just promised to marry the present Lord Greystoke. Now, though her deepest or ''primeval'' feelings prompt her toward Tarzan, her sense of honor toward "a good man" (244), who, like her mysterious suitor, also loves her, prompts her more strongly to keep her promise.

The irony of redundancy in Tarzan's proposal, that a man must be civilized in order to be civilized, is emphasized in Jane's refusal. For what can we say at the end of this romance but that Jane turns down Lord Greystoke to marry Lord Greystoke. In terms of the racial and class politics that structure the romance, in which readers, knowing the identity of Tarzan, can be titillated by the threat of racial, species, or class miscegenation (all of which are figures for one another in the novel) without ever facing the fact of miscegenation, Jane is safe in any case. Emphasizing this safety, a telegram from Tarzan's friend and mentor D'Arnot arrives just *after* the nick of time, with the final piece of proof of Tarzan's identity: "Fingerprints prove you Greystoke. Congratulations" (244). As in Twain's *Pudd' nhead Wilson* (1894), it is fingerprints, which appear under the aegis of the biological, that finally and apparently definitively separate the savage from the civilized, black from white, ape from man, commoner from noble; yet, as the fingerprinter in Burroughs's romance admits, fingerprints can distinguish individuals, "but the science has not progressed sufficiently to render it exact enough in such matters" (222) as species, or racial, identification. We should remember that in *Tarzan,* as in all racist ideologies, the line between race and species, between, that is, the human and the animal or the cultural and the natural is radically blurred. Although Tarzan now has "proof" of his noble identity, he must nobly suppress it for the sake of Jane, whom he has promised to help "bear the burden" of her "choice." He also realizes that if he were to make his noble identity public, it would not only dispossess William Clayton of "his title and his lands and his castles . . . it would take them away from Jane Porter also" (244). So in the final lines of the romance, when Lord Greystoke asks Tarzan, "If it's any of my business, how the devil did you ever get into that bally jungle?", Tarzan, nobly concealing his noble identity, replies, "I was born there. . . . My mother was an Ape, and of course she couldn't tell me much about it. I never knew who my father was" (245).

Caught up in a nostalgia for the noble individualism that Tarzan's act represents here, the reader, presumably, is not intended to worry about the politics of class that this individualism mystifies. And what could locate this romance in America more than the figure of individualism mystifying the figure of class? The reader, that is, is not intended to worry about the dispossession of either colonial subjects or the working class by the wealth-holding class—the kind of dispossession that U.S. domestic and foreign policy initiated at the time, and still does today, although we can no longer speak literally of "colonial subjects." Instead, the reader is implicitly involved in worrying about the dispossession of the rich by the rich, a worry that is not a worry, for it entails the same redundancy that Tarzan's proposal and Jane's refusal do. In the novel, what we witness is Lord Greystoke's noble refusal to dispossess Lord Greystoke, dispossession that in the ideological economy of the text is impossible. For if we see that this is a case of class and not of individuals, wealth, whatever Tarzan decides, remains in the hands of Lord Greystoke.

With my brief plot summary and comments on the ideology of class that drives the novel, I intend to suggest that *Tarzan of the Apes* is a romance of identity; it is identical in structure, significantly (if we are interested in revising the traditional, that is, phallo- and ethnocentric, view of the frontier as a site of individualism or of the triumph of "civilization" over "savagery") to Cooper's *The Pioneers* (1823), in which at the end of the novel we discover that Oliver Edwards, suspected of being a half-breed throughout, is only a figurative Indian (an adopted Delaware) but a literal white man, and a noble one at that. This "fact," the rhetorical fiction that *absolutely* severs the literal and the figurative, allows him to marry the judge's daughter and claim his property, deeded to his family by the Indians, who, as we recall, were judged legally incapable of such deeds by the Marshall Court in the same year in which Cooper published his formative frontier romance.[13] Such American frontier romances as Cooper's and Burroughs's, of which *The Tempest* might be seen as the prototype, act to literalize absolutely racial and class hierarchies (and, typically, race and class are confounded in these romances) when these hierarchies and their political agendas are needed to rationalize the policy of dispossession that I am describing, though these romances rationalize this dispossession with varying degrees of doubt (Cooper's and Shakespeare's are much more full of doubt than Burroughs's).[14] Or, more precisely, such romances argue the naturalization of the literal: For to sever the literal from the figurative absolutely is to naturalize it, in that such severance denies or represses the figurative basis of the literal—its constitution as an ideological or culturally specific formation. It is worth remembering here that among the oldest Western definitions of translation is one—"to use in a metaphorical or transferred sense" (OED)—that insists on an indissoluble and complex relationship between the literal and the figurative. In this naturalization of the literal, which attempts to defend certain ''places'' from the process of translation by attempting to control it, these romances of identity seek to erase the cultural or ideological basis of racial and class identity.

Furthermore, and here the romance of *Tarzan* works like U.S. foreign policy in Central America or the Middle East, the cultural function of *Tarzan* is radically to reduce or homogenize domestic political complexities by displacing them onto a foreign scene, whose own political complexities are thereby radically homogenized in the vision of the romance. To turn our attention obsessively as we have in the United States to that radically decontextualized figure the ''terrorist'' (a modern version of that other European projection, the ''cannibal,'' or Caliban) is a way of forgetting our homeless people, for example, by forgetting that what we call terrorism in the Middle East is itself the result of the political struggle against homelessness. The terrorist is the demonized specter of our own homeless people, just as Caliban, that ''born devil, on whose nature / Nurture can never stick'' (IV.i.188–89), is the demonized specter of Europe's lower classes, who were themselves beset by the violence of homelessness at the time of *The Tempest*. Following this pattern of transfiguring the domestic and the foreign in terms of one another, so that, ironically, the differential connections between them are repressed in a particular ideological representation of the foreign, the romance of racial, or national, identity that has dominated U.S. foreign policy (toward other than European peoples) throughout its history is inevitably a romance of translation, in which, like the Indians in the Marshall Court's decisions, the other is translated into the terms of the self in order to be alienated from those terms. We might say that at the heart of every imperial fiction (the heart of darkness) there is a fiction of translation.

Like his ideological forebear Leatherstocking, who, in the words of his Sioux antagonist Mahtoree in Cooper's *The Prairie*, ''can talk to the Pawnee, and the Konza, and the Omaha, and . . . his own people,''[15] Tarzan is a translator. Raised speaking the language of the apes, Tarzan teaches himself to read and write English by correlating pictures (fantasized implicitly in this fiction as a universal or ur-language) and words in the books that his father transported from England to Africa. Tarzan discovers these books as a boy among the apes, though he does not learn to speak his father's tongue until the very end of the romance, after he has become fluent in French, his first spoken European language, which his mentor, D'Arnot, taught him. Tarzan's search for identity, then, is a linguistic search, in which he is literally translated from ape into man; in learning to read, what Tarzan learns centrally is that "[h]e was a M-A-N, they were A-P-E-S" (50), a distinction that the language of the apes cannot make, "for in the language of the anthropoids there was no word for man" (85). Translated through the power of books from ape into English man or, more precisely, from the oral language of the apes into written English, Tarzan, with the aid of his father's knife (the mastery of a written, or European, language and of an "advanced" technology are identical in this romance), gains an imperial power over what appeared to be his kin, precisely because they cannot follow Tarzan or can only follow him partially in his translation: "So limited was their vocabulary that Tarzan could not even talk with them of the many new truths, and the great fields of thought that his reading had opened up before his longing eyes, or make known ambitions which stirred his soul" (91). Tarzan cannot fully converse with the apes because written English cannot be translated into their impoverished tongue, which Burroughs represents in that self-consciously metaphoric language that "savages" typically speak in European discourse. And unable to converse fully with the apes, Tarzan can only dominate them. The failure of dialogue, figured as a genetic inability in the other, rather than as a problem of cultural difference, is the imperial alibi for domination.

But this failure of dialogue, this systemic inadequacy of the language of the apes for translating the complexities of English, is represented throughout most of the novel not simply as a failure of communication *between* Tarzan and the apes, but also *within* Tarzan of the Apes. For, as noted, until the end of the novel, Tarzan cannot speak English; and then, we are told, he only speaks it in a rudimentary way. Furthermore, until the end of the novel, Tarzan, who enters English strictly through the letter, cannot understand spoken English. In the fantastic learning process that Burroughs imagines for his hero, fantastic in part because, paradoxically, Tarzan first grasps the superior English by translating it into the only language he knows (the inferior language of the apes), the sounds of English and the representation of the sounds are absolutely severed, converting the language, within Tarzan, into a foreign double of itself. This alienation of the oral from the written, an alienation in the West that becomes one rationalization of violent class and cultural hierarchies, is presented in Burroughs's romance of identity as a crux of the plot: the apparition of two Tarzans—one purely textual, the other purely physical—and their resolution into one.

The first Tarzan to appear is the textual Tarzan, the one who writes and reads English: Tarzan leaves a note on his cabin declaring his proprietary rights to it, after he finds it ransacked by the mutinous sailors, who are in the midst of abandoning Jane and her party on the island:

THIS IS THE HOUSE OF TARZAN, THE KILLER OF BEASTS AND MANY BLACK MEN. DO NOT HARM THE THINGS WHICH ARE TARZAN'S. TARZAN WATCHES. TARZAN OF THE APES. (103)

Thus Tarzan identifies himself to the newly arrived white people in ways that they have no trouble identifying with: asserting his property rights, casually equating beasts and blacks, and declaring his brutal dominance over them. In fact, the only problem that Jane and her party have with this note—they never comment on its politics—is with the name of the author:

"Who the devil is Tarzan?" cried the sailor who had before spoken.
"He evidently speaks English," said the young man [William Clayton].
"But what does 'Tarzan of the Apes' mean?" cried the girl [Jane]. (103)

The assumption that the figure who writes English and signs himself "Tarzan of the Apes" also speaks English (a logical enough assumption, given the way we typically learn languages) creates the context for the doubling, or splitting, of this figure into a foreigner to itself. When Tarzan first appears to the English-speaking party, it is to his cousin, William Clayton, whom the ape-man has just saved from an attacking lion:

Clayton spoke to the stranger in English, thanking him for his brave rescue and complimenting him on the wondrous strength and dexterity he had displayed, but the only answer was a steady stare and a faint shrug of the mighty shoulders, which might betoken either disparagement of the service rendered, or ignorance of Clayton's language. (113)

A moment later, however,

there dawned upon [Clayton] the conviction that this was Tarzan of the Apes, whose notice he had seen posted upon the cabin door that morning.
If so he must speak English.
Again Clayton attempted speech with the ape-man; but the replies, now vocal, were in a strange tongue, which resembled the chattering of monkeys mingled with the growling of some wild beast.
No, this could not be Tarzan of the Apes, for it was very evident that he was an utter stranger to English. (113)

Clayton's identification of his white savior as someone other than Tarzan of the Apes is, ironically, correct. For while the author of the imperialist text on property, blacks, and beasts and the killer of the lion are the same person, they are two people culturally, that is, linguistically: Greystoke/Tarzan is both familiar with English and "an utter stranger" to it. He is a figure constituted by problems of translation. Unable to speak to himself in English, unless he translates it into the language of the apes (which, as we have read, is inadequate for such translation), he is also unable to speak to other English speakers across the frontier of the language of the apes, though he is able to communicate with them, but only obliquely, through a writing that never identifies him, except as a figure completely foreign to himself. And it is, precisely, through writing that Tarzan becomes aware of this alienation. Having stolen a letter of Jane's, written to a friend back home—stolen it as a figure of Jane, a "precious treasure" (141) to the ape-man—he reads in the letter of the two strangers that compose himself: one who "speaks no English and vanishes as quickly and as mysteriously after he has performed some valorous deed," and another who "printed a beautiful sign in English and tacked it on the door of his cabin . . . warning us to destroy none of his belongings, and signing himself 'Tarzan of the Apes' " (146). Attempting to identify the two strangers as himself to Jane, the ape-man writes "beneath Jane Porter's signature": "I am Tarzan of the Apes" (147). But this written assertion of identity, isolated, as it is, from any referent but the text that has produced it, can only repeat the alienation of Tarzan from himself that it is intended to resolve. And so it is not until the end of the novel, when Tarzan can speak French and some English, that he resolves the two Tarzans into one for Jane and her party.

This process of identification, in which the problems of translation produced by textuality are finally resolved in the spoken word, is interwoven with the romance of identity in which, as I have noted, the textual, or literal, basis of racial identity is naturalized. What I want to note here is that the apparently evolutionary process by which Tarzan translates himself from ape into man, one that Burroughs reads as Darwinian, is contradicted by the process of translation, the process of textual doubling, that I have been describing. Indeed, the evolutionary, or "natural," process of translation exists as a repression and projection of the textual process of translation in a way that I have associated with the dynamics of reduction, homogenization, and displacement characteristic of U.S. foreign policy. That is, the political purpose, however unconscious, of the evolutionary process of translation is to figure *internal* problems of translation as simply a problem of translation between an inside (the domestic) and an outside (the foreign), in which the problem of communication is, typically, located exclusively in the outside. While the evolutionary process of translation has it that Tarzan cannot communicate with the apes because their language is naturally inferior to his newly evolved English, the textual process has it that the language of the apes is in the first instance inscribed within English, as a domestic ideological construct, alienating English from itself, rather than, of course, a literal foreign language. We might read the language of the apes, then, as a sign of problems of translation within a language, English in this case, which are produced by conflicts of race, gender, and class: Tarzan's translation into English is his translation into the identity of an upper-class, white male. When these intracultural problems of translation are projected onto an intercultural scene, then the problems of translation that would occur in any case are violently obscured.

Transformed from ape into man in this evolutionary romance of identity, Tarzan must nevertheless undergo a final transformation for the romance to be complete: that from man to nobleman, from Tarzan, which means "White-Skin" in the language of the apes, to Greystoke. And this final transformation requires a final translation. For the secret of Tarzan's identity appears in his father's African diary, which the senior Greystoke kept in French (a written language that Tarzan could not teach himself, we infer, because his father's library did not contain French picture books). So, speaking French but not reading it, Tarzan must rely on D'Arnot's translation, which comes as the two men approach the brink of civilization:

> To-day our little boy is six months old. . . . Somehow . . . I seem to see him a grown man, taking his father's place in the world—the second John Clayton. . . . There—as though to give my prophecy the weight of his endorsement—he has grabbed my pen in his chubby fists and with his inkbegrimmed little fingers has placed the seal of his tiny finger prints upon the page.

" 'Well! Tarzan of the Apes, what think you?' asked D'Arnot. 'Does not this little book clear up the mystery of your parentage?' " (212). But for Tarzan "the mystery of my origin is deeper than before" (212), because a crucial piece of physical evidence, which would ground the text of his putative identity, is missing: a baby's skeleton found in the crib in his father's cabin and buried along with his mother's and father's skeletons by Jane, her father, her father's assistant (Samuel T. Philander), and William Clayton. If the baby in the crib is the baby in the text, then who is Tarzan? That is the question that troubles the king of the apes.

The reader, of course, whose prime pleasure in this text may come from never being in doubt about the hierarchy of race, class, and gender that justifies the imperial system the romance projects, has known all along what Tarzan will learn from Philander just before he proposes to Jane and what will be confirmed shortly thereafter by D'Arnot's report of the fingerprints: that the baby in the crib is not the baby in the text (that is, that there is a natural place outside the text to solve or substantiate the literal), but the skeleton of a baby ape, who, having died, was left by its mother Kala in the place of the living baby, John Clayton the second, when, bereft, the ape claimed the baby for her own. "That the huge, fierce brute loved this child of another race is beyond question," Burroughs tells us, "and he, too, gave to the great, hairy beast all the affection that would have belonged to his fair young mother had she lived" (39). What can translate across racial boundaries, apparently, is the "natural" love of mother and child; the principal male apes on the other hand are entirely brutal to the child. This kind of sentimentality, which is a simultaneous universalization and alienation of races according to gender, typifies racist discourse.

In the plot of this imperial romance, biology, in the form of fingerprints and skeletons, solves a problem of translation: how can Tarzan identify himself absolutely in the text of his father so that the imperial reign of that particular race, gender, and class can be naturalized? How, that is, can the text of the father ground itself in a nature that escapes the alienating process of translation, like the skeleton of a baby that appears buried in natural ground, not grounded in a text? This is the problem of translation that confronts U.S. foreign policy throughout the history I have been sketching; for this policy wants desperately to conceive of itself as natural rather than textual, as beyond the problems of translation that the very notion of foreign policy entails.

Tarzan of the Apes both embodies and contradicts, against its will, this conception of foreign policy. For in this Anglo-American romance, biology, far from existing beyond the confines of translation, is a figure of translation itself, a figure, that is, not of cause and effect or of organic development, but of displacement, or figuration, the very marks of the rhetorical, the political interplay between the literal and the figurative.

Tarzan's fingerprints, apparently working against Burroughs's intent to naturalize white, or upper-class, male power, declare themselves not as natural signs but as an extension of the father's writing, "blurred imprints" "on the margin of the page" (212). Rather than being marks of a natural relationship between father and son, these imprints are signs, "prophecy" and "seal," of a political relationship, a displacement in which the son will "take[. . .] his father's place in the world," not because of an individual or biological relation to the father but because they belong to a class in which a particular title grants the son the "right" to maintain the force that the father maintained in dispossessing colonial subjects and the working class, a force the romance mystifies from its beginning, when it tells us that the first Lord Greystoke is traveling to Africa simply to protect the Queen's colonial subjects from the depredations of another European power (2).

Likewise, the skeleton of the baby ape, intended by Burroughs as the mark of a biological evolution that proves Greystoke's natural primacy over all "lower" forms of social life—whether apes or the "mob" for which they unabashedly stand—ironically gains its meaning in a primal scene that privileges not evolution but violent displacement as the motive force of the romance. This scene, in which Kala grabs the infant Lord Greystoke from his crib, displacing him with her own dead baby and transferring the living child lovingly into her arms, is neither a mark of the evolutionary difference between ape and human nor of their primal evolutionary identity as embodied in the mother, but a figure for the process of translation that, underwriting U.S. foreign policy, civilizes the other in order to savage her.

2

The Foreign Policy of Metaphor

Indian people *are* practical and spiritual. We don't horseshit around. We're not coy and cute. Occasionally we're difficult, but that's different. We don't believe in metaphor. Very few of us even understand what that term means in terms of what it means to the greater poetry community around us or to the critical establishment.

PAULA GUNN ALLEN

IN HIS INFLUENTIAL *The Machine in the Garden,* Leo Marx ends his chapter on *The Tempest* by suggesting that the play "may be read as a prologue to American literature" (72); for "in its overall design, [it] prefigures the design of the classic American fables, and especially the idea of a redemptive journey away from society in the direction of nature" (69). It is my purpose in what follows to read *The Tempest* as a prologue to American literature, but in a way that moves against Marx's reading. For I do not read the play or the American frontier tradition it can articulate as a conflict between nature and culture, between savagery and civilization. In *The Tempest* the garden is not a form of nature. The garden is the garden of eloquence. The garden is the machine. And so the conflict cannot be between the machine and the garden, but only between machines, between cultures, between, in this case, the culture of Caliban, which we will need to specify, and that of Prospero. When Prospero laments that Caliban is "a Devil, a born devil, on whose nature / Nurture can never stick" (IV.i.189–90), the conflict proposed, whatever Prospero's figuring of it may be, is not between nature and nurture but between two forms of nurture, a conflict of translation, as I will argue.

Further, *The Tempest* that I have in mind as a prologue to American

22

literature does not confine itself to figuring only "the classic American fables" (by which terms Marx refers to those white, male, middle-class, Protestant writings that compose what until recently has been the largely unquestioned American literary canon). In fact, when I use the term *literature* here I want to use it in the classical sense of everything that appears in letters, the written. I am not ignoring the oral, but simply noting that my emphasis in this book will be the violent politics through or within which Western European writing translated Native American oral cultures. Finally, I should add that just as I am interested in disrupting the integrity of the term "literature" by politicizing it, so I am equally committed to disrupting the integrity of the term "American." Frantz Fanon is my immediate inspiration for reading *The Tempest*. And his name should remind us that Shakespeare's play is the possible prologue not only for the literature of the United States, but for a significant body of Caribbean literature, which itself represents, among other things, the violent history of imperialism in the Americas, a history of crimes from which the United States has yet to disentangle itself.

At the time of one of the first productions of *The Tempest*, in 1611 for the court of James I, eloquence, so central to the Renaissance vision of the world, was still conceived of as the prime technology, the primary motive force in transforming the world. The West had not as yet entered the fully modern era, the era we are still part of, in which technology is the principal form of the West's eloquence. Literate men of the Renaissance, who because of the privileges of gender and class could aspire to the ideal of the classical orator of the writings of Cicero and Quintillian, saw true, or morally proper, eloquence—ideally the end result of a formal education centered in rhetoric—as the ability to translate words grounded in "wisdom," or "reason," into power in the world. "The humanists' stand on eloquence," Hanna Gray tells us, "implied an almost incredible faith in the power of the word,"[1] a faith we might liken to the West's current faith in the power of technology, which seems to find its apotheosis, indeed its macabre parody, in the American dream of dominion through technological perfection.

The Tempest conceives of power in terms of eloquence. Commenting on an identity between Prospero and Ariel, Harry Berger, Jr., notes:

> Spirit and master have much in common: each has both a histrionic and a rhetorical bent which he delights to indulge, and each savors his performances to the full. In the case of Ariel, this is perhaps unambiguously clear only in his opening speech, but it is marked enough there to set up the

analogy. Notice [in that speech] . . . how his obvious delight in magical performance is doubled by his pleasure in describing it.[2]

Berger goes on to quote the speech in which Ariel describes his pyrotechnics on board Alonso and company's tempest-tossed ship:

> I boarded the king's ship; now on the beak,
> Now in the waist, the deck, in every cabin,
> I flam'd amazement: sometime I'd divide,
> And burn in many places; on the topmast,
> The yards and boresprit, would I flame distinctly,
> Then meet and join. Jove's lightnings, the precursors
> O' th' dreadful thunder-claps, more momentary
> And sight-outrunning were not: the fire and cracks
> Of sulphurous roaring the most mighty Neptune
> Seem to besiege, and make his bold waves tremble,
> Yea, his dread trident shake.
>
> (I.ii.196–206)

Ariel's speech is intended to flatter Prospero with a vision of the master's magical power and to persuade him of his servant's faithfulness in translating this power "[t]o th' syllable" (I.ii.503); its eloquence is meant to persuade the audience of these powers as well, by summoning a vision of their effects that the available stage machinery, no matter how innovative for the time, could not have equaled. Thus Ariel's eloquence becomes the double of a technology yet to be realized, and therefore conceived of as magical in the sense that it is a figure of this technology and acts in its place. But, and this is crucial, the Renaissance audience would not have felt the discrepancy between technology and word that a modern Western audience would feel if it could witness and listen to the same spectacle. For the Renaissance audience would have conceived of the eloquent word *as* a powerful technology.

"Theatre in 1605," Stephen Orgel remarks, "was assumed to be a verbal medium. And acting . . . was a form of oratory; the Renaissance actor did not merely imitate action, he persuaded the audience through speech and gesture of the meaning of the action." And, I would add, in the case of a play like *The Tempest*, dependent as it was on an as yet unrealized technology, this actor had to persuade the audience of the action as well. "Obviously," Orgel continues, "much more than this was in fact being experienced in an Elizabethan theatre—for example pageantry, violence, symbolism—for which the visual sense was essential. But this did not render the drama any less a verbal form.''[3] Orgel then goes on to make the central point that unlike modern theater (theater from the late nineteenth century on), where the visual, or technological, and the verbal are opposed (and where the visual takes precedence over the verbal), the Renaissance theater operated under a different conceptual agenda:

> The distinction . . . between "verbal" theatres and "visual" theatres in this period is a false one. Both the Globe and the court theatre were spectacular, both were highly rhetorical; the visual and the verbal emphases in no way excluded each other. In fact, if we look at plays that were specifically written to be produced with scenes and machines, we shall find them far more elaborately rhetorical than plays for the public stage. (19)

The Renaissance theater is one of the spaces where we can "see" that the frontier between language and technology, a frontier that seems so familiar to the West today, had not yet been articulated. In the Renaissance, even granting the increasing voice of the bourgeois technical arts in their debate with the aristocratic liberal arts, technology remains predominantly within the territory of eloquence. At the time *The Tempest* was first performed, *nature*, which could be read as the very sign of an emergent technology that claimed experience (hence, *experiment*) rather than authority for its basis, was still predominantly contained within the figure of the Book, the very sign of eloquence.[4]

The Tempest is a figure of the map of Renaissance power as eloquence. When, as noted above, Ariel promises to carry out Prospero's commands "[t]o th' syllable," he emphasizes the verbal character of Prospero's art, which is grounded in the book. Caliban recognizes this source of Prospero's power, when, plotting with the commoners Stephano and Trinculo to usurp Prospero, who has usurped him, he tells his coconspirators

> Remember
> First to possess his books; for without them
> He's but a sot, as I am, nor hath not
> One spirit to command: they all do hate him
> As rootedly as I. Burn but his books.
>
> (III.ii.89–93)

The historic relationship between social class, literacy, and power in the West is simply asserted here. And Prospero implicitly reasserts it, when in the last act of the play he ends the speech in which he promises to abjure his magic by promising Ariel: "I'll drown my book" (V.i.57), a promise he never carries out in the play proper. Shakespeare conceives of Prospero's power in *The Tempest* as the magical literacy of eloquence. Prospero, for example, associates his magical power with "the liberal Arts" (I.ii.73), not the mechanical arts. And the play opens with a failure of the mechanical arts when pitted against the liberal arts of Prospero. For the technical skills of the sailors cannot save the ship from foundering in the storm, which, as we discover immediately in the second scene of the play, is not a natural phenomenon at all, but a cultural one: the literalization or translation of Prospero's figures of speech into power, the kind of power that Henry Peacham dramatizes in the 1577 edition of *The Garden of Eloquence:*

> For by Fygures, as it were by sundry streames, that great & forcible floud of Eloquence, is most plentifully and pleasantly poured forth by the great might of Figures which is no other thing then (wisdom speaking eloquently) the Oratour may leade his hearers which way he list, and draw them to what affection he will. . . . By figures he may make his speech as cleare as the noone day: or contrary wyse, as it were with cloudes and foggy mistes, he may cover it with darkness, he may stirre up stormes, & troublesome tempestes, or contrariwyse, cause and procure a quyet and sylent calmnesse.[5]

In *The Tempest* nature is not nature but culture, the culture contained within the norms of eloquence; that is, nature is a form or forms of language, conceived of like its sign, technology, within the territory of the Book. Indeed, the opening scene of the play on board the tempest-tossed ship, which the critical tradition has read as a scene of nature's power over social and political hierarchy, might well have been read by the royal audience at the performance of the play not as a scene of nature over culture, but as the most conspicuous figure of political life available to the Renaissance, the allegory of the ship of state. How, we might ask, given the ubiquitousness of the figure and the sensitivity of the audience to questions of political order and disorder, could this audience not have read it in this way, even before Prospero's appearance in the second scene, when the audience discovers that the storm is his invention, fabricated to help him regain the helm of his ship of state, which his brother Antonio had violently wrested from him in league with Alonso, king of Naples. Importantly, one of the documents that we know influenced Shakespeare in writing *The Tempest, A True Declaration of the Estate of the Colonie in Virginia,* of which the audience at court—among whom were investors in the Jamestown venture—would have been well aware, is structured by figures of the ship of state, comparing the political turmoil at Jamestown to the tempest that wrecked the *Sea Venture* in the Bermudas.

Not only was the ship of state a ubiquitous figure of political life, but it was typically the exemplary figure of allegory in the books of Latin rhetoric that the men in the audience would have gone to school with or could have read in translation. Alonso's storm-tossed ship, in which the "master" appears briefly only to disappear, and the common crew quarrels openly with the nobles, would have announced to the audience its figurative force, its structure as part of a rhetorical machine, rather than its transparency to a purely physical world. The opening scene of *The Tempest,* at the very least, would have appeared to its audience not simply as mimesis, but also as the Renaissance trope *translatio,* or metaphor, of which allegory was a particular kind. In this opening scene, and throughout the play, Ariel is Prospero's air articulated eloquently, transformed into the literally spellbinding orations that hold the figures on the island entranced so that Prospero can restore the political order that was disrupted by his usurpation in Milan. Prospero, like the poet-orator of Emerson's *Nature,* "forges the subtile and delicate air into wise and melodious words, and gives them wing as angels of persuasion and command. One after another his victorious thought comes up with and reduces all things, until the world becomes at last only a realized will, —the double of the man."[6] Or at least Prospero attempts such a reduction of all otherness to the terms of the self. We will return to the point that his imperial translation, like that of Emerson's poet-orator (as I have argued elsewhere[7]), meets significant resistance.

I synchronize *Nature,* published in 1836, with *The Tempest,* not least of all because Emerson's text is one of the best readings we have of the play, and it is particularly useful if one is interested, as I am, in interpreting the play within the context of the Jamestown colony, what Richard Beale Davis calls precisely "Britain's first major experiment in Empire" (14), an experiment that, as we know, would eventuate in the formation of the United States.

Nature is not a declared reading of *The Tempest.* Nowhere in his text or in his notebooks does Emerson declare that the purpose of his first book is to interpret the play, which is, perhaps, why no one, as far as I know, has brought the two texts into immediate relation before now, although Marx in *The Machine in the Garden* implies a relation between the two texts within the context of his vision of an American pastoral. Yet as Emerson implicitly tells us in *Nature,* he had *The Tempest* before him as he was writing his book; for he quotes portions of Prospero's long speech in Act V (wrongly attributing part of it to Ariel[8]), in which the magician eloquently evokes his magical powers even as he promises to abjure them (V.i.33–87). These quotes, Emerson tells us, illustrate the "transfiguration which all material objects undergo through the passion of the poet" (66), a passion exemplified for Emerson by Shakespeare, whose

> imperial muse tosses the creation like a bauble from hand to hand, and uses it to embody any caprice of thought that is uppermost in his mind. The remotest spaces of nature are visited, and the farthest sundered things are brought together, by a subtle spiritual connection. (65)

Emerson attributes to Shakespeare in this passage the same omnipotence that Shakespeare attributes to Prospero in the speech from Act V:

> I have bedimm'd
> The noontide sun, call'd forth the mutinous winds,
> And 'twixt the green sea and the azur'd vault
> Set roaring war: to the dread rattling thunder
> Have I given fire, and rifted Jove's stout oak
> With his own bolt; the strong-bas'd promontory
> Have I made shake, and by the spurs pluck'd up
> The pine and cedar: graves at my command
> Have wak'd their sleepers, op'd, and let 'em forth
> By my so potent Art.
>
> (V.i.41–50)

This speech, echoing Ariel's eloquent invocation of his pyrotechnics aboard Alonso's ship, embodies the "imperial muse" of Emerson's Shakespeare, who "tosses the creation like a bauble from hand to hand, and uses it to embody any caprice of thought that is uppermost in his mind." The sense conveyed in the passages from both *Nature* and *The Tempest* is of an imperial figure who acts absolutely, that is, immediately, or without resistance, on the world, even though this figure needs the world as words to express, or mediate, his thoughts (a potential contradiction to which I will return). This imperial figure dwarfs the world—the creation appears like a bauble in his colossal hands, which seize Jove's lightning and hurl it powerfully down to earth—and uses it to figure forth "*any* caprice of thought" that enters his consciousness. The world offers no resistance to the expression of this emperor's thought. "To him," Emerson tells us in the same passage, "the refractory world is ductile and flexible; he invests dust and stones with humanity, and makes them the words of the Reason." Finally, this imperial figure expresses his most "potent Art" through the conquest of time and space; he visits the "remotest spaces of nature" and brings "the farthest sundered things . . . together." And what could be more sundered than life and death, which Prospero unites in his waking of the dead.

The kind of immediate power that Emerson attributes to his poet-orator, of whom, I am suggesting, Prospero is the explicit prototype in *Nature,* can be read as the power to make metaphors—the power to bring sundered, or dispersed, things together—a power that from Quintillian to Emerson is the very secret of eloquence. And this metaphorical power can also be read as technological power. As Marx comments in *The Machine in the Garden,*

> No stock phrase in the entire lexicon of progress appears more often than the "annihilation of space and time," borrowed from one of Pope's relatively obscure poems ("Ye Gods! annihilate but space and time, / And make two lovers happy."). The extravagance of this sentiment apparently is felt to match the sublimity of technological progress. (194)

Marx's book has helped instruct us in the ways that the figure of the machine began to become the figure of the United States in the period between 1830 and 1860. "Again and again, foreign travelers in this period testify to the nation's obsessive interest in power machinery" (208), an obsession that was and is, no doubt, American, but might also be seen as the apotheosis of a European vision of immediacy, or absolute power, that was instrumental in founding the New World. Let us continue to work toward a figure of this founding vision, Prospero's vision, by continuing to look for a moment at Emerson's *Nature.*

As one example of what he calls "the rhetoric of the technological sublime" (195, 230), Marx cites the passage from *Nature* that I used to synchronize Emerson's text with *The Tempest.* Here is the passage as it appears in *The Machine in the Garden* (the emphases are Marx's):

> The exercise of the Will, or the lesson of power, is taught in every event. . . . Nature is thoroughly mediate. It is made to serve. . . . It offers all its kingdoms to man as the *raw material* which he may mould into what is useful. Man is never weary of *working it up.* He *forges* the subtile and delicate air into wise and melodious words, and gives them wing as

angels of persuasion and command. One after another his victorious thought comes up with and reduces all things until the world becomes at last only a realized will,—the double of the man. (231)

About this passage Marx makes the following brief but telling comments, which directly precede the passage in his book:

A measure of the depth to which machine power penetrates [Emerson's] imagination is the large part it plays in his figurative language. Here, in a later chapter of *Nature*, he is praising intellectual power in general, but, as the submerged metaphor indicates, the specific example he has in mind is technology. . . . (230)

We might note first that what Emerson is praising in the passage under consideration is not "intellectual power in general" but a specific form of intellectual power, the classical form of eloquence, which was of immediate interest to him, not only as a Lyceum lecturer and former preacher, who had received an education in classical rhetoric at Harvard, but also as a citizen of an antebellum, nineteenth-century America that took the oratorical genius of Daniel Webster, for example, as one of the primary symbols of its power. The specifics of Emerson's description of what Marx refers to as "intellectual power in general" point to the descriptions of eloquence in the Latin rhetorics of Cicero and Quintillian with which both Shakespeare's audience at the royal performance of *The Tempest* and Emerson's audience of New England intellectuals were familiar. It is "melodious words" based on wisdom and capable of "persuasion and command" that Emerson is evoking here (and we should note the conflation of wisdom with power in this representative discourse; it is a classic Western conflation). We can see, both in *Nature* and in the trajectory of Emerson's work from *Nature* to his two late essays on eloquence, that his emblem of absolute power is the "poet, the orator, bred in the woods" who uses nature as a language with which "the spells of persuasion, the keys of power are put into his hands" (52). Emerson surely sensed American affinities in the spellbinding eloquence of Prospero.

Emerson's language, I would argue then, as an alternative to Marx's vision, does not simply reflect or represent the powerful emergence of the machine in antebellum America; rather, it absorbs this modern lexicon of technological power, perhaps in part as a last desperate act of containment, into the traditional yet still potent figure of eloquence as technology. In *Nature* it is explicitly "eloquence," not the machine, that

Emerson gives as one of the "examples of the action of man upon nature with his entire force," one of the "examples of Reason's momentary grasp of the sceptre; the exertions of a power which exists not in time or space, but an instantaneous in-streaming causing power" (79). In *Nature*, as in *The Tempest*, the imperial figure that conquers time and space is not technology but eloquence.

Marx, although he is not at all interested in the figure of eloquence as a force that cannot be separated from the history of technology, testifies implicitly to the lingering force of this figure in antebellum America, when he describes for us how until the 1850s in the United States the mechanical arts sought to justify themselves in terms of the literary arts. In one example that Marx gives among several of a similar cast, a writer argues for the "genius" of the machine by asserting its intellectual equivalence to the very epitome of eloquence, "an oration of Cicero" (199). But, as Marx tells us, "By the 1850's the celebrants of the machine take the offensive" (202). Hereafter, as we know quite well today, it will be the literary, or rhetorical, arts that will have to justify themselves in terms of use, or practicality, which the machine will have appropriated to itself from the historic realm of language's potency.

David Noble succinctly articulates this struggle between rhetoric and technology in his description of shifts in the curricular emphasis of higher education in nineteenth-century America:

> In the early nineteenth century the colleges were firmly in the hands of the classicists and the clerics, and there was considerable academic disdain for the study of experimental science and even more for the teaching of the "useful arts." Technical education in the United States, therefore, developed in struggle with the classical colleges, both inside and outside of them. One form of this development was the gradual growth of technological studies within the classical colleges, resulting from the reorientation of natural philosophy toward the empirical, experimental, scientific search for truth and from the pressures of some scientists and powerful industrialists for practical instruction; the other was the rise of technical colleges and institutes outside of the traditional colleges in response to the demands of internal improvement projects like canal-building, railroads, manufactures, and, eventually, science-based industry.

But it was not until 1862, Noble continues, that

> the big leap forward in technical education in America came . . . when Congress passed the Morrill Act granting federal aid to the states for the support of colleges of agriculture and the mechanic arts. State legislatures

that had been deaf to all appeals for technical instruction now quickly accepted the federal grants and voted to create the new type of school, while established colleges caught the spirit and added departments of engineering. In the first decade following the passage of the Morrill Act, the number of engineering schools jumped from six to seventy. By 1880 there were eighty-five, and by 1917 there were 126 engineering schools of college grade in the United States. Between 1870 and the outbreak of the First World War, the annual number of graduates from engineering colleges grew from 100 to 4300; the relative number of engineers in the whole population had multiplied fifteenfold.[9]

Before the Civil War, despite the flowering of the machine (the steamboat, the railroad, the cotton gin, the telegraph, and the improved printing press), the principal form of technology was still eloquence, whereas after the war, marking the decline in the idea of a classical education as normative, technology became the principal form of eloquence. If literary texts are any guide to shifts in cultural forces or emphasis, we might note that the texts that are occupying a good deal of the revisionary attention of Americanists at the moment are these that express their technological vision in terms of eloquence. We have been looking, of course, at Emerson for whom language is *the* technology. But we could introduce other texts here. The narrative power of *Uncle Tom's Cabin*, for example, is based on an already waning yet still potent figure of eloquence, the preacher (a figure that is, apparently, still waning and still potent). Stowe aims to convert her audience, and the figures within her text that she offers for her reader's admiration, Tom and Little Eva, work, however we may take them, through this particular power of eloquence as well. In *Moby Dick*, "a book . . . intoxicated with rhetoric," Ahab is "the greatest orator of all," as Myra Jehlen so precisely puts it.[10] As the business-minded Starbuck sees early on in the voyage, the trip aboard the floating factory of the *Pequod* will be one in which the ideally rational terms of technology (the efficient aegis of profit and loss) will be wildly skewed in the imperial muse of Ahab's eloquence. This voyage can suggest as well that technology does not represent any absolute break from eloquence, but is a particular manifestation of it. Look, for example, at Mark Twain's *A Connecticut Yankee in King Arthur's Court* (1889), written during a period of the growth of corporate power through the linking of science and technology, when the tradition of eloquence might seem to have been superseded by that of technology. Here Twain conceives of his hero, apparently the epitome of technological rationality, as a Prospero-like figure whose technological expertise does not rationalize the culture of the thaumaturgic word (the culture of those "white Indians,"[11] sixth-century Britons, whom the Yankee comes to "civilize"), but is an absolutely deadly version of it.

In his 1845 *Narrative*, Frederick Douglass, ironically I think, but in a way that opens up the most complex entanglements of black and white identity in America, founds his liberation from slavery on a *mastery* of the master's word, a mastery he associates with "a book entitled 'The Columbian Orator,'" in which "[a]mong much of other interesting matter, [he] found in it a dialogue between a master and his slave" (83). In this dialogue the slave through the eloquence of his argument defeats his master's argument for slavery and wins his emancipation (83). Like Caliban, Douglass's narrator realizes that the central act of rebellion (a rebellion that this narrator envisions as a revolution) must be "to possess [the master's] books." Unlike Caliban, however, and the difference is not simply that between a seventeenth-century and nineteenth-century text but between a text by a free European and one by a fugitive black slave, Douglass's narrator wants to possess the books not to burn them, but to learn to read and write from them.

Douglass conceives of the mechanics of slavery in the *Narrative* precisely as Shakespeare does in *The Tempest*, as a differential in the power of language possessed by master and slave. Both Prospero and Caliban curse each other in the same language, the language that Prospero through his daughter and disciple Miranda has taught Caliban. But the absolutely crucial difference is that whereas Caliban's curses remain mere figures of speech, Prospero's figures have the power to literalize themselves, to act immediately, if Prospero chooses, as engines of torture in Caliban's flesh. When Caliban appears reluctant to continue his work, Prospero threatens a curse:

> If thou neglect'st, or dost unwillingly
> What I command, I'll rack thee with old cramps,
> Fill all thy bones with aches, make thee roar,
> That beasts shall tremble at thy din.
>
> (I.ii.370–73)

To which severe stricture (the command that Caliban must do his slave's work willingly tells us much about the fantasies of omnipotence of slave-owners), Caliban responds in an aside: "I must obey: his Art is of such pow'r, / It would control my dam's god, Setebos, / And make a vassal of him" (I.ii.373–76), thus confirming the power of Prospero's verbal art to literalize litself. When Caliban responds to Miranda in what are by now quite famous lines: "You taught me language; and my profit on't / Is, I know how to curse" (I.ii.365–66), we might well notice a certain irony in the lines. For there is no profit for Caliban in learning the Europeans' language; though he knows how to curse, he does not know how to curse in the eloquent, or lethal, manner of his master. This, as we will read in Chapter 5, is a matter of the politics of decorum. And I would emphasize here that the "rack" of language on which Prospero threatens to torture Caliban is not simply a figure for, or mystification of, that engine of torture employed in Shakespeare's time, but is an expression of an aristocratic *belief* in an incalculably more efficient, an absolutely persuasive, machine of eloquence: one that not only convinces the other to be a slave but to be one willingly. How far is it after all from a belief in Prospero's threatened curse in the text of a Renaissance "romance" to a passage we have already looked at in part from Richard Hakluyt's *Discourse of Western Planting* (1584), in which we find a similar, if ostensibly more benign, belief in the technology of eloquence?

> This people [the Iroquoian-speaking Indians whom Jacques Cartier encountered on his second trip to Canada in 1535] beleve not at all in God but in one whome they call Cudruaigny. . . . And yet notwithstandinge they are very easie to be perswaded . . . and were very desirous to become christians. . . . It remayneth to be throughly weyed and considered by what meanes and by whome this moste godly and Christian work may be perfourmed, of inlarginge the glorious gospell of Christe, and reducinge of infinite multitudes of these simple people that are in errour into the righte and perfecte waye of their salvacion: The blessed Apostle Paule the converter of the Gentiles . . . writeth in this manner: Whoesoever shall call on the name of the Lorde shall be saved: But howe shall they call on him in whom they have not beleved? And howe shall they beleve in him of whom they have not hearde? And howe shall they heare withoute a preacher? and howe shall they preache excepte they be sente? Then it is necessarie for the salvation of those poore people which have sitten so longe in darkenes and in the shadowe of deathe, that preachers should be sent unto them. . . . Nowe the meanes to sende suche as shall labour effectually in this busines ys by plantinge one or twoo Colonies of our nation uppon that fyrme, where they may remaine in safetie, and firste learne the language of the people nere adjoyninge (the gifte of tongues beinge nowe taken awaye), and by little and little accquainte themselves with their manner, and so with discrecion and myldenes distill into their

purged myndes the swete and lively liquor of the gospell. (Taylor, 2, 214–15)

The piece at once recognizes cultural difference as linguistic difference (we will have to learn their language) and obliterates this difference in a belief in the power of eloquence to act immediately on the Indians, a contradiction that is characteristic of the documents of early "discovery" from Columbus's journals onward.

For Douglass, the archetypal slave-driver is one named, allegorically enough, "Austin Gore, a man possessing, in an eminent degree, all those traits of character indispensible to what is called a first-rate overseer." And the first-mentioned of Gore's "powers" is his ability, his absolute power, as a translator of both the body language and the language proper of the slaves: "He was one of those who could torture the slightest look, word, or gesture, on the part of the slave, into impudence, and would treat it accordingly" (65). The process that Douglass describes here, the forcible displacement of what the slave could properly claim, if he or she could claim anything, as proper meaning into the figurative sphere (of the overseer's desires in this case), is quite precisely translation in the sense of the Greek *metaphora* or its Latin derivative *translatio*. When Peacham in the 1593 edition of *The Garden of Eloquence* calls rhetoric "this excellent Art of translating,"[12] he not only points to the central place that metaphor holds in the history of eloquence, but also epitomizes this history as one in which the notion of translation and of metaphor both etymologically and ideologically are inseparable: the notion, first formally defined by Aristotle in his famous and still basic definition of metaphor, of *transporting* a term from a *familiar* to a *foreign* place, from, that is, its so-called "proper" signification to a "figurative" sense, with the idea of "resemblance," or "similitude," determining the decorous limits of such transportation.

"Metaphor" (*metaphora*), Aristotle tells us in the *Poetics*, "is the application of an alien [*allotriou*] name by transference [*epiphora*] either from genus to species, or from species to genus, or from species to species, or by analogy, that is, proportion" (XXI.4–5). *Metaphora* comes from the verb *metaphero* (literally, "to carry across"), which, as Liddell's and Scott's *Greek-English Lexicon* notes, contains among its other meanings the sense of translation from one language into another. Yet that the same word, *metaphero,* can refer to either the translation of one language into another or the transference of sense within a language is not simply what brings the idea of metaphor within the context of translation or the idea of translation within the context of metaphor. For as Aristotle's definition of metaphor suggests with its notion of the "transference" of an "alien name" into a familiar context, the very idea of metaphor seems to find its ground in a kind of territorial imperative, in a division, that is, between the domestic and the foreign.

In Chapters XXI and XXII of the *Poetics,* Aristotle develops his definition of metaphor, which rests upon a division of language into "current or proper word[s] [*kurion onamaton*]," those "in general use among a people" (XXI.2–3), and "unusual words [*tois xenikois*]," under which, among others, Aristotle places "strange (or rare) words [*glottan*]" and those that are "metaphorical [*metaphoran*]" (XXII.1). What I want to note immediately is that the word S. H. Butcher translates as "unusual" is *xenikos,* which means "strange" or "foreign." Thus, while Aristotle first appears to distinguish between the "metaphorical" and the "foreign" when in Chapter XXI he defines a "strange" word as any word "which is in use in another country" (XXI.3), he subsequently makes the metaphorical a species of the foreign, as the terminology of his definition suggests and as he makes clear in Chapter XXII when he classifies metaphor under "unusual words."[13]

So, as Roland Barthes points out in his essay "L'ancienne rhetorique," Aristotle's theory of metaphor "rests [*repose*] on the idea that there exist two languages [*deux langages*], one proper and one figurative [*un propre et un figuré*]." And, Barthes continues, this division into a proper and a figurative language cannot be separated from the division "national/foreign" (*national/étranger*) and "familiar/strange" (*normal/étrange*).[14] Within Aristotle's theory of metaphor, then, a theory that has exerted and continues to exert, whether explicitly or implicitly, a controlling force on the way Westerners think about language, the figurative becomes the foreign, or strange; the proper becomes the national, or normal. Thus, within this context, a language becomes foreign to itself. At the same time, the division between the proper and the figurative can govern the division between foreign languages, with the national language becoming the proper language, and the foreign, the figurative. Here it is worth remarking that the word *kuria,* which Butcher translates as "current or proper," has among its most immediate senses those of *authority* and *legitimacy.*

In *The Arte of English Poesie* (1589), George Puttenham defines "*Metaphora,* or the Figure of transporte," as "a kinde of *wresting* [my emphasis] of a single word from his owne right signification, to another not so naturall, but yet of some affinitie or conveniencie with it.''[15] If Gore's translations break the bounds of all "affinitie or convenience" in wresting the slaves' language absolutely from them, these translations nevertheless point to what Puttenham suggests: the very activity of translation, no matter how decorous, based as it is on a certain foreign policy, is an act of violence. Abraham Fraunce, defining *trope* in *The Arcadian Rhetoric* (1588), also evokes the violence in metaphoric displacement, or translation, and with a figure that suggests the master/slave relationship: "A trope or turning is when a word is turned from his naturall signification . . . so convenientlie, as that it seeme rather willinglie ledd, than driven by force to that other signification.''[16] The key word in Fraunce's definition, I take it, is *seeme*. The skilled translator, or rhetorician, like the skilled overseer with a slave, must use force in transporting a word from its proper, or "natural," place, but conceals that force, or tries to, under the semblance of the word's willingness to give up its property in itself.

As Douglass describes Gore's translations of the slaves' language, they are a form of torture. And just as Gore can "torture" this language into any form he desires, so, as Douglass describes him, can he translate his own language *immediately* into torture: for a slave "to be accused [by Gore] was to be convicted, and to be convicted was to be punished; the one always following the other with immutable certainty" (66). Whereas, confronted with the overseer, the slave's word can only exist in the overseer's translation, that is, figuratively, the overseer's word, as we read here, literalizes itself with "immutable certainty" in torture on the body of the slave, who has no chance to translate this word; for "there must be no answering back to him [the overseer]; no explanation was allowed a slave, showing himself to have been wrongfully accused" (65). Under these circumstances, to say of the overseer "his words are the whip" is, virtually, to speak quite literally, so little space is there (no room for the displacement of deflection) between accusation, conviction, and punishment. What on the other hand could we say of the slaves' words in relation to power that would not have to be read figuratively?

The whip and the gun, those emblems of slave-owning technology, do appear and exert an obviously terrible force in Douglass's *Narrative*. But Douglass and his largely white abolitionist audience do not primarily understand power in their terms (the *Narrative* is prefaced by William Lloyd Garrison, who authorizes Douglass's humanity, with unselfconscious irony, in terms of this black man's abilities in eloquence). Rather, as I have been arguing, and Douglass does much more than suggest, the terms of power in the world of the *Narrative* are terms themselves. In this world, the ideal, though not abstract, overseer is defined by a strict economy of literalization:

> Mr. Gore was a grave man, and, though a young man, he indulged in no jokes, said no funny words, seldom smiled. His words were in perfect keeping with his looks, and his looks were in perfect keeping with his words. Overseers will sometimes indulge in a witty word, even with the slaves; not so with Mr. Gore. He spoke but to command, and commanded but to be obeyed; he dealt sparingly with words, and bountifully with his whip, never using the former where the latter would answer as well. (66)

Figurative language, of which metaphor, or translation, is the model, is the driving force of interpretation, that is, of language itself. For this language within language that is the force of language opens up a space between signified and signifier, a rupture of identity, where the conflictive play of dialogue takes place that constitutes the speakers (writers/ readers) for and significantly through each other. Historically in the West, eloquence developed in Greece and retained both a dialogic, or "democratic," component (democratic within the upper class) and an imperial component. That is, eloquence is conceived of both as what makes the *polis* the free marketplace of ideas, the place of open debate in the law courts and in councils, and, contradictorily enough, as what can mesmerize the other into silent assent. In *De Oratore* Cicero evokes these two aspects of eloquence, though not apparently with any irony, when he describes the orator's art as both "kingly [*regium*]" and "worthy of the free [*liberale*]" (I.viii.32).[17] Emerson's entire oeuvre can be read within this dual figure of eloquence.

Now in respect to the passage concerning the overseer Gore, we might say that as the imperial force of eloquence comes to repress the dialogic, or democratic, force, language (which can never be anything but political) loses its figurative, equivocal, or conflictive play and rigidifies into the literal, proper, or univocal. In the equivocal play of language, the literal and the figurative operate as continual translations of each other. For every literal term is only provisionally, or contextually, literal or proper; that is, it is continually open to interpretation, a process that emphasizes the figurativeness of the literal, the impropriety of the proper. In the equivocal play of language, and let us understand *equivocal* in both its literal and its figurative sense, no single voice prevails because there is no univocality. Rather, the precarious coherence of each voice can only constitute itself in translation *between* other voices. When this equivocality is repressed, the literal and the figurative aspects of language become hierarchized into absolute and oppositional entities, with the masters occupying the territory of the literal or proper and consigning the slaves to that of the figurative.

Gore is the very figure of this literalization, a man purged of equivocality, or otherness, a monologist of brutal orations. In Gore the space of interpretation that the figurative opens up has vanished. His words and his looks are one. And his only words are commands. Imperious, Gore speaks only in imperatives that must be obeyed. The only language he utters is language that insists on literalizing itself; no jokes for Gore, only words that are whips or, what amounts to the same thing but is even more efficient, whips that "answer" the words of slaves. These are the words of Gore.

Confronted with this monopoly of the literal, the slaves are left in possession of the figurative, which, as we have seen in the translations of their language by Gore, is used to dispossess them. And yet what is a sign of their dispossession, figurative language, also invests them with an ironic, or potential, power. For, as Douglass tells his story, he bears witness to the slaves' most profound language, the language that escapes the overseer's translations, the language, that is, of their songs, structured by the tropes of irony and aenigma. The slaves "would sometimes sing the most pathetic sentiment in the most rapturous tone, and the most rapturous sentiment in the most pathetic tone"; and they would sing "words which to many would seem unmeaning jargon, but which, nevertheless, were full of meaning to themselves" (57), a meaning that was decidedly subversive. "Every tone was a testimony against slavery, and a prayer to God for deliverance from chains. . . . To those songs [Douglass tells his readers] I trace my first glimmering conception of the dehumanizing character of slavery. I can never get rid of that conception. Those songs still follow me, to deepen my hatred of slavery, and quicken my sympathies for my brethren in bonds" (58). Cut off from the language of the literal by the dangers and legalities of the slave system (not only must slaves refuse to speak their truth to masters, but, as Douglass reminds his readers, they must be wary of spies in their own ranks [62] and have no voice at all in the letter of the law), the slaves must cultivate a foreign language of the figurative, an "unmeaning jargon" (to outsiders), which, if it is a mark of powerlessness, also contains within it and transmits from slave to slave and generation to generation of slaves the power of a critique, an alternative eloquence, that waits for its opportunity to translate itself into literal rebellion.

3

Translating Property

THE NAME OF *Caliban* appears in *The Tempest* through an imperial and colonial act of translation. The name itself, so the critical consensus has it, is an anagram, a kind of translation itself for that matter, of *cannibal*. And *cannibal*, as we know, entered English (and other European languages) in the early sixteenth century as a precisely literal translation of the Spanish *caníbales*. It appears for the first time in Columbus's journal on November 23, 1492, where, sailing between Cuba and the island that he would name Española, he noted that

> those Indians [Arawaks] whom he had with him called [Española] "Bohio." They said that this land was very extensive and that in it were people who had one eye in the forehead, and others whom they called "Canibals." Of these last, they showed great fear, and when they saw that this course was being taken, they were speechless . . . because those people ate them and because they are very warlike.[1]

The origin of the word *can(n)ibal* remains in doubt, except that it apparently is a European deformation of a Native American term, either Arawakan or Cariban. We can't say which, or, of course, what the original term meant. *Canibal* may be a deformation of the word *Carib*, which, after Columbus, came to be the self-ascription of the native inhabitants of the lesser Antilles. Roberto Fernandez Retamar argues that *caníbales* is a direct deformation of *carib*, which occurred because Columbus, searching for the Asia of the Great Kahn (*El Gran Can* in Spanish), had a vested interest, no matter how phantasmal, in hearing "n" for "r," which would confirm the imminent discovery of the Asia of gold and spices he longed for. Yet it is possible that *n* and *r* are dialectical variants of the Arawakan and Cariban languages, in which case Columbus's phantasy of Asia would only be a coincidental component of his translation. However, *carib/Carib* itself may be a Spanish deformation of

41

another native word, perhaps, as Peter Hulme suggests, *Karina* or some variant of it, a self-ascriptive term used by mainland Indians who spoke and still speak a Cariban language. But, as Hulme also suggests, "It seems possible that Columbus's *canibal* was the native *kanibna,* meaningful in Arawakan languages but probably not in Cariban."[2]

Whatever the actual linguistic case may be, however, we have cause to wonder, as Columbus himself apparently did from time to time, at Columbus's association of the cannibals with eating human flesh. He did not have any empirical evidence, and his assertion that the Arawaks themselves told him is contradicted by Columbus's own admission that neither the Indians nor the Europeans knew the other's language. If we try to imagine the use of gestures in this case, we have not gotten around the problem of translation, but only embedded ourselves more deeply in it. For gestures are already translations of the culturally specific signs that compose linguistic phenomena, although Columbus and the European voyagers who later followed him appear to have believed from moment to moment in the power of a universal gestural language to transcend the frontiers of translation that frustrated their efforts to communicate.[3]

After the association Columbus elaborated in his journal, *cannibal* will come to mean one thing in Western languages: a human who eats another human's flesh. For Europeans this term will be part of a diverse arsenal of rhetorical weapons used to distinguish what they conceive of as their "civilized" selves from certain "savage" others, principally Native Americans and Africans. Certainly, Europeans, following Columbus, will not conceive of all Indians (and Africans) as cannibals, nor, as we know, will they/we necessarily conceive of those who don't fall under the category of "cannibals" as "civilized," for the rules of the game are nuanced not to include but to exclude. Yet the term, as Hulme has shown, will prove useful in colonial discourse as a means of distinguishing the "good" Indians from the "bad," those who, like the historical Caribs, fiercely resisted European expansion in the Caribbean. (In actuality the "good," or initially friendly, Arawaks also turned to organized resistance once the Spanish under Columbus tried to enslave them to hunt for the largely illusory gold of Española.)

We can understand, then, that the missing Arawak/Carib term that Columbus translates as *caníbales* follows a particular ideological trajectory; cut off from its proper (cultural) meaning in Native American languages, it becomes a purely political figure in European tongues, a figure that tries to erase its own rhetoricity by claiming a proper, or ethnographical, referent—the "fact" of cannibalism—which, even if it could be proved, would not justify or explain the colonial/imperial process of translation that displaces the original native term.

In fact, if we reread the entry from Columbus's journal in which the term *caníbales* appears for the first time, we can understand that the figure of the cannibal, far from being the legitimate signifier of a particular Native American culture, is the figure of another, earlier European man-eating figure, or fiction, that of the *anthropophagite* (literally, "man-eater"), which Columbus's term, taking on the aura of ethnographic accuracy over the years, would gradually displace in Western languages. For in the journal entry, Columbus claims that the Arawaks described not only human-eating humans to him, but also "people who had one eye in the forehead." Thus, we gather that Columbus's source was not the Arawaks but certain classical, or Mediterranean, stories, in which barbarian lands are peopled by monsters such as the Cyclops, anthropophagi, and dog-headed men. (On November 4, Columbus recorded in his journal that the Arawaks had described the latter monstrosity to the admiral [52]).

The name *Caliban* in *The Tempest*, then, appears as the translation of a translation of a translation" *Caliban* translates *caníbal,* which translates an unknown Native American term through the European term *anthropophagi.* And in this case the translation is a pure translation, or *translatio,* for it has lost its place in its proper, or domestic, meaning. It is wholly alienated in a foreign tongue. This process of translation, initiated by Columbus and perpetuated by the European voyagers who follow him, prepares the way for and is forever involved in the dispossession by which Native American land was *translated* (the term is used in English common law to refer to transfers of real estate) into the European identity of *property.* As noted briefly in Chapter 1, the kinship-based cultures I have in mind were (and in important ways, where they still exist, are) societies where the land was held not as *property* to be alienated, but in common to be used. Correspondingly in these cultures, identity was (and is) not conceived of as the autonomy of the *individual* (term)—a kind of tyranny of the semantic or the univocal or the proper—but in a syntactic, relational, figurative, or quite literally, equivocal way. I should, perhaps, say that lacking any direct knowledge of Native American languages I am forced in my description of kinship economies to use the process of translation that I am criticizing. Hence, and here I refer my reader back to the discussion of Douglass's *Narrative,* my use of the term *figurative* must remain equivocal, referring at times to a particular communal play of language (though this play is by no means an entirely, or idealized, free play; that is, it has its cultural constraints) and at times to the relative rigidification of that play into the individualized and opposed poles of the *proper,* or *literal,* and the *metaphoric.*

The English world in which *Caliban* entered *The Tempest* as the translation of a translation of a translation was a world where social identity and land ownership were inseparable: the copyholder, or customary tenant, whatever the strength of the lease, had a less secure hold on social place than the freeholder, as the sixteenth-century crisis of enclosures was to prove, setting a significant part of the population to wandering aimlessly, who had once been settled by tenures they felt were secure.[4] It has long been a commonplace in the literature on the West's colonization of the Americas that the idea of a Golden Age, when there had been no *meum* or *tuum* in respect to the land or its fruits, influenced the early settler's perceptions of the place of American Indians in the land. Nostalgia for a mythic past of common land, and anxiety over the increasing privatization of commons to profit from a growing market economy in agriculture and wool, both conflict with and conceal the English project of converting this new land into the alienable places that property constitutes. When these English settlers met the native inhabitants of that place the West had named America, they possessed ideas of place that, though they were finally subsumed under the notion of property, nevertheless, also conflicted with it, even as these Western notions of place ultimately and destructively came into conflict with Native American notions.

I want to begin to articulate a figure of the Western notion of place by turning to a particular context: the conflicting ideas of land held by Puritans and Indians in seventeenth-century New England. As a preamble to this excursion and, indeed, to what follows it in this book, I would do well to quote from Lévi-Strauss's *The Savage Mind:* "[A]ll thought," the thought of all cultures, he reminds us, "is founded on [the] demand for order." As an illustration of this demand Lévi-Strauss cites the translated remarks of a Pawnee, recorded by A. C. Fletcher at the beginning of this century: "All sacred things must have their place," the Pawnee is reported to have said. And Lévi-Strauss elaborates on this "penetrating comment": "It could even be said that being in their place is what makes them sacred for if they were taken out of their place, even in thought, the entire order of the universe would be destroyed."[5] All cultures, Lévi-Strauss suggests, have notions of place. And it should not surprise us if this were true. For whatever the culturally specific ideas of place that must abound in the world, which of us can imagine a culture that does not contain and is not contained by certain ideas of place? Further, he suggests—and this should not surprise us either if it were true—that these notions of place are fundamental to the coherence and incoherence of cultures. It is, of course, then not my purpose in what follows to suggest that only Western thought is dominated or structured by a notion of place. Rather, I am interested in locating certain figures of place in the West that are contained, not always obviously, within the figure of place as alienable land, or property, or conquerable territory that can be claimed (typically through colonies), and then in articulating the impact of these figures, as they come into conflict with the figures of place of native cultures, on the European settlers' frontier experience in what was to become the United States.

"The popular idea that Europeans had private property, while the Indians did not, distorts European notions of property as much as it does Indian ones," William Cronon writes in *Changes in the Land,* his important and problematic study of the influence of European and Indian contact on the ecology of colonial New England. And, Cronon continues,

> The colonists' property systems, like those of the Indians, involved important distinctions between sovereignty and ownership, between possession by communities and possession by individuals. They too dealt in bundles of culturally defined rights that determined what could and could not be done with land and personal property. Even the fixity they assigned to property boundaries, the quality which most distinguished them from Indian land systems, was at first fuzzier and less final than one might expect. They varied considerably depending on the region of England from which a group of colonists came, so that every New England town, like every Indian village, had idiosyncratic property customs of its own.[6]

As I read it, Cronon's purpose in this passage is to complicate any simple, or absolute, opposition between European and Indian conceptions of land use during the period in question (roughly 1620 to 1800, although Cronon focuses more on the seventeenth century). He wants to emphasize regional and local differences within cultures, as well as cultural changes over time, so that the similarities as well as the differences between cultures can be recognized. So, for example, Cronon reads the colonists' land economy in the period as changing from one with a more or less communal emphasis (depending on the region from which the emigrant came in England) to one with a decided property emphasis, as the economy of New England moved into a more market-oriented, or capitalist, phase. And thus he invites us to consider both the ways in which the earliest colonial conceptions of land might translate or be translated into Native American conceptions, as well as the ways in which this translation might be impossible.

But even as Cronon invites us to be sensitive to the fact and problem of translation in the land transactions between the Indians and the English (and to their cultural and historical particularities), his call to such sensitivity, which must be heeded and which he heeds in significant ways, is constituted by a problem of translation. For in the passage under discussion (and this is characteristic of Cronon's entire discussion of land use), it is assumed that the words "property," "sovereignty," "ownership," and "possession" can be used to describe Indian as well as English conceptions of land in seventeenth-century New England, when in fact these are English terms whose relationship to each other within a discourse about the use of land cannot be separated from the legal system of English common law, within which the English idea of land is bounded by such terms. It must be stated here that initially Cronon seems well aware of this problem of translation. He remarks that "we must be careful about what we mean by 'property,'" for "it is actually a . . . complicated social institution which varies widely between cultures." And he adds the crucial comment: "To define property is . . . to represent boundaries between people" (58). Yet, as I want to suggest now, Cronon's use of the term *property* for both the English and Algonquian systems of land use (even with the care he takes to differentiate between them) does not take sufficient account of its cultural specificity. And this leads him to universalize, or naturalize, the term in ways that threaten to erase the boundaries between Indians and Europeans that the term defines.

Within the context of the common law, the terms *ownership* and *possession*—which themselves derive through complex mediations of French feudal law and English custom from the Roman legal concepts of *dominium,* or *proprietas,* and *possessio*—are inseparably linked to each other and to the term *property* through the legal concept of *title. Title,* according to Blackstone's authoritative definition, "is the legal ground of possessing that which is our own; or, it is the means whereby the owner of lands hath the just possession of his property." And:

It is an ancient maxim of the law, that no title is completely good, unless the right of possession be joined with the right of property; which right is then denominated a double right. When to this double right the actual possession is also united, then, and then only, is the title completely legal.

In English common law, title to land is that relation between a person or persons and a piece of real estate which allows the individual or individuals the lawful "translation of [that] property," to use a phrase out of Blackstone that itself translates as the legal term "alienation."[7]

By the middle of the seventeenth-century in England, this "translation of property," typically, we must remember, represented after the thirteenth century in written forms such as the deed and the will, was to all intents and purposes free of feudal entanglements, so that the absolute individualization of land ownership was virtually a fait accompli. Yet, as we know, this process of individualization, in which a "peasant" economy characterized by household rather than individual ownership of land was transformed into a modern free-market economy, had begun much earlier. Alan Macfarlane writes that Marx, for example, "considered that there was a tenurial revolution [in England] centering on the late fifteenth to the end of the sixteenth centuries. No longer was land held by lords and peasants on conditional tenures that prevented them from doing what they wished to do with it. . . . Economic activities were torn away from social life and modern individualistic property law, as it was to be observed in the eighteenth century [in the rest of Western Europe], was gradually developed." Macfarlane tells us: "Almost all our authorities agree that the [English] peasantry had in practice vanished by the late fourteenth century. They all, however, look back to an earlier period when a peasantry really *did* exist. . . ." Rejecting the notion of a "'golden age' of English peasantry" during the thirteenth century and the evolutionary theory of tenurial change offered by Marx, Weber, and Tawney, Macfarlane himself offers a radical theory of the origins of English individualism and of the kinds of land tenure that both grew out of it and constituted it: "What now seems clear is that England back to the thirteenth century was not based on either 'Community' or 'communities.' It appears to have been an open, mobile, market-oriented and highly centralized nation, different not merely in degree but in kind from the peasantries of Eastern Europe and Asia, though only further research will prove whether this was the case." Thus Macfarlane's working hypothesis is that "the majority of ordinary people in England from at least the thirteenth century were rampant individualists, highly mobile both geographically and socially; economically 'rational,' market-oriented and acquisitive, ego-centered in kinship and social life.'' His major argument for this hypothesis is that at least as early as the second half of the thirteenth century, when court rolls commence, land owner-ship was located in the *individual*, not a person's household or the lord of the manor, in the case of both freehold tenures, where individual ownership was upheld de jure, and customary tenancies, where it was allowed de facto.[8]

It is not my purpose here to debate the history of property in England. It is, however, my purpose to suggest that the use of the *English* terms *property, possession,* and *ownership* to refer to the Algonquians' land usages in seventeenth-century New England risks collapsing the cultures and histories of these peoples into the English histories I have been sketching, which was precisely the prime mode of expropriation that the colonists used in their "legal" dealings with the Indians. Since the risk entailed is quite specifically that of ignoring or obscuring the problem of translation, we must remember that the cultures and histories of these peoples are represented by the diverse Algonquian languages we can know so little about, since, as Cronon is aware, we are dependent on European translations and fragmentary transcriptions. I also want to emphasize that the English histories of property that I have just brought into play are themselves represented by diverse languages (Latin and French, for example, cannot be avoided if one is to think about English law) and by diverse English dialects that in the second half of the sixteenth and the beginning of the seventeenth century were becoming marginalized as a national English language was being formed, based on the language spoken at court in London. I will have more to say about this formation in Chapter 5. Let me only note now what I want to stress throughout this book: that the absent voices of history abound, even in the very proliferation of histories now being written in the West intended to articulate or suggest the articulation of these voices.

We need to ask ourselves, then, turning back to Blackstone's definition of "title," what words or phrases or sentences in the Algonquian languages under consideration (absent from Cronon's study and from my own) could translate "the right of possession," "the right of property," and "actual possession," explaining the always potential disjunction between the three phrases, such that the three have to be united *in one person* for a fully legal "title" to exist? In Chapter 1, we read in the

Marshall Court's opinion in *Johnson and Graham's Lessee v. M'Intosh* that, while the Indians "were admitted to be the rightful occupants of the soil, with a legal as well as just claim to retain *possession* of it, the original fundamental principle [of] discovery gave exclusive *title*" (my emphasis) to the colonists. We can read in this decision how in the tradition of English common law, title overrides "legal" possession, how those who appear to possess are dispossessed. We might ask ourselves, then, how the absent Algonquian languages might have translated this paradox of Western legality. And how might these languages translate the pun in Blackstone's definition when he tells us that a "title is the legal *ground* of possessing that which is our own" (my emphasis). The English colonists and the Indians stood, apparently, on the same ground, in the same place. And they didn't. Here is the heart of the conflict. For, *we* might say, this ground, this place, was grounded on different grounds.

And how, we might ask, would these Algonquian languages translate the English term for the ground of ground, *property,* whose legal and linguistic history is inseparable from its history as a key term in Western logic and rhetoric. In Aristotle's *Topics,* a text that for us initiates the crucial discussion of the place of place (the ground of ground) in Western thought, *property* emerges in a division of identity, "what is peculiar to anything" (I.4.19), into "essence" (of which "definition" is the *topos*), and into that "which does not indicate the essence of a thing, but yet belongs to that thing alone, and is predicated convertibly of it" (I.5.17–19). One may speak, Aristotle tells us, of "temporary" or "relative" property (property that only belongs to the subject in an immediate context, or under the circumstances [I.5.26]), but then one is deforming the proper sense of *property,* which deals in the absolute.[9] In a proposition, when the predicate is identical to the subject and to that subject alone, and so is really in the place of the subject, we can say that the predicate is a property of the subject. Property is not essence, which is the very heart of identity in Western metaphysics; yet it is the sign of essence, in the sense that within this system of metaphysics it is only through an elaboration of properties that we can define, or indicate, a perpetually transcendent identity. Paradoxically, property is the language of an always silent essence, its figure in the world. In the metaphysical realm, property is the shadow of substance. But as we translate property across the frontier into the physical realm, it becomes substance itself. And those who own it and who in this system of property must inevitably ground their identities on it become its shadow. In the West's system of things, we are the shadows of property; and if we own nothing, then even this obscure visibility is denied to us.

In the West, property, in that tangled space where the physical and the metaphysical mix, is the very mark of identity, of that which is identical to itself: what we typically call a "self" or an "individual," indicating the absolute boundaries that are predicated of this entity. The *self,* like *property,* has its history, or, rather, histories (and, of course, I am suggesting that the histories of *self* and *property* are inseparable). Jean-Pierre Vernant, for example, locates the emergence of the notion of the individual in fifth-century Athens, where it grew out of a conflict between a rather recent legal notion of responsibility and an ancient idea of divine justice, or fate. In this context, Oedipus's guilt for a crime he unknowingly committed becomes the paradoxical dramatization of this conflict: the paradox of someone guilty and not guilty of a crime, or guilty of it in one historical framework—that of an emergent legal system, of which property is the basis, that can try *individuals*—and not guilty of it in another (or at least guilty of it in a significantly different way), in which the idea of an individual who wills and owns has not been clearly formed. By the time of Aristotle, Vernant suggests, the boundaries of the self had become defined, grounded in an idea of the absolute rather than the relative, of individual identity, we might say, rather than kinship.[10]

In making these remarks about the possible histories of the self and property, I want to be careful to speak not in absolutes but in emphases. I do not want to suggest a linear, or evolutionary history, but a complex of interacting, still open-ended histories in which certain figures at certain times gain more or less articulation. If, for example, something we recognize as a modern self emerges in fifth-century Athens or the property-holding Rome of the Republic, it may seem only a shadow of itself throughout the Middle Ages, only to gain clarity again, albeit in new forms, during the Renaissance. Nevertheless, there are directions. And in every history values are asserted. So, while kinship does not die in the West, while communal forms persist, while, that is, we all recognize our relatives, the question that remains is not whether but how we recognize them. How is this recognition represented in the social rather than the psychological sphere? It seems clear now that by at least the beginning of the sixteenth century in England, and perhaps much earlier, the social recognition of kinship was losing ground rapidly to the recognition of property in the social sphere, and that this recognition of property would proceed apace in the West, coming to take its most extreme forms in that part of North America that would become the United States. Do not mistake me here. I have no nostalgia for—that is, I do not believe in—a pastoral vision of some stable feudal past. Raymond Williams has criticized effectively the kind of historical violence this kind of myth conceals.[11] Nor do I think that we can *simply* translate kinship forms in the West, at whatever stage of development, with kinship forms in the Indian cultures of North America, precisely because these Western forms have developed in relation to hierarchical forms of property, ownership, and possession, and to the hierarchical political forms contained in the term *sovereignty*. That ideas of kinship, of the common holding of land, extend themselves in sixteenth- and seventeenth-century England into more or less radical critiques of property is witnessed both in the "commonwealth literature" of the sixteenth century and the revolutionary communist groups of the seventeenth. Yet to read Native American cultures of the time as no more than idealized figures of these Western political movements is to practice the kind of translation that I oppose in this study. Still, there are no neutral readers. And it is a critique of *place* as *property* that I am pursuing. Let me place myself for the moment in a section of Lévi-Strauss's *Tristes Tropiques*, translated by John and Doreen Weightman:

> Other societies are perhaps no better than our own; even if we are inclined to believe they are, we have no method at our disposal for proving it. However, by getting to know them better, we are enabled to detach ourselves from our own society. Not that our own society is peculiarly or absolutely bad. But it is the only one from which we have a duty to free ourselves: we are, by definition, free in relation to the others. We thus put ourselves in a position to embark on the second stage, which consists in *using* all societies—without adopting features from any one of them—to elucidate principles of social life that we can apply in reforming our own customs and *not those of foreign societies:* through the operation of a prerogative which is the reverse of the one just mentioned, the society we belong to is the only society we are in a position to transform without any risk of destroying it, since the changes, being introduced by us, are coming from within the society itself.[12]

The issue of getting to know other societies better is deeply problematic, dependent as it is on the problems of translation that I am trying to make excruciating. And the issue of "using" other societies to reform our own, even if in this process we somehow never use them, bothers me. But that is probably because "use" in this context is the honest word. Even if we were to disavow the attempt to make other societies into our property, vowing only to get to know them better in order to reform the institution of property in our own, we would remember, as Lévi-Strauss does, that the history of this knowledge, the history of anthropology, cannot be separated from the history of the West's appropriation of these societies.

Thinking of the possible histories of *property* in the West, then, let us return to the question of how the seventeenth-century Algonquian cultures might translate an English term that at the time combined within it the complex relations between individuality and title to land that had been developing in the West for centuries. Wolf, as noted, gives us a useful vocabulary with which to pursue this question, one that scrupulously tries to avoid the typical and univocal Western notion of cultures developing from the "savage" to the "civilized," or the "simple" to the "complex" (figures for a classic opposition by which the West has traditionally justified its destruction of certain other cultures in the name of "progress").[13]

Following Wolf (and his vocabulary is the best I have found, though no terminology is going to be rinsed of its ethnocentrism), we can discuss cultures in terms of "three modes" of production: the "kin-ordered" mode (of which North American Indian cultures are the ones that will interest us), the "tributary" mode (of which Western feudalism is a prime example), and the "capitalist" mode, which was emerging or had emerged from the tributary mode, depending on one's point of view, in sixteenth- and seventeenth-century England. These modes, Wolf cautions, are "neither types into which human societies may be sorted nor stages in cultural evolution." Rather, "They are . . . constructs with which to envisage certain strategic relationships that shape the terms under which human lives are conducted," or "instruments for thinking about the crucial connections built up among the expanding Europeans and the other inhabitants of the globe, so that we may grasp the consequences of these connections" (100).

Kinship, clearly, functions in all three of Wolf's modes of production; "appeals to filiation and marriage, and to consanguinity and affinity" (91) operate in the tributary and capitalist modes, as well as in the kin-ordered. Yet the crucial difference between the former two modes and the latter is that in the kin-ordered mode kinship in its extended forms is the very ground of society, of society's juridical, political, and economic relations, as well as of its more intimate institutional arrangements (92–93). In the tributary mode of production, the terms *lord* and *tenant,* for example, define the central complex of juridical, political, and economic relations, and in the capitalist mode the terms *capital,* or *owner,* and *labor,* or *worker,* define them, whereas in the kin-ordered mode family terms articulate these relations. But we would do well to remember that although we may translate these family terms into such Western equivalents as *father, mother, brother, sister,* the translation is not a sign of any simple equivalency. For the terms themselves are given meaning by the various modes of production in which these terms are part of a complex syntax. In discussing the Iroquois's treaty-making with the Dutch, French, and English, Francis Jennings gives us some striking examples of the translation problems that occurred in the case of family terminology:

> Metaphorical terms of address were used by Indians [in treaties] to distinguish relationships of parity or subordination. *Grandfather* expressed ceremonial deference but no obligation to obey; it was used by Algonquians and Iroquoians alike in referring to the Delawares and appears in some records as addressed by mixed tribesmen to the Hurons, but no one called the masterful Iroquois grandfathers. *Father* is a more difficult word. Among the Iroquois, fathers had no power to command children, but among Europeans they did. The Iroquois quickly came to understand this difference. Colden tells of an incident when a suspicious governor of New York reproached the Iroquois with their formal behavior when treating with New France's governor. "How came you to call him Father? For no other Reason, they replied, but because he calls us Children. These names signify nothing." In fact, however, the names signified much. The real reason behind the *father* image in New France was that French governors would not treat at all without it. The Iroquois refused the same term of address to English governors. They understood the statuses implied to Europeans in father-children terminology, and they knew that the English needed their alliance too badly to force the issue.[14]

In contrast to the tributary and capitalist modes of production, the kin-ordered mode is *relatively* nonhierarchical, or egalitarian, and decentralized. Thus, while what we term "hierarchies," or "oppositions," such as, for example, ranks according to gender and age, appear to exist in kin-ordered societies, these "oppositions as they are normally played out are particulate, the conjunction of a particular elder with a particular junior of a particular lineage at a particular time and place, and not the general opposition of elder and junior as classes" (95). Further, "[t]he kin-ordered mode inhibits the institutionalization of political power, resting essentially on the management of consensus among clusters of partici-pants," who are geared to flexibly concentrate or disperse their labor "when changing conditions require a rearrangement of commitments. At the same time, the extension and retraction of kin ties create open and shifting boundaries of such societies" (99).

> In contrast to the kin-ordered mode, both the tributary and the capitalist modes divide the population under their command into a class of surplus producers and a class of surplus takers. Both require mechanisms of domination to ensure that surpluses are transferred on a predictable basis from one class to the other. Such domination may involve, at one time or another, a wide panoply of sanctions based on fear, hope, and charity; but it cannot be secured without the development of an apparatus of coercion to maintain the basic division into classes and to defend the resulting structure against external attack. Both the tributary and the capitalist modes, therefore, are marked by the development and installation of such an apparatus, namely the state. (99)

In contrast to tributary and capitalist societies, kin-ordered societies possess relatively "open and shifting boundaries" (a point that Cronon makes as well) in the juridical, political, and economic realms. And, although Wolf does not explicitly discuss the relation of his modes of production to land use, I want to emphasize that the more flexible boundaries of kin-ordered societies are grounded in a relation to the land (as place) that is opposed to that contained in the term *property,* which is grounded in a notion not of shifting and open boundaries, but of fixed and closed ones, both of the self and physical property. Thus when Wolf tells us that in kin-ordered societies "social labor is 'locked up,' or 'embed-ded,' in particular relations between people" (91), it is the notion of "between" here that for me stresses the horizontal, or reciprocal, form, or figure, of this labor, which claims a title neither to itself nor to the land it works. Commenting on the kin-ordered Bororo Indians of South America, Lévi-Strauss notes that "for them, a man is not an individual, but a person. He is part of a sociological universe" (*Tristes Tropiques,* 234). The same comment could be made of all kin-ordered societies. That is, we can imagine the members of these societies thinking of themselves predominantly in terms of reciprocal *relations* rather than as opposed *entities,* existing prior to or outside of any set of relations, whether these entities are conceived of as classes or as mobile individuals or as both at once. Following Lévi-Strauss, we might say that kin-ordered societies, in contrast to tributary and capitalist ones, do not naturalize, or absolutize, cultural places. And in Western thought, it is the figure of property that performs this naturalizing function. Locke's *The Second Treatise of Government* is exemplary here. For, as Locke figures it, property in the produce of the earth and in the earth itself precedes social life. And this property is founded on the primal fact that to begin with "every man has a property in his own person" (5.27), which, when invested through labor in the originally "common" things of the earth and the earth itself, converts the common to the proper. In the beginning, if we follow Locke, the earth was populated with *individuals,* an individual being someone who is "proprietor of his own person" and has "in himself the great foundation of property" (5.44). And these individuals were created by "one omnipotent and infinitely wise Maker . . . they are his property whose workmanship they are" (2.6). As Cronon's seventeenth-century Puritans were meeting his seventeenth-century Algonquians, the Puritan's God, we might say, was becoming truly American (as opposed to Native American): the ultimate individual, the infinite proprietor. And the Bible was undergoing an implicit translation: in the beginning was property.[15]

For Locke, who summarizes the history of Western thought on the subject, the very mark of property is the enclosure: the defining, or bounding, of a place that signals the *perceived* settling, or cultivation, of that place. In both these writers it is this figure of enclosure that marks the frontier between the savage and the civilized; for, in Locke's words, "the wild Indian . . . knows no enclosure and is still a tenant in common" (5.26) (although, ironically enough, this same Indian, in Locke's scheme of things, would have a property in himself and thus be as psychologically or metaphysically enclosed as the enclosed and enclosing Europeans). Cronon records some remarks of John Winthrop, the first governor of the Massachusetts Bay Colony, that also articulate this frontier of enclosure: "As for the Natives in New England," he wrote, "they inclose noe Land, neither have any setled habytation, nor any tame Cattle to improve the land by, and soe have noe other but a Naturall Right to those Countries," a right, as Cronon points out, "superseded" by what the colonists *recognized* as the civil rights of cultivation (56).

As we know, the southern New England Indians were cultivators.

And, as Cronon attests, the colonists were aware of this. Yet looking at this "savage" cultivation, facing what for them was a contradiction in terms, they could continue to deny what they affirmed. In May of 1607, for example, on their first trip up the James river from the newly settled Fort James, a group of colonists arrived at Powhatan's village. In the account of this journey attributed to Gabriel Archer, the narrator remarks of the village that "it is scituat vpon a highe hill by the water syde, a playne betweene it and the water . . . whereon he sowes his wheate, beane, peaze, tobacco, pompions, gowrdes, Hempe, flaxe &c. And were any Art vsed to the naturall state of this place, it would be a goodly habitatyon . . ." (Barbour, 1, 85). Cultivation, the sign of the civil as opposed to the natural, is at once perceived and denied; Powhatan "sowes," and yet the "place" remains unimproved by "any Art."

We can agree with Cronon that statements like Winthrop's and Archer's are "little more than an ideology of conquest conveniently available to justify the occupation of another people's lands" (57). Yet we must also note that ideologies are not consciously constructed at a moment's notice, but are the deep places cultures are founded on through the complex production, projection, and reading of signs. And the sign that the English colonists did not find in the Native American landscape, the sign that for them was (and for us is) the very sign of cultivation, the sign of the civil, the sign of place (as property), the sign, that is, of enclosure, was the fence, "which to colonists," Cronon tells us, "represented perhaps the most visible symbol of an 'improved' landscape" (130). The English colonists had come from a place where fences were absolutely crucial both in defining one *individual's* property vis-à-vis another's and in defining the internal economic and ecological functions of a piece of property (dividing arable land from pasture, for example [Cronon, 137]). They confronted a place that they would rapidly and violently *re-mark* with the fence (for this place, although unfenced, was certainly marked in places by the native inhabitants): a place or, rather, places that seemed to those colonists, even as they noticed its cultivation, a no-place, both in the sense of that golden age of commons that Thomas More had evoked in his *Utopia,* and in the sense of a wilderness that needed the improvements that a system of fences would signal.

Cronon's study of New England land use during the colonial period forcefully articulates for us the importance of the fence in defining the sense of the frontier between the colonists and the native inhabitants. I diverge from Cronon when, having distinguished between Europeans' and Indians' relation to the land, he continues to apply the term *property* on both sides of the fence, threatening to enclose the Indians in the very "legal" terminology that the colonists eventually enclosed them in through the compulsion of the treaty and land sale. Commenting on such early "sales," Cronon shows us why the application of the term *property* to the places of the Indians will not do:

> Because Indians, at least in the beginning, thought they were selling one thing and the English thought they were buying another, it was possible for an Indian village to convey what it regarded as identical and nonexclusive usufruct rights to several different English purchasers. Alternatively, several different Indian groups might sell to English ones rights to the same tract of land. Uniqueness of title as the English understood it became impossible under such circumstances, so colonies very early tried to regulate the purchase of Indian lands. (70)

We can only talk about the *sale* of *property* in such cases, if, like the deeds themselves, we talk about these cases exclusively in English terms. For from the Indians' perspective there was in the first place no place to *translate* (to use the legal terminology from Blackstone). That is, the land that the Indians negotiated to share with the English was in Algonquian, or kin-ordered, terms not alienable in individualized places that could be traded in a market economy. The Indians' land, then, was unfenced, which is not to say that it wasn't marked or bounded, that is, placed, but only to say that from the contemporary Western perspective of Wolf and Cronon these boundaries were "open" and "shifting," and from the perspective of the English colonists they were virtually invisible or untranslatable. So, for example, Cronon notes that "the great bulk" of Algonquian place names "related not to possession but to use," whereas the English "most freqently created arbitrary place-names which either recalled localities in their homeland or gave a place the name of its owner" (65, 66). The problem here, it seems to me, is not the translation of the reasonable into the "arbitrary" (or vice versa); the notion that English ideas of place were arbitrary or "abstract" (another term Cronon uses) in contrast to Indian conceptions risks placing the Indians back in the natural world as noble savages (all naming is arbitrary or abstract, that is, cultural, when one thinks of it in terms of some unmediated natural realm). Rather, the problem is how does one translate ideas of place grounded in conceptions of communal or social labor into ideas of place grounded in the notion of *identity?* The problem is not, as Cronon suggests, how does one translate radically different systems of *property* into one another. But can one translate the idea of place as *property* into an idea of place the terms of which the West has never granted legitimacy?

4

Translation, Transportation, Usurpation

THE EUROPEAN PROCESS of translation I am describing displaced or attempted to displace (for there was and still is enduring resistance) Native Americans into the realm of the proper, into that place where the relation between *property* and *identity* is inviolable, not so these Americans could possess the proper but so that having been translated into it they could be dispossessed of it (of what, that is, they never possessed) and relegated to the territory of the figurative. *A Good Speed to Virginia* (1609), a representative propaganda pamphlet of the time of *The Tempest*, focuses one form of this displacement for us: "Savages have no particular propertie in any part or parcell of that countrey, but only a generall residencie there, as wild beasts have in the forests."[1] Not to have "propertie," then, is to lose, from a European perspective, a significant part of one's humanness. No other *legitimate* mode of relation to the land—no other mode of identity—is imagined in the preceding passage. A complementary if apparently opposed form of this process of translation into property is articulated in the propaganda pamphlet *A True Declaration of the Estate of the Colonie in Virginia* (1610), which we have considered and which we will have occasion to return to in considering its relation to *The Tempest*. In arguing the legal grounds for colonization, the pamphlet declares that such grounds obtain "chiefly because *Paspehay*, one of their [the Algonquian-speaking Indians] Kings, sold vnto vs for copper, land to inherit and inhabite. *Powhatan*, their chiefe King, received voluntarilie a crown and a sceptre, with a full acknowledgment of dutie and submission." In the first instance the English translate Paspehay into English property relations (and into English political relations as well, with his nomination as a

59

"king," a typical English translation of the Algonquian *weroance*) so that the English can recognize him as having "sold" "his" land to the English, who following the "legal" logic of their language can thus claim "title" to this land. The English convert the land that Paspehay and his people use and that nobody "owns" (at least not in Algonquian languages) into Paspehay's "property" so that the English can alienate the land from these people (in words only, at the moment of *A True Declaration,* but only because the English did not yet possess the force to translate the words of the pamphlet into deeds). From that point in history, until, in the twentieth century, the Indians themselves had recourse to lawyers and courts, the translation of the Indians into property relations and their exclusion from them are identical or complementary moves in a Western strategy of dispossession.

In the second instance, Powhatan, whom the English, with their own dream of empire exerting terrific force, typically nominated "Emperor" of the Algonquians inhabiting the Jamestown area, was translated into English political terms, where he becomes a power subject to the English crown. This, as Alden Vaughan notes, "would not give the English title to *his* lands [my emphasis; note that Vaughan himself assumes Powhatan's property in the land], but it would justify action in the King's name when disputes over boundaries, treaties, trade, or jurisprudence occurred" (43), thus effectively circumscribing the Indians within the English civil code, which was grounded on the idea of land as property. The coronation ceremony that the *True Declaration* adduces in its argument for the legitimacy of colonization took place, as we have read, in the fall of 1608 at Powhatan's village of Werowocomoco. Captain Christopher Newport officiated at the ceremony. In his *A Map of Virginia* (1612), in a passage that we have read in part, Captain John Smith, who at the time was president of the council at Jamestown, leaves us a kind of slapstick account of the coronation in which the Virginia Company's claim that Powhatan "received voluntarilie a crown" is contradicted:

> All things being fit for the day of his coronation, the presents were brought. . . . But a fowle trouble there was to make him kneele to receaue his crowne, he neither knowing the maiestie, nor meaning of a Crowne, nor bending of the knee, indured so many perswasions, examples, and instructions, as tired them all. At last by leaning hard on his shoulders, he a little stooped, and Newport put the Crowne on his head. (Barbour, 2, 414)

Smith's description of Newport forcibly placing a crown on Powhatan's head is an apt figure for the translation process I have been describing. It is the process of translation that places *Caliban* in *The Tempest,* dispossessing the term of its proper identity, or rather dispossessing the term of its cultural relations by translating it into the realm of property and identity. And it is this process that historicizes the play. For, as we have just read, the name could not have appeared in any text before Columbus's contact with the Arawaks in 1492–1493. More importantly, the name's appearance marks *The Tempest* as an utterance in the colonial/imperial process of translation that I am describing and that, I will argue, the play itself describes. Upon seeing Caliban for the first time, Trinculo, whom along with Stephano, Caliban will lead in an abortive rebellion to dispossess Prospero of his "crown," immediately thinks of transporting the "savage" back to Europe, where if "they will not give a doit to relieve a lame beggar, they will lay out ten to see a dead Indian" (II.ii.32–34); the jester reminds us that *The Tempest* itself, playing before the court of James I, which was economically and politically invested in the Virginia experiment, was one way of transporting Indians back to a Europe that was eager to see signs that its investments had a ground.

But before describing a particular historical process *in* the play, I want to rehearse some moves in the traditional historicizing of *The Tempest* (moves that have long connected the play through the "Bermuda pamphlets" to the founding of Jamestown). For while these moves have provided us with material that is crucial to understanding the colonial/imperial context of the play, scholars, until very recently, have considered this material in ways that have left it external to the form and meaning of *The Tempest,* so that its historicizing force has been neutralized, because the play is typically read as transcending its immediate historical context. This traditional historicizing of the play, exemplified particularly well by the influential readings of Frank Kermode and Leo Marx, and most recently by Stephen Orgel's introductory essay to the Oxford edition of *The Tempest,* takes into account the colonial context of the play, and then renders this context effectively superfluous by translating the play out of it, that is, by reading *Caliban* not as a name produced by a colonial history of translation, but as a pure figure of the European imagination (of "nature," for example, or the "unconscious," or "savagery" as expressed in the figure of the "wild man"). These readers read *Caliban* in the way that Columbus translated that unknown Arawak term into *caníbal*. Kermode, for example, in his introduction to the Arden edition of *The Tempest* (published in 1954 and last reprinted in 1983 without a change in the following information), tells us that "Caliban's name is usually regarded as a development of some form of the word 'Carib,' meaning a savage inhabitant of the New World" (xxxviii). Because cultural perspective is not a problem for Kermode, the crucial question of the construction of this meaning is not raised here. Kermode reads the play entirely within the confines of Western culture to the point, as we can see in his translation of *Caliban*, that Western meaning becomes all meaning. In a gesture that is homologous with Kermode's reading of the play, Marx asserts that *The Tempest* "is not in any literal sense about America" (34). Thus, it follows inescapably that Marx, like Kermode, will read *Caliban* not as a proper name inscribed within a violent history of translation, a history of crowning Powhatans, but as a pure figure that names those "dark, hostile forces exhibited by the storm [and emblematic of 'instinct']. . . . the repression of [which is] necessary to the felicity Prospero and Miranda enjoy" (54). Perhaps we can understand at this point that the implicit model of interpretation that Marx and Kermode employ is the same model that governs the overseer's reading of the slave in Douglass's *Narrative:* a model in which the figurative and the literal are cut off from one another—denied, that is, their dialogic relation of translation. My purpose is to restore this relation and, in restoring the dialogic relation of translation between what we conventionally refer to as text and context, or the figurative and the literal/proper, to insist on the political, that is, the ethnohistorical, character of this relation in the West and in the West's relations with the peoples it has invaded during its colonial expansion. Whether or how translations of this relation obtain in cultures outside of the West, while ultimately crucial to the work I am doing, is not my immediate concern here, though I will have occasion to speculate upon it when I discuss Montaigne in the last chapter.

Since Edmond Malone first called attention in 1808 to the relation between *The Tempest* and the Jamestown colony,[2] the historicizing of the play in relation to the colony has proceeded apace, until today there is a scholarly consensus on the links of Shakespeare's text to Jamestown, links which depend on the wreck of the *Sea Venture* in the Bermudas on July 28, 1609.

The *Sea Venture* was the flagship in a fleet of nine vessels, transporting about five hundred colonists, that were on their way from Plymouth,

England, to resupply the colonists at Jamestown for the third time. The two-year-old colony was foundering because of internal political dissension and conflicts with the Indians, on whom the colonists, ignorant of the new environment, depended for basic material survival. Among the one hundred and fifty passengers on the flagship were Christopher Newport, who commanded the *Sea Venture* and had been, until that voyage, in charge of the colony's maritime operations; Sir George Somers, Newport's replacement as admiral of the Jamestown fleet; and Sir Thomas Gates, newly appointed interim governor of the colony, pending the arrival of the governor general, Lord De La Warr. Gates carried with him a new charter for the colony, shifting it from "direct royal control . . . to [the] private control [of a corporation], under a royal charter" (Barbour, 2, 249), and a set of instructions from the colony's governing council in London. The instructions, which were intended to give Gates firm direction in dealing with the internal and external political problems of the colony, ordered him to take "full authority" (Barbour, 2, 264) in the governance of Jamestown. (The system of a local council that elected a president as its head had proved too divisive.) As for relations with the Indians, the London council ordered Gates to form alliances with Indian peoples distant from Jamestown and hostile to Powhatan, on whom the settlers were extremely dependent because of his hold on the balance of power in the area, and whose own political goals did not guarantee the English an unambiguous welcome. (The specifics of these proposed alliances appear, at points, terribly blurred because problems of translation lead to both a skewed geography and the transcription of some Indian names that seem to have no referents.) In addition to the proposed alliances, the instructions from the council, as we read in Chapter 1, ordered Gates to institute a plan, using force if necessary, to educate the children of *weroances* (Indian leaders) "in your language, and manners"; for "if you intreate well and educate those which are younge and to succeede in the government in your Manners and Religion, their people will easily obey you and become in time Civill and Christian." A design of translation is advanced here: the Indians will become English by first of all learning to speak English. That the English men fabricating this design saw no contradiction between treating the Indians well and "seis[ing them] into . . . custody" in order to educate them should they flee the English (or in imprisoning or killing their "priests," if they impeded this education) is an example of the need for violence being simultaneously acknowledged and ignored (rationalized) in the process of colonization. Ironically, this new policy of translation was meant to be a humane replacement for Captain John Smith's policy, which was based on the *display* of force as a negotiating tool. (And yet in the 1609 instructions Smith was named a member of Gates's advisory council and was to be retained in case certain military dealings with the Indians became necessary [Barbour, 2, 266]. His return to England in the fall of 1609 preempted his participation in the governance of the colony.) I emphasize "display" because we should be clear that these English strategies for winning the Indians over or winning *over* the Indians are rhetorical, not technological or, rather, that the rhetorical and the technological are inseparable here. Lurie has argued that the colonists' "argument of technological superiority at that time was a weak one; despite guns and large ships the Europeans could not wrest a living from a terrain which, by Indian standards, supported an exceptionally large population" (39). And comparing the bow and arrow to the gun, Kupperman, extending Lurie's comments on technology, suggests that while "[i]t is undeniable that the Indians were impressed by the colonists' guns and wanted them for themselves," the bow and arrow, in the early phase of colonization, was a more effective weapon than the gun "in frontier warfare" (102). These speculations are strengthened when we consider, for example, the *Instructions Given by Way of Advice* from the Virginia Company's London Council to the first settlers in the winter of 1606, before their voyage. In this document, we find, among other directives, the following:

> And whomsoever any of Yours Shoots before them [the Indians] be sure that they be Chosen out of your best Markesmen for if they See Your Learners miss what they aim at they will think the Weapon not so terrible and thereby will be bould . . . to Assailt You. Above all things Do not advertise the killing of any of your men that the Country people may know it if they Perceive they are but Common men and that with the loss of many of theirs they may Deminish any part of Yours they will make many Adventures upon You if the country be Popalous. . . . (Barbour, 1, 52)

The English, it appears from the preceding passage, felt it necessary to advertise or display their guns for maximum technological efficiency, and to try to make themselves appear to be not the "Common men" they were, but invulnerable. I am reminded here of Cooper's *The Last of the Mohicans*, when Leatherstocking speaks of a gun fight he and a group of Hurons had as a "conversation."[3] Let us say that what we have in the present case is not a conversation between guns (for the Indians do not as yet possess this method of speech), but an English oration, in which the gun is a prime piece of eloquence, pronounced to persuade the Indians, and the English themselves, no doubt, of English power. In this context, the momentary force of Captain John Smith is as much a matter of oratorical, or dramaturgical skills, as it is of military strategy. Or, rather, in this context, military and oratorical skills are inseparable. The success of his "eloquence," we should remember, depended entirely on his audience's, that is, Powhatan's, perception that the English could be of use to him in his own political maneuverings with neighboring tribes. And so in these early moments of contact, Algonquians and English struggled to translate each other, barely knowing a word of each other's language.

On July 24, 1609, a tempest, or hurricane,[4] struck Gates's fleet. One vessel sank with all hands; seven reached Jamestown. The *Sea Venture* went aground on the coast of the Bermudas, but all of its passengers got ashore safely, salvaging needed stores, and discovering the Bermudas to be not the storied "devils' islands" but a fruitful place to live. After a nine-month stay on the islands, the peace of which was interrupted briefly by the staging of three abortive rebellions, the company, aboard two vessels the members had constructed, sailed for Jamestown. They arrived there, after a two-week voyage, on May 23, 1610. What they discovered was a disaster. Of the five hundred colonists that had been at Jamestown in October 1609, when John Smith, deposed as president by political intrigue, returned to England for good, sixty remained. Most of the others had died of disease and starvation as a result of their alienating the Indians, on whose technology they were so dependent. The rest the Indians killed. We have, of course, only English accounts from which to infer the reasons for this violence. Faced with what appeared to be the unsalvageable wreckage of Jamestown, where political and physical turmoil prevailed, Gates, with his people and the remaining settlers, prepared to abandon the colony and return to England on June 7, 1610. But just as the *Sea Venture* had been saved by what appeared to the English as providential circumstances, so the wreck of Jamestown was salvaged by the arrival of Lord De La Warr, which coincided, providentially enough (from the English point of view), with the moment of Gates's departure. De La Warr, bringing with him three hundred colonists and enough stores for a year (although he brought virtually no meat), stayed Gates's departure and took over control of the colony.

These events—the wreck of the *Sea Venture,* the sojourn of its company on the Bermudas, the return of the castaways to Virginia, and the state of the colony there—provoked a flurry of narratives in the months following De La Warr's assumption of authority in the colony. We now accept that Shakespeare read three of them: a letter, sent from Virginia to a noblewoman in England in July of 1610 (but not published until 1625), written by William Strachey, a passenger on the *Sea Venture* and secretary to the council in Virginia under De La Warr; the pamphlet *A True Declaration of the Estate of the Colonie in Virginia,* published in November of 1610 under order of the Council of Virginia; and the first published work on the wreck and its aftermath, *A Discovery of the Bermudas,* published in October of 1610 and written by Sylvester Jourdain, who, like Strachey, had also been a passenger on the *Sea Venture.*[5] Unlike Jourdain's account, which, omitting the strife both on the Bermudas and in Virginia, presents a brief, harmonious tale of salvation on the surprisingly pleasant isles and a safe return to the colony, Strachey's letter and *A True Declaration* (which appears in part to be taken from Strachey's letter) relate narratives of conflict. Of the three documents, Strachey's letter gives the only account of the rebellions on the Bermudas, praising Gates highly for his restoration of civil order: "In these dangers and devilish disquiets . . . , thus enraged amongst ourselves to the destruction each of other, what a mischief and a misery had we been given up had we not had a governor with his authority to have suppressed the same?" (45–46) But the letter was not published until 1625, perhaps because it portrays the Virginia colony, even after De La Warr's arrival, in open-ended conflict with Powhatan, who does not seem as susceptible to English authority as the Bermuda rebels. On the other hand, because its purpose is clearly propagandistic, *A True Declaration,* while describing the conflicts with the Indians and within Jamestown (including a case of alleged cannibalism, in which a settler was accused and convicted of murdering and eating his wife), portrays the resolution of the colony's civil and foreign conflicts by De La Warr's administration: "This Oration and direction [of the lord governor] being received with a generall applause, you might shortly behold the idle and restie diseases of a divided multitude, by the vnity and authority of this gouernment, to be substantially cured. . . . [and] Our forces are now such as are able to tame the fury and treachery of the Sauages: our Forts assure the Inhabitants, and frustrate all assailants" (20).

Since Malone, but particularly beginning with the work of Morton

Luce at the beginning of this century,[6] scholars have noted verbal parallels between the texts and *The Tempest*. Thematic parallels, particularly with Strachey's letter and *A True Declaration,* are quite conspicuous and have been noted but not pursued to any significant degree. The theme of rebellion, by "savages," commoners, and nobility, and the restoration of order in a colonial outpost governed by a figure of imperial force, is a motif that Shakespeare would have found in both the Strachey and *A True Declaration.* Prospero has been identified with Sir Thomas Gates. In De La Warr, whose oration had the power to restore civil order after what *A True Declaration* calls "the tempest of dissension" (15) in Virginia, Shakespeare might have found a possible figure for the eloquent governor of his island, as he might have in John Smith, whose *True Relation* he also read.

There are, certainly, other thematic parallels between *The Tempest* and the narratives that we could develop. When Prospero, for example, expresses his angry despair at Caliban's rebellion by referring to the island's first inhabitant as a "devil, a born devil on whose nature / Nurture can never stick; on whom my pains, / Humanely taken, all, all lost, quite lost" and vows to "plague" the rebels "[e]ven to roaring," his words echo the complaint and threat of Sir Thomas Gates upon seeing one of his men, sent to retrieve a boat that had drifted away from Algernon Fort, murdered by Indians. Strachey recorded Gates's sentiments in his letter:

> It did not a little trouble the lieutenant governor, who since his first landing in the country (how justly soever provoked) would not by any means be wrought to a violent proceeding against them [the Indians] for all the practices of villainy with which they daily endangered our men, thinking it possible by a more tractable course to win them to a better condition. But now, being startled by this, he well perceived how little a fair and noble entreaty works upon a barbarous disposition and therefore in some measure purposed to be revenged. (88–89)

The whole hope and failure of Prospero's "civilizing" mission to Caliban is condensed in the preceding passage. And in a *True Declaration* the reference to the Indians as "humane beasts" (6) suggest the ambiguity that surrounds the identity of the "monster" Caliban.

Or, seeking another parallel between narratives and play, we could turn to the opening of Act II where the ideologically opposed pairs of Gonzolo and Adrian and Antonio and Sebastian, standing, apparently, on the same ground of the island, describe it as if it were two islands, which they figure as two stereotypes of women, the nurturing and the deceiving, the fertile (sexually open) and the barren (sexually scheming), the natural, sweet-smelling mother and the whore, stinking with the disguise of cosmetics:

> ADR. Though this island seem to be desert—
>
> . . . .
>
> It must needs be of subtle, tender and delicate temperance.
> ANT. Temperance was a delicate wench.
> SEB. Ay, and a subtle; as he most learnedly deliver'd.
> ADR. The air breathes upon us here most sweetly.
> SEB. As if it had lungs, and rotten ones.
> ANT. Or as 'twere perfum'd by a fen.
> GON. Here is everything advantageous to life.
> ANT. True; save means to live.
> SEB. Of that there's none, or little.
> GON. How lush and lusty the grass looks! how green!
> ANT. The ground, indeed, is tawny.
>
> (II.i.34–52)

Shakespeare might well have found the figurative basis for the preceding colloquy of contradictions in a rhetorical question from *A True Declaration* concerning the unwholesome climate of Jamestown: "How is it possible that such a virgin and temperat aire, should work such contrarie effects, but because our fort (that lyeth as a semy-Iland) is most part inuironed with an ebbing and flowing salt water, the owze of which sendeth forth an vnhwolsome & contagious vapour?" (14) And he might well have found the thematic basis for his colloquy in a passage, directly following the one just cited, which acknowledges the conflicting testimony about the estate of the colony in Virginia:

> If any man shall accuse these reports of partiall falshood, supposing them to be but Vtopian, and legendarie fables, because he cannot conceive, that plentie and famine, a temperate climate, and distempered bodies, felicities, and miseries can be reconciled together, let him now reade with judgment, but let him not judge before he hath read. (14)

Both the passage from the play and that from the pamphlet represent one land that is two, hostile and nurturing at the same moment. And both the literary work and the work of propaganda propose solutions to this apparent paradox that are quite similar.

In the scene preceding the conflictive colloquy, Shakespeare has had

Caliban inform the audience in passing, through a conversation with Prospero (which is essentially a history lesson of the latter's dispossession of the former) that as far as the environment of the island goes it is not a case of either/or but of both/and; that is, the island is composed of "fresh springs, brine-pits, barren place *and* fertile" (I.ii.340; my emphasis). Thus, when we arrive at the opposing descriptions of the place in the verbal duel of Gonzalo/Adrian with Antonio/Sebastian, we should be attuned to the rhetorical, or ideological, grounds of these descriptions, their very partial perspectives. For Adrian/Gonzalo's perception of the land as essentially nurturing is a figure of Gonzalo's nurturing relationship to Alonso in the scene (or his attempt at such a relationship, which Alonso rebuffs). When the scene opens and as it progresses, we find Gonzalo trying to find a ground for or buoy up the hope of Alonzo, who is drowning in the despair of the double loss of his son Ferdinand, whom he believes has drowned, and his daughter Claribel, whose marriage to the King of Tunis he is now regretting. Gonzalo's attempts to nurture Alonso's hope recalls the crucial nurturing role that Prospero assigns the "noble Neapolitan," when in his long recounting of their past to his daughter, Miranda, the rightful Duke of Milan tells his child, "Some food we had, and some fresh water," which Gonzalo, "Out of his charity, who being then appointed / Master of this design [of setting father and child adrift] did give us, with / Rich garments, linens, stuffs and necessaries, / Which since have steadied much; so, of his gentleness, / Knowing I lov'd my books, he furnish'd me / From mine own library with volumes that / I prize above my dukedom" (I.ii.160–68). Gonzalo, then, nurtures Prospero and Miranda not only by providing what is necessary to sustain life but also what is necessary to sustain their noble identity: rich garments, prime symbols of rank, and books, which, even as Prospero opposes them to temporal power in the passage just cited (prizing them above his dukedom), he is using to regain that temporal power. (He has told Miranda in a previous part of the speech that it was his retirement to study and his ceding of administrative power to Antonio that led to his usurpation.) Life itself and noble identity become equated through the word *necessary* (we are reminded of Lear's famous speech, "O, reason not the need! . . ." [II.iv.259–281]). Thus Gonzalo's nurturance becomes equated with upholding constituted authority, though not without some irony. For Gonzalo is both the master of the plan to destroy Prospero and his savior. He is also both Alonso's follower and his opponent, a conflict that appears reconciled through the betrothal of Ferdinand and Miranda, for it is their projected marriage that promises to unite Milan and Naples.

In contrast to Gonzalo's optimism, Antonio and Sebastian's pessimistic view of the island is equated with the subversion of authority. The scene ends with their plotting Alonso's assassination, and, leading up to that plot, which is thwarted by an omnipresent Prospero/Ariel, they goad Alonso to despair, presenting him first with a dismal view of the island and then encouraging him to blame himself for the loss of his children (a guilt that he has just assumed of his own accord): "Sir," Sebastian tells him, "you may thank yourself for this great loss, / That would not bless our Europe with your daughter, / But rather loose her to an African" (II.i.119–21). In this malign reasoning it follows that if Alonso had not sailed to Tunis to marry his daughter to an alien (not nearly as alien as Caliban but not European) there would have been no shipwreck to drown (apparently) Ferdinand.

A True Declaration uses the same rhetorical strategy that the debate between Gonzalo and Antonio/Sebastian figures. The pessimistic view of the Virginia colony is equated with political subversion, with that "tempest of dissension" that undermined the traditional political hierarchy and, it is strongly implied, threatened to subvert class structure at Jamestown. Thus unregulated, so the story goes, the settlers could not organize themselves to appreciate the virtues of the virgin land. The optimistic view of the colony on the other hand is equated with political order, with the arrival of Gates and De La Warr and the institution of "an absolute and powerfull gouernment" (18) that allows for the effective exploitation of Virginia.

In the last paragraph of his letter, Strachey figures Virginia as a fallen woman whose honor, he hopes, has been restored by the new regime; "bungerly" though he is, he has "presumed . . . to present" the "shadow" of Virginia to the gentlewoman he is writing, whose "graces still accompany the least appearance of her and vouchsafe her to be limned out with the beauty which we will beg and borrow from the fair lips" (95). Ambiguities of pronominal reference merge the feminine correspondent with the feminized land. Following what I have referred to as "parallels" between play and the Virginia narratives, but which I would prefer to call ideological "entanglements," we can understand how common tropes, the trope of woman/land being immediately before us, fabricate these texts. So, for example, we might read *Miranda* not as a character in a play by Shakespeare—and we might note in passing that

The Tempest in a sense is devoid of characters, or is not a study of individual psychology as *Lear* and *Hamlet* are—but as a figure or name that articulates a complex of masculine attitudes toward the British settlement of the New World.

If we were to pursue such a reading, we might begin by noticing that the conflicting attitudes expressed toward the island in the argument of Gonzalo/Adrian with Antonio/Sebastian are doubles of and are doubled by Prospero's attitude toward Miranda. Antonio's characterization of the island as "a delicate wench" recalls Prospero's use of "wench" to address Miranda on two occasions in the second scene of the first act (lines 139 and 415). Now at the beginning of the seventeenth century, *wench* contained a range of meanings. At what we might think of as the least inflected end of the ideological scale, it could refer to "a female child," or it could be used as "a familiar or endearing form of address" for "a daughter, wife, or sweetheart." It could refer in the language of class distinctions to a "girl of the rustic or working class" or to a "female servant." Finally, *wench* could mean a "wanton woman," that is, I take it, any woman that a man from the same or a higher class perceived as a "whore" (OED). In the first scene of *The Tempest,* Gonzalo uses the term in this way when he crudely refers to the sinking ship as "an unstanched wench" (I.i.48). And Prospero's use of the term in addressing Miranda, however affectionate, cannot be separated from his angry obsession with her purity or from the political fact that she exists to serve him.

When Antonio responds to Adrian's positive characterization of the island as a land "of subtle, tender and delicate temperance" with the figure of temperance, or the land, as "a delicate wench," we understand immediately from Antonio's function in the play, that of a foil to the nurturance of proper political order, that he is using *wench* derisively. We can hear an actor repeating Antonio's line with sarcasm. Moreover, we can understand that when Antonio repeats Adrian's "delicate" (just as, immediately following this repetition, Sebastian will sarcastically repeat Adrian's "subtle"), he is subverting or attempting to subvert the meaning that Adrian, given his nurturing function in the play, must attach to the word (just as "subtle" in Adrian's mouth must be a synonym for his sense of "delicate" [OED]): the positive meaning, particularly when it modifies "temperance," of "delightful," "charming," or "pleasant" (OED). But at the beginning of the seventeenth century *delicate* could also suggest sensual overindulgence or indolence or debility (in the sense of effeminacy), just as *subtle* could mean cunning or crafty (OED). And it is in these senses that Antonio/Sebastian must be using the adjectives "delicate" and "subtle" with the term "wench."

We can understand that what we have before us is a scene of translation, in both senses of the term that have concerned us. For in this symbolic struggle between Gonzalo/Adrian and Antonio/Sebastian to control the island through naming it (and we remember here that a crucial part of the Western imperialist project was to rename the peoples and places being conquered), what is at stake is first of all the proper meaning of a set of terms (*wench, delicate,* and *subtle*), which, due to the conflict, are torn away from any proper meaning, remaining in translation between the two factions, and reminding us that the inescapable process of politics is precisely a struggle for the control of meaning in which we are confronted with the foreignness of our own language. We have noted how the opposed pairs of Gonzalo/Adrian and Antonio/Sebastian, standing on the same island, describe it as if it were two. We might add, then, that what makes this scene a scene of translation is that these pairs, while speaking the same language, are in effect speaking two.

We have understood in our reading of this scene up to now how the meaning of the island, its figuration as a delicate and subtle wench, is entangled, as is the figure of Virginia in *A True Declaration,* with ideas of political order and subversion. In *The Tempest* perhaps the principal, certainly the most conspicuous, figure of the relationship between political order and subversion is the figure of usurpation. In Florio's introduction to his translation of Montaigne's essays (1603), which, as we know, Shakespeare read and used in part in *The Tempest,* the translator figures translation, among other things, as "usurpation," reminding his readers implicitly of how translation works through displacment.[7] It will be useful to keep this figure of translation as usurpation in mind.

Antonio's usurpation of Prospero is the action "outside" the action proper of the play that sets the action going. And this action, until at the end of the play Prospero, like De La Warr in the *True Declaration,* puts everyone in his or her proper place (proper from Prospero's perspective, that is), is a continual process of actual or projected usurpation: Prospero's usurpation of Caliban ("This island's mine, by Sycorax my mother, / Which thou tak'st from me" [I.ii.333–34]); the sailors' usurpation, during the opening scene, of the nobles' prerogative of command (even the boatswain's displacement of the master might be read as a figure of the figure of usurpation that drives the play); Ferdinand's unknowing usurpation of his father, Alonso (Ferdinand believes his father drowned and so believes himself, by right of succession, the king of Naples, but Prospero knows better and tells the son, "thou dost here usurp / The name thou ow'st not" [I.ii.456–57]); Caliban's foiled attempt to usurp Prospero; and Antonio/Sebastian's foiled attempt to usurp the usurper Alonso (Alonso, we know, aided Antonio in his usurpation of Prospero).

This driving force of usurpation, of the displacement of the proper (of the seizing of what someone else conceives of as his or her property), is entangled with another powerful figure of displacement in the play, that of transportation from domestic to foreign shores. In a well-known speech from Act V, Gonzalo catches the interplay of the domestic and the foreign in trying to make sense of the strange world of Prospero's eloquence from which he has just been released, along with the rest of Alonso's company:

> Was Milan thrust from Milan, that his issue
> Should become Kings of Naples? O, rejoice
> Beyond a common joy! and set it down
> With gold on lasting pillars: in one voyage
> Did Claribel her husband find at Tunis,
> And Ferdinand, her brother, found a wife
> Where he himself was lost, Prospero his dukedom
> In a poor isle, and all of us ourselves
> When no man was his own.
>
> (V.i.205–13)

The passage suggests the paradoxical or ironic way that alienation, figured in the form of voyaging to foreign shores, leads to domestic union in the political, familial, and personal spheres and echoes in its own way England's dream of American empire, in which voyaging to foreign shores was intended to resolve pressing domestic problems such as unemployment, overpopulation, and shrinking markets (particularly for wool). So Milan's being thrust from Milan (Prospero's usurpation and exile on foreign shores) combined with the voyage of Alonso and his company to make a foreign alliance with Tunis through the marriage of Alonso's daughter, Claribel, to the King of Tunis has led, finally, through all of its alienations, to the domestic stability of marriage, the domestication through marriage of foreign conflict (Naples/Tunis and

Naples/Milan), and the domestication, or remarriage, of selves estranged from themselves, as each "man" becomes "his own" property once again. Even that "deformed slave," Caliban, it is suggested shortly after Gonzalo's speech, will be left to himself on the island, for, Prospero promises, all the Europeans are going home in the morning.

It may seem quite possible to accommodate the traditional reading of the play, one that understands it as a romance of reconciliation, within the figures of usurpation and transportation that I am exploring. It seems certain enough, within a reading of reconciliation, that the action of *The Tempest* is circumscribed by a movement from home to foreign places and back to home again (from Milan/Naples to the island to Milan/Naples), a movement from political order to usurpation to political order (from Prospero as duke to Antonio as duke to Prospero as duke again). We might even accommodate something we might identify as Caliban's perspective within this clearly Prospero-centered reading by acknowledging that Prospero's denouement to the drama restores the "savage" to home and rule, if only by a kind of default—the promised departure of Europeans when the morning comes.

But if we entertain a reading of reconciliation, from either Prospero's or what we might take to be Caliban's perspective, we might acknowledge that morning never comes in *The Tempest*. The Europeans' departure remains a promise, never fulfilled within the confines of the play. And when the audience last sees Prospero in the epilogue, he is still confined on the "bare island," now as dependent on the "spell" and "prayer" of the audience for his release to Europe, as Caliban and Ariel, indeed all the figures of the play, are dependent on his eloquence for their liberty within the confines of the drama.

With the figure of transportation on our minds, we might want to modify at this point the dramatic trajectory of home to foreign shores to home. For all of the visible, or present, action of the play takes place, from a European perspective, on the *foreign* shores of the island. Milan and Naples are the scenes only of past action, which Prospero narrates for us in the second scene of Act I; about the future we neither see nor hear a thing. From Caliban's perspective the trajectory of home to foreign shores to home needs rethinking as well. In what we might be tempted to call a literal reading of the figure of transportation, just as none of the Europeans are ever at home, Caliban never leaves home, although at the same time he is never at home either; for his home is alienated in Prospero's usurpation and enslavement of him. At the end of the play, the promised end of this alienation (Caliban's return home in the return of his home to him) remains, as noted, only a promise—and in terms of the language of the fifth act, with which Caliban is regarded, a rather hollow one at that. When Ariel "drive[s]" (V.i.255) the "savage" and his two common cohorts, their rebellion ended, into the place where Prospero has gathered the entire company for the revelation of his design, Antonio, who has not seen the islander before, views him immediately and only as "marketable," echoing Trinculo's remarks about the marketability of dead Indians in Europe. In a similar, if apparently more refined, spirit of ownership, Prospero, returning Stephano and Trinculo to their master, Alonso, who "[m]ust know and own" them, asserts his own property in Caliban with the declaration: "this thing of darkness I / Acknowledge mine" (V.i.275–76). And, finally, bound by figures of property in this final act, Caliban is compelled to give up what identity he has left in confessing the foolishness of his rebellion: "I'll be wise hereafter, / And seek for grace. What a thrice-double ass / Was I, to take this drunkard for a god, / And worship this dull fool!" (V.i.294–97). The tone is flat, transparently so. If, in earlier speeches, Shakespeare invests Caliban with some dignity of difference—in his recitation of his own history, for example (he is the only figure allowed such a recitation; in all the other cases Prospero is the narrator), or in his early display of anger against Prospero (he is the only figure allowed a direct display), or in his lyric descriptions of the island—here in the end the dramatist dispossesses his savage figure of such dignity.

Just as an exploration of the figure of transportation must complicate the figure of reconciliation, or home, with conflict, or foreignness, so an exploration of transportation's twin figure of displacement, usurpation, must complicate the trajectory from usurpation to restoration with the reoccurrence of usurpation. We have just grasped how, from Caliban's purchase, this is so. And from Prospero's as well, we have grasped how the epilogue of the play renders him powerless, his position usurped by the audience he addresses. But even within the boundary of the play proper, Prospero's power is never simply his own; it is never simply proper to him. And in the sense that what appears to be absolute power is dependent on others and so in a sense is possessed by them as well, this power is exercised only in a state of usurpation. This state of usurpation presents us with a contradiction between Prospero's apparently absolute, or immediate, power and its compromised, or mediated, state. We notice, for example, that for Prospero to regain his dukedom in Milan he must forge a political alliance with Alonso through the mediation of Miranda's marriage with Ferdinand—a conventional arrangement that is in striking contrast to Prospero's apparently immediate power on the island with which he effects the arrangement. Thinking with "hope" of witnessing "the nuptial / Of these our dear-belov'd soleminized" in Naples and then of his retirement to Milan, Prospero expresses a disquieting note of despair, with which the epilogue will harmonize, when he tells the gathered company that once home, "Every third thought shall be my grave" (V.i.308–11). Just as dreams of immediate, or absolute, power are inseparable from dreams of immortality, the specter of mortality appears here as Prospero evokes the marriage scene that mediates his power.

But even on the island, before the arrival of the Europeans, where Prospero's power might seem to find an interlude from his usurpation in Milan or the mediation of alliance, there are contradictions of this apparently absolute power. At the opening of scene ii of Act I, Prospero tells a distressed Miranda, who believes that the "[p]oor souls" aboard Alonso's ship have just "perish'd" (9) in the storm, that "[t]here's no harm done" (14), suggesting that Prospero has events under absolute control. Yet later in the scene, when Ariel is introduced, we find that Prospero has an agent and that the relationship between master and servant is not necessarily univocal. For Prospero must ask Ariel the same question that he has just answered for Miranda: "But are they, Ariel, safe?" (217). And while Ariel's answer ("Not a hair perish'd" [217]) confirms what Prospero has told Miranda, Ariel's subsequent request for the "liberty" (245) that, he tells his master, his master has "promis'd" (243) him and Prospero's enraged response reasserts the equivocality of their relationship. Ariel may carry out Prospero's orders "[t]o th' syllable," but the master is not the absolute master of this syllable. The power of eloquence has its limits.

When Prospero claims a property in Caliban with the declaration "this thing of darkness I / Acknowledge mine," he seems to acknowledge this equivocality, or limitation, his implication in an otherness that he has failed to "reduce from darkness to light" (to borrow a figure for converting "savages" that was typical during the first stage of England's imperial project in America).[8] The language of possession simultaneously speaks of dispossession here, of the dislocation of the self in the place it imagined as other. When, a moment later, an apparently repentant Caliban promises Prospero that he will "seek for grace," the promise may seem empty precisely because it casts a false light on the despair of Prospero's "dark" claim, a claim that alienates or suggests the alienation of any domestication or restoration the play may appear to propose.

In considering Caliban's mediation of Prospero's apparently immediate power, we must turn to a moment in *The Tempest* that has perplexed critics of the play, precisely because it appears to contradict without apparent reason the immediacy of his power. It is the moment when Prospero, *"suddenly"* remembering the "foul conspiracy / Of the beast Caliban and his confederates" (IV.i.139–40), calls a halt to the masque he has ordered to celebrate the betrothal of Miranda and Ferdinand, to "prepare to meet with Caliban" (IV.i.167). As Hulme has noted in an especially productive analysis, we cannot help but "note the ludicrousness of elaborate preparations to deal with a woefully inadequate force who could be immobilized on the spot" (119). Prospero's sudden fear of usurpation by Caliban appears to contradict Prospero's apparently absolute power.

In order to understand this moment, which, like the figure of Ariel we have just summoned, appears to usurp belief in Prospero's absolute power, we should remark that earlier in the play, a moment before the audience first sees Prospero and Caliban together, the master expresses a dependency on the slave that anticipates the contradictory moment before us. Responding to a reluctance, indeed a revulsion, on Miranda's part "to look on" Caliban (I.i.312), Prospero informs his daughter:

> We cannot miss him: he does make our fire,
> Fetch in our wood, and serves in offices
> That profit us.
>
> (I.ii.313–15)

The question raised here is: why does the immediate power of the master need the mediacy of the slave to operate? Hulme has seen in this situation "a precise match with the situation of Europeans in America during the seventeenth century, whose technology (especially of firearms) suddenly *became* magical when introduced into a less technologically developed society, but who were incapable (for a variety of reasons) of feeding themselves" (128). In this reading, I take it, the contradiction between Prospero's immediacy and Caliban's mediacy represents an ironic gap between (what Hulme understands as) the fact of English technological superiority over the Indians and English dependency for survival on the technology of Indian agriculture, hunting, and fishing.

As my discussion of technology and eloquence makes clear, I do not agree with Hulme's conception, for the only way he can claim English technological superiority, it seems to me, is by the ethnocentric move of abstracting technology from the ecologies of particular cultures, so that he can talk of Western technology as if it were a universal. The Indians' methods of producing food, which gave them a crucial edge on the settlers in the initial stages of colonization, do not seem to be counted as technology by Hulme, else we might see the Indians rather than the English possessing the more developed technology. Further, there is the implication in Hulme's formulation, if I read him right, that the Indians translated this putatively superior technology into the terms of magic. I take it that his somewhat ambiguous *"became* magical" means "magical for the Indians," since the English, as our earlier discussion of the Virginia Council's instructions on the use of firearms shows, appear to have been aware of the shortcomings of their technology (although no doubt they too, as we can today, could erase at crucial moments, when the national psyche needs to feel invulnerable in the face of its own vulnerability, the facticity of their own reports). The question of what conceptual apparatus these particular Algonquian-speaking Indians initially used to understand English technology, some aspects of which, as Lurie shows, were clearly more familiar to them than others (38), is difficult if not impossible to answer. For, as we know, we only have English reports on the subject, and all the problems of translation (of cultural perspective coupled with political and psychological motive) bring into question such reports, which typically display the Indians in awe of the magical power of Western technology. So, to take a prime example, in *A Map of Virginia,* a text we have already examined in part, we find that "those Salvages [with whom John Smith lived at Werowocomoco and neighboring villages as a captive for about a month during the winter of 1607–1608] admired him as a demi-God" (Barbour, 2, 388). For

> he had inchanted those poore soules . . . in demonstrating vnto them the roundnesse of the world, the course of the moone and starres, the cause of the day and night the largenes of the seas the qualities of our ships, shot and powder, the devision of the world, with the diversity of people, their complexions, customes and conditions. All which hee fained to be vnder

the command of Captaine Newport, whom he tearmed to them his father; of whose arrival, it chanced he so directly prophecied, as they esteemed him an oracle; by these fictions he not only saved his owne life, and obtained his liberty, but had them at that command, he might command them what he listed. (390)

What the English express confidence in the superiority of here is not simply their technology—"the qualities of our ships, shot and powder"—but Smith's rhetorical ability to marshal this technology, along with the accompanying "fictions" of Newport's global and his own oracular power, as dramatic and/or verbal effects that enchant the Indians. Smith (as a representative of the English) is presented here to an English audience not as a consummate technician (in our sense of the word) but as a consummate storyteller or dramatist, as a man of eloquence, which would have made him a consummate technician in the audience's understanding. The power that Smith is portrayed possessing over the Indians—and it appears to be absolute power, for he can "command them what he listed"—is the power to persuade of power (the entangled power of ships and guns, Western forms of knowledge, and fictions of English dominion over the natural and the supernatural). Smith must have been quite an orator, quite a magician of persuasion, for, as we learn from his *True Relation,* he enchanted the Indians with only a compass and a pistol that broke during one of his demonstrations, hardly a reassuring sign of English technological superiority (Barbour, 1, 181, 184).

We know that this portrait of Smith as a grand manipulator of fiction, as an eloquent orator of absolute command, whose eloquence was grounded ultimately in the "wisdom" of English colonial policy, is a fiction. And no doubt many of Smith's readers, and even Smith himself, knew it, which does not mean that they did not still believe it; we can simultaneously know and not know matters of this kind, such are the linked imperatives of our psychological and political economies. We know that this portrait of Smith, and by extension the English, is a fiction because clearly enough Smith could not command the Indians as he listed. The particular scene reproduced in both *A True Relation* and *A Map of Virginia* that we have before us translates into a fantasy of absolute control, whereas complex dependencies existed between the Algonquians and the English. Powhatan did not have Smith executed, we speculate, because the Algonquian leader felt he needed the English to help him maintain the power of his "confederacy" vis-à-vis hostile tribes; and Smith had been captured in the course of a trip to procure desperately needed food from the Indians for a colony on the brink of famine. Further, and here we can only imagine a purely ironic scenario, as the Smith of *A True Relation* and *A Map of Virginia* believed he was dazzling his initial captor, Opechancanough, Powhatan's brother, with the magic of his compass, the Pamunkey may well have been telling his compatriots in quite practical terms how the machine worked. For, and here I quote Hulme's summary,

> Around 1560 a Spanish ship . . . picked up an Algonquian who was probably Pocahontas's uncle. He was baptized Don Luis de Velasco, educated in Cuba and Spain, and taken back with a group of Jesuits to the York river to establish a mission. His family called him Opechancanough, "he whose soul is white." In 1572 he defied his name by organizing and leading the massacre of the Jesuits and the destruction of their mission. (142)

If this is true, then we can imagine Don Luis feigning amazement (perhaps out of politeness, but certainly enjoying the joke) at a machine that was no surprise to him.

Finally, and most important for my purposes, we know Smith's portrait of his oratorical power is a fiction because of the unspoken or repressed problem of translation. How can Smith fabricate persuasively complex cultural fictions of power for an audience with whom he could have communicated only in the most fragmented way? An annotated copy of Smith's *True Relation* reminds us how little of any Algonquian language Smith probably knew: "This Author I fy[nde] in many errors whic[h] they doe impute to h[is] not well vndersta[n]dinge ye language . . ." (Barbour, 1, 189). And even *A Map of Virginia* acknowledges Smith's "want of the language" (Barbour, 2, 385). In his *True Relation*, which gives us an extended account of the captivity mentioned only briefly in *A Map of Virginia*, Smith renders accounts of complex conversations with the Indians, as if there were no problems of translation whatsoever (the English and the Indians ritually exchanged what the English term "orations," before either side could possibly have understood the other). However, Smith implies his "want of the language" when he writes of his initial encounter with Opechancanough's forces that not he but his Indian guide "treated betwext them and me of conditions of peace" (an enormous euphemism, considering Smith tells us he was outnumbered two hundred to one) and when he remarks that in presenting the compass to the Pamunkey he had to "describ[. .] . . . the vse" of the machine "by my best meanes" (Barbour, 1, 181), suggesting that language was not adequate. At the time Smith was captured the English had been in Virginia for only seven months. After the initial month of what appears to have been largely amicable and sustained contact with the Indians leagued with Powhatan, when there was at least a limited exchange of people across cultural boundaries (the situation that typically produced translators), hostilities broke out and contact with the Indians became sporadic. It remained so until Smith's captivity established the basis for a temporary peace, which was arrived at when Smith and Christopher Newport visited Powhatan early in 1608, just after Newport's return from England with the first shipment of supplies. It was at this meeting that Newport ceremoniously sent the English boy Thomas Savage to live with Powhatan and Powhatan reciprocated with his kinsmen Namontack, who would return to England with Newport in April of 1608 and come back to Virginia on Newport's second supply voyage in September of the same year. Savage (an ironically appropriate name, given the task of this translator) and Namontack were the first known translators that the Jamestown experiment produced. *A Map of Virginia* notes the presence of the newly returned Namontack at the coronation of Powhatan, which we have inspected, where he "perswaded [Powhatan] they would doe him no hurt" (Barbour, 2, 414). Savage's presence at the event is not mentioned, though it would appear from the duration of his stay with the Indians that he must have been there too.[9] Perhaps, we might imagine, one or both of these translators explained to Powhatan the meaning of a crown, so that the Algonquian's recorded resistance to the ceremony came not from ignorance, but from a certain uneasy knowledge of intensifying entanglements. We can only speculate, indeed we must speculate, in order to complicate the entire problem of intercultural "knowing" in the scenes of translation we are interpreting. Within this context of extremely tentative translation, a context within which Smith can contradictorily be described both as wanting a knowledge of native languages and as Powhatan's and Newport's "interpreter" (Barbour, 2, 392) at the meeting just described (a contradiction common to the early American travel narratives, where ignorance of native languages is simultaneously acknowledged and repressed, the sign of a telling anxiety), Smith's narrative of fluid intercultural communication must announce itself, precisely because of the seamless way in which it is presented, as a fiction of an understanding that never existed, a fiction that conveys the power of eloquence to the English.

Lastly, in this particular discussion of the problem of translation between Algonquians and English, we should note that, as Kupperman has pointed out, magic was a conceptual category common to both Algonquian and English culture at the time of *The Tempest;* and, reversing the typical view of these matters, she has offered us some evidence of ways in which the English translated Indian power into terms of magic (114–17). I would only add in this regard what may appear obvious: that while magic was common to both cultures, the term "magic" is English, and so until we study its translation into the Algonquian languages involved (if this is even possible any longer) we cannot assume any univocality of forms. As I have already suggested, for example, magic in Renaissance England can be included within the category of eloquence, a category that appears important to native American cultures as well, while not necessarily having either the same relation to magic or the same cultural force as it did in English society. And, of course, the relation of magic to religion in European cultures and Indian cultures is crucial. In Europe, particularly in Protestant Europe, the relation at best was highly ambivalent and ultimately antagonistic. Can the same be said of the relation of "magic" to "religion" in Algonquian-speaking cultures? Indeed, are there or were there two terms corresponding to these European words?

Hulme's explanation of Prospero's declaration, "We cannot miss him," I am suggesting, cannot be understood in the traditional terms of Western technological superiority, but must be comprehended within the problematic of translation, within the problematic of a fiction of understanding, of the kind that we have read John Smith fabricating in his relations with the Algonquian-speaking Indians, and of the kind that I want to explore now in *The Tempest.*

5

The Frontier of Decorum

The first grief of my life was when we reached the mission. They took my buckskin dress off, saying I was now a little Christian girl and must dress like all the white people at the mission. . . .

My next serious grief was when I began to speak the English, that they forbade me to use any Cree words whatever.

E. PAULINE JOHNSON

THE FICTION, or scene, of translation I have in mind begins at the end of Prospero's "We cannot miss him" speech, where Prospero commands Caliban to "speak." It is the first order that Prospero gives Caliban in the play; and it finds its focus in Miranda's claim that it was the Europeans who brought language to Caliban. I want to move toward an exploration of this claim, but in a measured way that will allow me to accumulate details necessary to my exploration of it in Chapter 7. Considering that the order comes precisely at the end of a brief speech in which Prospero is apparently expressing an absolute material dependence (for fire and wood and, by extension, food) on Caliban, the order may strike us as strange, somewhat anomalous. Wouldn't it be more logical for Prospero to *order* Caliban to *fetch* wood, or fire, or food for himself and his daughter, the order being a way of denying this particular dependence, and of dealing with the anxiety of this dependence, even as it expresses the dependence? Indeed, Caliban's response ("There's wood enough within" [I.ii.316]) implies the logical form of the absent order, as if this were a ritual, which it no doubt is. All Prospero has to do is say "speak," and Caliban knows what to say. In this way the form of the ritual, the order to speak and the response of speech, is stressed over and above the content, which has to do with material dependence.

Now, there is no doubt that the English were dependent on the Indians for food, not only at the time of *The Tempest* but well into Jamestown's second decade, as Sheehan describes (104). And Shakespeare reflects this clear dependency, when, shortly after Prospero's admission of dependency, Caliban, recalling his first encounter with the Europeans, reminds Prospero how the islander showed the deposed duke "all the qualities o'th' isle" (I.ii.339) necessary to survival. Yet, as we have seen in examining Gonzalo's role of nurturer, *The Tempest* defines Prospero's and Miranda's survival on the island not simply as physical survival, but also as psychological or sociological survival: the essential need the Europeans have to maintain the class status that supports their identities. Thus, when Prospero tells his daughter, who does not love to look on the "villain" Caliban, that "[w]e cannot miss him" for he "serves in offices / That profit us," we understand that crucial to these offices is the office of serving itself, which defines Caliban as a "villain" (in the feudal sense of the word, which is inseparable from the "moral" sense) and, in defining him this way, defines Prospero and Miranda as nobility. In understanding the way the slave mediates the master's power, we cannot separate the food that Caliban serves from the fact that he serves it. For in terms of the logic of Prospero's power in the play, it makes no sense at all that someone who can summon up a tempest and wake the dead with his eloquence cannot materialize his daily bread with the same technology. Yet no amount of technology, no amount of eloquence, can in and of itself make Prospero a noble. For that he needs others to play the role of the lower classes. Commenting on the contradictory nature of Prospero's power, Hulme notes that "he cannot, or will not, chop wood, make dams to catch fish or do the washing up, all tasks for which Caliban's services are required" (128). Hulme's argument emphasizes the "cannot"; mine emphasizes the inseparability of the "cannot" and the "will not," noting here John Smith's complaints about the nobles at Jamestown (Vaughan, 54) who would not get down to performing the bare tasks of survival because to perform such tasks would have contradicted their identity as nobles. In fact, when De La Warr restored order to Jamestown, the basis for such order was, according to *A True Declaration,* the restoration of the proper class division entailed in the separation of manual and intellectual labor (20). Considering the class relationship as crucial in any equation involving food and power in *The Tempest* explains the seeming contradiction to Prospero's power not only in terms of the contemporary historical situation in America but also in terms of the play itself, which inescapably are the historical terms of class.

For Kupperman "neither savagery nor race was the important category for Englishmen looking at Indians [in the sixteenth and seventeenth centuries]. That is, English colonists assumed that Indians were racially similar to themselves and that savagery was a temporary condition which the Indians would quickly lose. The really important category was status'' (2). Kupperman is certainly right about race in this instance, if we understand the term in our modern sense of it, that is, biologically. For the biological sense of the word did not begin to gain hold until the end of the eighteenth century. And there is evidence in the Jamestown documents that the early colonists saw skin color, which in any event was not the most crucial "racial" category to them (the early documents of voyaging from Columbus onward suggest that language and clothing, for example, were more significant cultural definers), as a cultural rather than a natural acquisition.[1] Although, if we understand *race* in a cultural rather than biological sense and "savagery" as a particular racial characteristic projected by the early colonists onto the Indians, Kupperman's assessment of how the colonists viewed themselves and the Indians seems overly optimistic, there is still no doubt that the category of status was crucial, precisely because it was a focal point for intense anxiety in English society of the time, where, with the intensification of the transition to capitalism as the mode of production, status as a function of wealth rather than family made the class structure practically and potentially volatile. When Miranda calls Caliban a "villain," the word evoked, perhaps, in the noble audience watching one of the first performances of *The Tempest* a nostalgia for England's feudal past, vestiges of which were rapidly disappearing at the time of Shakespeare's play. MacFarlane, as we have read, dates its end to the thirteenth century, when in effect the feudal economy was replaced by a market-oriented economy centered on individual, rather than on certain common forms of land ownership.

At the time of *The Tempest,* and here I quote Kupperman for her summary is to the point,

Europe was in the midst of a century and a half of very rapid population growth and economic inflation. Use of farmland showed the effects of this as landholders consolidated their holdings into sizeable fields which could be farmed more efficiently than the small plots formerly worked by tenants and copyholders. Consolidation, along with the use of new scientific agricultural techniques, helped to feed the enlarged population, but at the price of sending many people off the land. These people, "masterless men," looked for work in the towns and cities or became reliant on poor relief. . . . Humble people in general found themselves squeezed as food prices rose disastrously. Many people of all walks of life looked back nostalgically, and with a good deal of romanticism, to a settled past where everyone had had a place in society and money meant less than place. This nostalgia had an impact on colonization. Gentry or aristocratic colonial leaders sometimes came to America looking for a chance to recreate such a society, organized semifeudally around the lord of the manor, the proprietor of the colony. At the other end of the social scale, the rank and file colonists were often made up of these poor people who lacked any other place to go or who felt they lacked economic opportunity in England. In some cases they were sent against their will. Others were skilled farmers or artisans who came looking for a chance to use their skills. (8–9)

The threat to *place* posed by an emerging capitalism and its accompanying social upheavals is well represented both in the Bermuda pamphlets that we have been reading, where we have touched on the "tempests of dissension" caused by class conflict in the early colonizing venture, and in *The Tempest,* where we are in the process of considering the force of displacement figured in the tropes of transportation and usurpation. In arguing that "there is nothing in *The Tempest* fundamental to its structure of ideas which could not have existed had America remained undiscovered, and the Bermuda voyage never taken place," and in supporting this argument by noting that "Shakespeare is at pains to establish his island in the Old World [and that this 'fact'] may be taken to indicate his rejection of the merely topical" (xxv–vi), Kermode with unintentional irony focuses on the fundamental structure of the play, which is, precisely, as I have been arguing and want to continue to argue, the "merely topical."

The figure of *topos,* or place, drives *The Tempest.* Indeed, considering first two aspects of this figure, before turning to its linguistic dimension, which, as I will argue, is contained within Prospero's ordering Caliban to speak, we might characterize *The Tempest* precisely as a play obsessed with putting people in what the ruling class understands as their proper places, both geographical and social. The action of the play first gathers the dispersed figures of the drama into one place, the island, and then, after dispersing them there, regathers them in Act V in a more concentrated place in that place, where Prospero through the agency of his power can finally appear to put them in their proper social places.

The island is *the* place in the play; and the criticism of the play has addressed the problem of place as that of the island's location. Kermode's gesture of placing the island beyond the territory of the "merely topical" by locating it in the Old World is a sign of this problem, even as it tries to solve it with such an unequivocal placement. As Leslie Fiedler, Jan Kott, and most recently Hulme (89–134) have argued, the location of the island is equivocal, lying somewhere between the New World and the Old.[2] Because while Shakespeare has literally (in the letters of the play) placed the island in the Mediterranean, somewhere between Tunis and Naples, the literal and the proper here are not identical. That is, the literal cannot escape its entanglement with the figurative in this case. In *The Tempest*, the island has no proper place, just as in the earliest travel writings the New World is not seen as opposed to the Old, a different place, but as a place where the Old will be reformed or perfected, both geographically (in terms of its material yield) and socially (in terms of its political yield). The island's "somewhere" is perpetually ideological, or rhetorical, as, for example, the exchange between Gonzalo/Adrian and Antonio/Sebastian about its topographical features attests. The island may literally lie in the Mediterranean, but in this Mediterranean distance is measured figuratively not properly. Antonio suggests this when he defines the relatively short distance (even by Renaissance standards) between Tunis and Naples as "[t]en leagues beyond man's life" (II.i.242). Kermode points out in a footnote that here Antonio, describing Claribel's distance from her father's throne, is playing the "orator, persuading" Sebastian, with the use of "hyperbole," of the feasibility of usurping Alonso. And we can agree, adding only that in *The Tempest* all distances of place from place must be measured within the boundaries of the figure of eloquence. Thus the island is located between competing claims, the claims of two names, one Latinate in origin, *Prospero*, with its connotations of hope and prosperity, the other Native American in origin, *Caliban*, with its native meaning, its claim, lost to us, because of a violent history of European translation.

It is this violent history of translation, marked by the name *Caliban*, that *The Tempest*, along with other colonial documents of the kind we have been exploring, records. When Kermode tells us that "Caliban is the ground of the play" (xxv), strangely echoing Prospero, who refers to the savage as "[t]hou earth" (I.ii.316), he places, or grounds, the play with unintentional irony in this history of translation, in the "merely topical," that is, precisely where he does not want to place it. For to acknowledge the play's complicity in this history is to call into question the Western category of "great art," grounded, as this category is, in an idea of universality or transcendence. And it is this category that Kermode's interpretation of *The Tempest* is implicitly driven to preserve. D. D. Carnicelli, commenting on the relation of the Bermuda pamphlets to *The Tempest*, makes Kermode's implicit anxieties explicit: "To ask how these texts contributed to the creation of *The Tempest* is not to diminish the brilliance of the playwright's invention or the scope of his achievement, rather it is to attempt to understand how the creative imagination transforms the cultural commonplaces of its time into great art."[3] But what of the opposite? What if "great art" is no more than a cultural commonplace, no more, that is, than the "merely topical?" In this hypothesis, it is not Caliban, the transcendent *translatio*, but *Caliban*, the translated name, that is the ground of *The Tempest*. In this hypothesis, *Caliban* is the historical and intercultural place within which we *must* (and this compulsion is political not natural) read *The Tempest;* for we may be able to repress history in our rhetoric about "great art" (to consign it to the realm of the "merely topical"), but we cannot contain or escape its imperatives.

If, then, *Caliban* is the place of *The Tempest*, and if, as I have been arguing, the notion of place, or of displacement, is the driving force of the play, as it is of the colonial and imperial history of which the play is merely a particular sign, then I would say that *Caliban* is the place of place in the play. We have been considering the social and geographical force of place in the play as it articulates itself in the twin figures of transportation and usurpation. What I want to do now is suggest that these twins are triplets, by discussing the linguistic dimension of place in the play, in order to argue that this dimension is the place of translation. Simply put, if *Caliban* is the place of *The Tempest* then this place is that violent history of translation, which is the ground of Anglo-American letters in the New World.

The centrality of the idea of place (*locus* or *topos*) to Renaissance conceptions of logic and rhetoric, and hence of language, is well known to us, and I will have more to say about this particular idea of place in the next chapter. But to begin with I want to take another look at Aristotle's theory of metaphor, which, as we have understood, is a theory of translation, in order to begin to elaborate the place of place-as-language in *The Tempest*, where Prospero orders Caliban to speak.

Aristotle's theory of metaphor, as we have noted, is inseparable from an idea of place that draws frontiers between the "domestic" and the "foreign." What determines such naming of places is not a metaphysical matter, but a historical/political one, a matter of foreign policy, which, however, presents itself to us metaphysically or, at least, neutrally, because of the translation of Aristotle's charged terminology into the vocabulary of the "literal," or the "proper," and the "figurative." Since the Renaissance, the force of this translation, in fact, has been to obscure or erase the political relationship between translation and figurative language. But in Renaissance languages, and in the Greek and Latin that informed them (most explicitly Latin, but Greek in a powerfully implicit way because Latin carried its figures in translation), this relationship is striking, at least one reason being that the figure of the foreign was so volatilely present to these societies, less repressed than in the United States' current liberal discourse, which insinuates rather than expounds its xenophobia.

So, in Chapters XXI and XXII of the *Poetics*, Aristotle develops his notion of metaphor by analogy with two notions of the foreign. The first notion appears when Aristotle defines a "strange word, [as] one . . . in use in another country." For the example he gives is not from a "barbarous" language (anyone who was *barbaros* was a non-Greek-speaking person), but from the Cyprian dialect of Greek (XXI.3). Here, in an atmosphere of intense political differentiation, we become aware of how a language can be alienated from itself, as dialect and political difference (the difference of one *polis* from another) coincide. We have read a figure of this kind of alienation in the scene of translation between Gonzalo/Adrian and Antonio/Sebastian. But this first notion of the foreign extends its boundaries into the notion of the barbarous, when in Chapter XXII Aristotle tells us that "a style wholly composed of ['strange (or rare)'] words is . . . a jargon" (XXII.2). For the Greek word that Butcher translates as "jargon" is *barbarismos,* which could not help but evoke in the Greek ear "people who make [unintelligible] noises like 'bar bar' instead of talking Greek,"[4] that is, *foreigners,* as we typicaly understand the term in contemporary parlance. It is at this point in the text that Aristotle once again makes a distinction between the metaphorical and the strange. For while a style wholly composed of strange words is a jargon, one wholly composed of metaphors is "a riddle [*aenigma*]" (XXII.2). But because, as we noted when I first introduced Aristotle's theory of metaphor, the boundaries between the metaphorical and the strange have already been blurred in the term "foreign" (*xenikos*), and because we along with Aristotle are already operating within a territory where metaphor by analogy is being pursued, it is not difficult for us to talk of a riddle, which, after all, first presents itself in the guise of unintelligibility, as a kind of jargon, or barbarism.

From its theoretical beginnings, then, metaphor comes under suspicion as the foreign, that which is opposed to the "proper," defined inescapably, as we have noted, as the *national*, the *domestic*, the *familiar*, the *authoritative*, the *legitimate*. And yet just as the foreign is never simply that which is outside the national, but is also that by which the national constitutes, or defines, its own identity through acts of startled recognition that entail projection and introjection ("this thing of darkness I / Acknowledge mine"), so our theories of metaphor from Aristotle to Emerson have not understood metaphor simply as a displacement of proper language but simultaneously as the place of proper language itself, whether as ur-language or as that which supplies necessary words to a language in which certain meanings lack signs (*catechresis*), or as the heart, the very motor, of eloquence.

Because of metaphor's doubleness—its foreignness that is paradoxically and ironically quintessentially national—the Western rhetorical tradition has attempted to master or domesticate metaphor, to translate it, like Tarzan translating himself from ape to human, under the rules of *decorum*, rules grounded in the notion of the absolute, or essential, relation between identity and proper place, between, that is, the identities that constitute a class system. In the Western rhetorical tradition, the idea of decorum is inseparably linked to the conception that for order to be maintained, with certain allowances made for the place, time, and purpose of a discourse, each class must speak, be spoken to and about in its proper speech. For, it is implied, if the lower class were to speak, be spoken to or about in terms of the upper class (that is, eloquently) or vice versa, then the hierarchy of identities would be overthrown. The crisis envisioned here is the same crisis that sixteenth- and seventeenth-century sumptuary laws were meant to arrest. Puttenham implicitly reminds his sixteenth-century aristocratic readers of the connection between the order of language and that of fashion, when in the course of his discussion of decorum, or "decencie," as he translates the Latin, he brings up the matter of clothing:

> And in the vse of apparell there is no litle decency and vndecencie to be perceiued, as well for the fashion as the stuffe, for it is comely that euery estate and vocation should be knowen by the differences of their habit: a clarke from a lay man: a gentleman from a yeoman: a souldier from a

citizen, and the chiefe of euery degree from their inferiours, because in confusion and disorder there is no manner of decencie. (283)

Thus, it is no coincidence that within the tradition we are exploring the principal metaphor for metaphor (as for language generally) is that of the garment. In *The Tempest,* as we have read, Gonzalo supplies the usurped Prospero with both "[r]ich garments" and books, in order to insure his noble identity in any new world he may reach.

The decorous use of metaphor plays a crucial part in maintaining this class system, as Puttenham points out to his readers (and as we proceed, we should understand that in the classical tradition both "figure" and "ornament" are synonyms for metaphor, precisely because, while metaphor may be conceived as a kind of figure or ornament, an understanding of the workings of all figurative language is based, first of all, on a conceptualization of the movement of metaphor):

> But as it hath bene alwayes reputed a great fault to use figuratiue speaches foolishly and indiscretly, so is it esteemed no lesse an imperfection in mans vtterance, to haue none vse of figure at all, specially in our writing and speaches publike, making them but as our ordinary talke, then which nothing can be more vnsauourie and farre from all ciuilitie. (138–39)

It is a breach of decorum, Puttenham remarks, "to use figuratiue speaches foolishly and indiscretly." In his discussion of decorum, Puttenham uses an example of such a breach that is to the point in our discussion of the relation between linguistic decorum and class:

> Another of our vulgar makers, spake as illfaringly in this verse written to the dispraise of a rich man and couetous. Thou hast a/misers minde (thou hast a princes pelfe) a lewde terme to be spoken of a princes treasure, which in no respect nor for any cause is to be called pelfe, though it were neuer so meane, for pelfe is properly the scrappes or shreds of taylors and of skinners, which are accompted of so vile price as they be commonly cast out of dores, or otherwise bestowed vpon base purposes: and carrieth not the like reason or decencie, as when we say in reproch of a niggard or vserer, or worldly couetous man, that he setteth more by a little pelfe of the world, than by his credit or health, or conscience. (274)

Although, we might argue, what Puttenham objects to in the metaphor of "princes pelfe" is a literal discrepancy in quantity (a prince's treasure, no matter how paltry, could never be the equivalent of "the scrappes or shreds of taylors and of skinners"), we can also understand that he deems such a literal discrepancy improper precisely because it violates, or blurs, a figurative, or class, distinction, that between the gentlemanly classes (nobility and gentry) and working people. (That it was becoming possible for the merchant class to buy their way into the upper classes through the purchase of land and the royal granting of peerages no doubt motivates the anxiety that Puttenham's language expresses about the proximity of "prince" and "pelfe.")

If, however, an improper use of metaphor can violate the decorum of class distinctions, metaphor itself is absolutely essential in maintaining this decorum; for it is "no lesse an imperfection in mans vtterance, to haue none vse of figure at all, specially in our writing and speaches publike, making them but as our ordinary talke, then which nothing can be more vnsauourie and farre from all ciuilitie." What in matters of speech distinguishes the civil from the savage, the upper classes from the lower, ordinary talk from eloquence, if it is not metaphor, properly clothing the impropriety of naked words? And yet, as we have just noted, if metaphor is the very figure of decorum, it is also the figure of decorum's disfigurement. For, to emphasize a previous point, metaphor is elaborated within a double history, where the frontier between the national and the foreign, or between one class and another, is at once asserted and uncertain.

In matters of metaphor, the frontier of decorum, following the dictates of Western foreign policy, is traditionally marked under the sign of the "far-fetched," or "alien." In *De Optimo Genere Oratorum,* Cicero gives us a typical formulation:

> For as eloquence consists of language and thought, we must manage while keeping our diction faultless and pure—that is in good Latin—to achieve a choice of words both "proper" [*propriorum*] and figurative [*translatorum*]. Of "proper" words we should choose the most elegant, and in the case of figurative language we should be modest in our use of metaphors and careful to avoid far-fetched comparisons [*alienis*]. (II.4–5)[5]

Rhetorical decorum demands that in the name of propriety the domestic dominate the alien, difference must be sacrificed to similitude. But such domination, traditionally, proves difficult, because metaphor is duplicitous, playing the part of a double agent in a game of foreign intrigue. In a discussion of figures, Puttenham's language suggests that my metaphor for metaphor of "foreign intrigue" is not so far-fetched:

As figures be the instruments of ornament in euery language, so be they also in a sorte abuses or rather trespasses in speach, because they passe the ordinary limits of common vtterance, and be occupied of purpose to deceiue the eare and also the minde, drawing it from plainnesse and simplicitie to a certaine doublenesse, whereby our talke is the more guilefull and abusing, for what els is your *Metaphor* but an inuersion of sence by transport; your *allegorie* by a duplicitie of meaning or dissimulation vnder couert and darke intendments: one while speaking obscurely and in riddle called *Aenigma* . . . and many other waies seeking to inueigle and appassionate the mind: which thing made the graue judges *Areopagites* . . . to forbid all manner of figurative speaches to be vsed before them in their consistorie of Iustice, as mere illusions to the minde, and wresters of vpright iudgement, saying that to allow such manner of forraine & coulored talke to make the iudges affectioned, were/all one as if the carpenter before he began to square his timber would make his squire crooked: in so much as the straite and upright mind of a Iudge is the very rule of iustice till it be peruerted by affection. (154)

We understand immediately that what Puttenham refers to as the Areopagites' ban on "all manner of figurative speaches" must be read as a *figure* of the desire to domesticate the far-fetched, or alien, figure, all "forraine & coulored talke." We understand this because we know that it is literally impossible to banish figures from language, precisely because figuration is the mechanism that makes language move with the force of language. And Puttenham, precisely because he is within the Western rhetorical tradition, understands this too, when he tells his readers at the very beginning of the passage that "figures be the instruments of ornament in euery language." For within the classical and Renaissance tradition of rhetoric, "ornament" does not suggest the superfluous or the exterior; rather, derived from the Latin verb *orno,* which means both "to provide with necessaries" and "to embellish," it articulates that place where the interior and the exterior, the necessary and the contingent are inseparable.

Metaphor, the figure of figures (Quintillian calls it "the supreme ornament of oratory" [VIII.2.6]),[6] is, indeed, a double agent, at once the "instrument [. . .] of ornament," and an "abuse [. . .] or rather trespasse [. . .] in speech." Metaphor works simultaneously for two governments, at once upholding the civility of domestic speech, but doing this, in "forraine & coulored talke," by "pass[ing] the ordinary limits of common vtterance," sometimes, like a spy, "vnder couert and darke intendments," sometimes "speaking obscurely and in riddle." Metaphor marks the frontier between the domestic and the foreign precisely by blurring that boundary. And that is why, in the rest of the chapter from which I have been quoting, Puttenham goes on to tell his readers what is a commonplace in the Western rhetorical tradition: that in matters of metaphor, or figurative language, the frontier between "vertue" and "vice," between the domestic and the foreign, is difficult to mark (see, for example, Quintillian, VIII.3.7, 58).

Because of the politics of metaphor (its paradoxical structure), decorum must inevitably declare itself not as the mark of natural frontiers, but as the inscription of political ones. Matters of decorum are matters of arbitration, as Puttenham suggests:

> So albeit we before alleaged that all our figures be but transgressions of our dayly speach, yet if they fall out decently to the good liking of the mynde or eare and to the bewtifying of the matter or language, all is well, if indecently, and to the eares and myndes misliking (be the figure of it selfe neuer so commendable) all is amisse, the election is the writers, the judgement is the worlds, as theirs to whom the reading apperteineth. But since the actions of man with their circumstances be infinite, and the world likewise replenished with many iudgements, it may be a question who shal haue the determination of such controuersie as may arise whether this or that action or speach be decent or indecent. . . . (262–63)

Because "all our figures be but transgressions of our dayly speach" (translations, or foreigners), it is not the figure itself but the context in which it is used that decides its decorum. And whether or not the figure is being used decorously, or properly, or decently, or domestically, in that context is a matter of judgment. The question is, then, who makes that judgment? While Puttenham poses the question, his answer only returns us to the question. The arbiter of decorum should be "he who can make the best and most differences of things by reasonable and wittie distinction" (263), a man who "obserueth much," rather than one who "spends all his life in his owne vaine actions and conceits"; for "one man of experience is wiser than tenne learned men, because of his long and studious obseruation and often triall" (264). But how can we recognize such a man unless we can also recognize "the best and most differences of things," in which case we have fallen back on the kind of individual judgment that Puttenham wants to avoid, and that clearly won't do in cases when common usage is to be enforced. Puttenham appears to have this predicament in mind when he recommends "example" as the arbiter of decorum:

> The case then standing that discretion must chiefly guide all those businesse, since there be sundry sortes of discretion all vnlike, euen as there be men of action or art, I see no way so fit to enable a man truly to estimate of [*decencie*] as example, by whose veritie we may deeme the differences of things and their proportions, and by particular discussion come at length to sentence of it generally, and also in our behaviours the more easily to put it in execution. (263)

The question, of course, remains: who chooses and upholds these examples? I trace the circular reasoning of Puttenham's argument to suggest that he is either avoiding or assuming the answer to the question of decorum that he poses, an answer that is implicitly contained in the examples of decorum that Puttenham provides (one of which, the example of the prince's pelfe, we have already read). For the situation in these examples is, typically, that in which someone of a lower class is speaking to or about or in the presence of a ruler, and in which all speech is judged decorous or indecorous according to the *difference* between the ruler and the class of the person speaking. The question of decorum, then, is a question of power and authority, of authority derived from the power of particular institutions, the monarchy in this case, and of power derived from this authority. The question of decorum, of what are the proper figures of speech, is inevitably answered by locating the most powerful, the most authoritative, figures in a particular society and by listening to how these figures speak, by studying what they write. Prospero's order to Caliban to speak articulates itself within this formulation of decorum, as we will read in Chapter 7.

We have read in the course of our discussion how in matters of decorum, the frontier of translation (as *translatio,* or metaphor) is defined, in the Western rhetorical tradition, both in terms of the "farfetched," or "alien," and in terms of the differences between social classes, inscribed within a particular hierarchy. Clearly, this double definition suggests a relation between domestic and foreign policy that needs to be specified.

For England, the initial period of expansion into the Atlantic and Caribbean regions, the period during which Puttenham wrote and of which *The Tempest* marks a terminus (for with the founding of Jamestown a "new" period of expansion begins), corresponds, as it did for England's European competitors, with a powerful surge in the formation of a national identity. The formation of this identity, as writers of the time instruct us, was particularly dependent on the formation of a national language. The articulation of ideas about such a language registers acutely how volatile definitions of the native and the foreign were at the time, when the line between internal and external frontiers was not nearly as clear-cut as it is in the political schemes of today.

In the 1530s, for example, dialectical differences in English prompted one writer to comment: "Our language is also so dyverse in yt selfe that the commen maner of spekynge in Englysshe of some contre can skante be understondid in some other contre of the same londe."[7] In contemporary English, to refer to another "country" is to refer, unequivocally, to a foreign place. But in sixteenth-century usage, as we can read, the term is equivocal, referring to a foreign place that is simultaneously domestic. And in the alienation of English from itself in the example at hand, we can read a parallel to those historical circumstances, which, as we have understood, compelled the Western definition of metaphor in terms of translation. Writing almost sixty years after the time of this example, Puttenham gives us an idea of how shifting notions of the domestic and the foreign played a crucial part in constructing the figure of a national English language. And I want to quote Puttenham at some length to give a sense of how obsessively he returns to the threat that forces identified as foreign under various guises pose to the identity of the newly forming English language:

> [A]fter a speach is fully fashioned to the common vnderstanding, & accepted by consent of a whole countrey & nation, it is called a language, & receaueth none allowed alteration, but by extraordinary occasions by little & little, as it were insensibly bringing in of many corruptions that creepe along with the time. . . . Then when I say language, I meane the speach wherein the Poet or maker writeth be it Greek or Latine, or as our case is the vulgar English, & when it is peculiar vnto a countrey it is called the mother speach of that people . . . so is ours at this day the Norman English. Before the Conquest of the Normans it was the Anglesaxon, and before that the British, which as some will, is at this day, the Walsh, or as others affirme the Cornish: I for my part thinke neither of both, as they be now spoken and pronounced. This part in our maker or Poet must be heedly looked vnto, that it be naturall, pure, and the most vsuall of all his countrey:

and for the same purpose rather that which is spoken in the kings Court, or in the good townes and Cities within the land, then in the marches and frontiers, or in port townes, where straungers haunt for traffike sake, or yet in Vniuersities where Scollers vse much peeuish affectation of words out of the primitiue languages, or finally, in any vplandish village or corner of a Realme, where is no resort but of poore rusticall or vncivill people: neither shall he follow the speach of craftes man or carter, or other of the inferiour sort, though he be inhabitant or bred in the best towne and Citie in this Realme, for such person doe abuse good speaches by strange accents or ill shapen soundes, and false ortographie. But he shall follow generally the better brought vp sort, such as the Greekes call [*charientes*] men civill and graciously behauoured and bred. Our maker therfore at these dayes shall not follow *Piers plowman* nor *Gower* nor *Lydgate* nor yet *Chaucer*, for their language is now out of vse with vs: neither shall he take the termes of Northernmen, such as they vse in dayly talke, whether they be noble men or gentlemen, or of their best clarkes all is a matter: nor in effect any speach vsed beyond the /river of Trent, though no man can deny but that theirs is the purer English Saxon at this day, yet it is not Courtly nor so currant as our Southerne English is, no more is the far Westerne mans speach: he shall therfore take the vsuall speach of the Court, and that of London and the shires lying about London within lx myles, and not much aboue. I say not this that in euery shyre of England there be gentlemen and others that speake but specially write as good Southerne as we of Middlesex or Surrey do, but not the common people of euery shire, to whom the gentlemen, and also their learned clarkes do for the most part condescend, but herein we are already ruled by th' English Dictionaries and other bookes written by learned men, and therefore it needeth none other direction in that behalfe. Albeit peraduenture some small admonition be not impertinent, for we finde in our English writers many wordes and speaches amendable, & ye shall see in some many inkhorne termes so ill affected brought in by men of learning as preachers and schoolemasters: and many straunge termes of other languages by Secretaries and Marchaunts and trauailours, and many darke wordes and not vsuall nor well founding, though they be dayly spoken in Court. Wherefore great heed must be taken by our maker in this point that his choise be good. And peraduenture the writer hereof be in that behalfe no lesse faultie then any other, vsing many straunge and vnaccustomed wordes and borrowed from other languages: and in that respect him selfe no meete Magistrate to reforme the same errours in any other person, but since he is not vnwilling to acknowledge his owne fault, and can the better tell how to amend it, he may seeme a more excusable correctour of other mens: he intendeth therefore for an indifferent way and vniuersall benefite to taxe him selfe and before any others. (144–46)

In Puttenham's description of the constitution of English, the term "countrey" does not mark a division within the land, as it did in the 1530s, rather it is identified with the land or, more specifically, with the "nation." What this identification tells us is that we are at the beginning of a period, the "early modern" period, when Western Europeans will attempt to erase the equivocal distinction between the domestic and the foreign through the legal fiction of the *nation-state,* that political and juridical entity in which (and this is the chief sign of the nation-state's existence as well as a principal mode of its formation) "a speach . . . fully fashioned to the common vnderstanding, & accepted by consent of a whole . . . is called a language." This is the state in which a speech domesticates or becomes familiar to itself, we might say. But we can recognize in Puttenham's formulation—in which the term "nation" hovers equivocally between an older "racial" meaning and a newer political one (see the OED)—a fiction of unanimity. For in the account of current English that follows this formulation, we are aware of the social and political differences that render this univocal language an equivocal speech: the difference between Norman and Anglo-Saxon English—the difference, that is, between the English spoken at court, and that spoken in other regions of the realm; or the difference between the English spoken "in the good townes and Cities *within* the land" and that spoken "in the marches and frontiers, or in port townes, where straungers haunt for traffikes sake"; or the difference between the English spoken in the urban south and that spoken "in any vplandish village or corner of a Realme, where is no resort but of poore rusticall or vncivill people"; or, within "the best towne[s] and Citie[s]," the difference between the English spoken by "the better brought up sort" and that spoken by "the inferiour sort" (the working classes); or the difference between the English of Chaucer's day and that of the present; or, finally, the difference between a putatively pure, or native, English and an English corrupted by "many darke wordes," the "many straunge termes of other languages," both "primitive" (Latin and Greek) and current.

The figure that governs these pairs of oppositions, in which we can read the alienation of English from itself at the moment of its national formation, is that of center and periphery, of power and of the threat to power, in terms of time (the threat of older English and classical languages to the shaky prestige of the contemporary idiom), and, more importantly, in terms of place, where the geographical, the social, and the political intersect. The Tudor court, as we know, was in conflict with the "foreign," not only abroad, where it was beginning to compete with other European powers for colonial jurisdiction in America, but at "home" as well, where militant, colonizing efforts proceeded against militant opposition in Wales (finally joined to England in 1543), Ireland, and Scotland. Rebellions in the North in 1536 and 1569, and in the South-West and Norfolk in 1549 remind us that there were still countries within the nation where even a person from another manorial district was termed a foreigner.[8] These regional rebellions reflected the radical displacements taking place at the time that forged the national figure of center and periphery: the displacement of the old nobility by the new, who were created by the Tudor monarchs and wielded power over the realm from London (the Northern rebellions, in part, were the result of such a displacement); the displacement of small landholders by large holders (gentry and nobles), part of the economic dislocations associated with the enclosure movement, and the increasing centralization of the economy in London (the Norfolk, or Ket's, rebellion was the result of this class antagonism); and the displacement of Catholicism by Protestantism. The Southwest rebellion of 1549 was provoked by the national institution of Cranmer's prayer book, which, in translating the mass from Latin into English, attempted, for the first time, to impose a single form of worship on the Church of England.[9]

Puttenham's description of the formulation of a national English language implies the conflictive movement of these displacements. And in the developing figure of the center/periphery, we can read how notions of the foreign and of social class, which, as we have understood, are central to the idea of rhetorical decorum, intersect. For just as English becomes increasingly foreign the farther it moves geographically from the court in London (the farther West or North it moves from its Southeastern "center"), so the "farther" it moves from the English of the upper classes (those who actually or potentially—if they give up their opposition to it—have access to the court), the more foreign it becomes. At the farthest reaches of the frontier forged by the figure of center/periphery, the reaches of the far-fetched, the English of the lowest class (those who hold virtually no property) and the "savage" languages of Native Americans (those who hold no property) can become a single foreign tongue in the perception of those in power. *Caliban,* who "wouldst gabble like / A thing most brutish" (I.ii.358–59) before Miranda taught him the language of her father (a problem in decorum to which we will have to return in Chapter 7), is associated from the moment they are introduced in the play with those of the lowest class, Stephano and Trinculo, with whom he plots a rebellion against Prospero.

The movement of metaphor and the movement of the English language in its national formation are, then, governed by a particular dynamics of displacement from periphery to center, in which the rules of decorum attempt to master an essentially equivocal relationship between the foreign or lower class and the domestic or upper class. This rule of decorum, as we have understood, is the rule that states simply: proper speech is the speech of the most powerful. That is, proper speech is eloquent speech.

The significance of eloquence to English during the period of its national formation is a particularly crucial one; and it is one that is mediated by translation, by the dynamics of the domestic and the foreign that we have been exploring. In the first three quarters of the sixteenth century, according to the generally accepted account given us by Richard Foster Jones, "Eloquence inhered not in the native elements in the language but only in the words introduced into it from the classics. That the English language per se was considered uneloquent may be easily deduced from the adjectives most frequently used to describe it: rude, gross, barbarous, base, vile" (7). Eloquence, then, and proper speech, as we have been defining it, are synonymous. Eloquent speech is speech that is native, not foreign, or "barbarous" (and the Renaissance was well aware of the Greek derivation of the term); it is speech that is of the city or manor, not of the country or surrounding villages ("rude" and "vile" would have been associated with the peasantry at the time); it is the speech of mind or spirit, not the body (it is not, that is, "gross" speech); and it is the speech of the upper, not the lower classes (the classes to which all these adjectives would apply). Projected, during the period of its national development, onto the international scene, both temporally (in relation to classical languages, principally Latin) and spatially (in relation to the prestigious contemporary languages, principally Italian and French), English was regarded by the privileged, or highly literate, who have left us the written record, as profoundly alienated from, or beneath, itself.

The problem, then, for English at this juncture, or rather, for the sixteenth-century English men whose writings represent the language for us, was how it could be domesticated, or civilized. It was the problem of how the language could colonize itself, or be colonized by its most powerful users. To use the figure of colonization here is not far-fetched, first because, as we have read, English colonization at the time was not simply a process of settling a territorial exterior, but of settling an interior as well, or, rather, one in which the frontier between exterior and interior was blurred, just as Caliban's New-World island appears to float in an Old-World sea; and, secondly and centrally, because the tool of colonization, whether we are discussing New World colonization or colonization ''within'' Britain, was translation.

Without connecting the force of translation in colonizing America with the force of translation in colonizing, or civilizing, English itself, scholars have certainly recognized the connection between conquest abroad and translation at home. ''A study of Elizabethan translations,'' F. O. Matthiessen tells us,

> is a study of the means by which the Renaissance came to England. The nation had grown conscious of its cultural inferiority to the Continent, and suddenly burned with the desire to excel its rivals in letters, as well as in ships and gold. The translator's work was an act of patriotism. He, too, as well as the voyager and merchant, could do some good for his country: he believed that foreign books were just as important for England's destiny as the discoveries of her seamen, and he brought them into his native speech with all the enthusiasm of a conquest.[10]

In linking, not incidentally, the voyager and the translator—two figures of transportation—Matthiessen's statement also points to the fact that the ''conquest'' of foreign books, their translation into English, was also the means of the conquest of English itself, its translation from barbarity into civility.

Translators, Julia G. Ebel tells us, ''exemplify that quest for cultural and national identity which lies at the heart of Elizabethan literary activity.''[11] This quest for national identity played in the prefaces of translations, like Florio's of Montaigne, and in some of the most popular English rhetorics, like those of Peacham and Puttenham. And translation was the central figure in the play. For consistently, as these texts testify, the test of the vernacular's identity was seen in its ability (or lack thereof) to adequately translate not only prestigious modern languages like French and Italian, but the great classical languages of Latin, Greek, and Hebrew. And this test, if passed, was continually figured as proof of the English language's (and hence the English nation's) civilized status, of the vernacular's emergence from barbarism, in the same way that Cicero in *De Optimo Genere Oratorum* implicitly understands Latin's ability to translate Greek (over and against those who doubted that ability) as a proof of its civility. In his dedicatory introduction to his translation of Pliny's *Natural History* (1601), Philemon Holland, linking this Roman past of translation to the English present, both remembers the period of England's barbarism and celebrates its civilized emergence when he writes of the translation of Latin texts into English as a "requitall" for Rome's conquest of Britain.[12]

But if English translations of classical texts marked a moment of triumph in England's conquest to civilize what it saw as its own savage past, these translations simultaneously posed a threat to this emerging, civilized identity. It was not that the translations were seen as failures (they weren't, except by an opposed group of scholastics who saw their professional identity, their control of the classics, threatened), nor simply because of the perceived danger, which Holland's introduction also shows, that the pagan religious ideas of the classical authors might subvert the Christian purity of English (for translation was also a means of Christianizing the classics), but because of a fear in certain vocal intellectual circles that the vernacular's contact with foreign languages in the translation process would alienate it through a "borrowing of other tunges," as Sir John Cheek put it in a prefatory letter included in Thomas Hoby's translation of *The Courtier* (1561). Cheek, along with others like Puttenham (252) and Roger Ascham, wanted the language written "cleane and pure, unmixt [with] and unmangeled [by]" foreign idiom.[13]

A crucial point should be stressed here. These scholars were not opposed to translation, quite the contrary, as their activities in behalf of it insist. Rather, we might say, they were for a certain kind of translation, one that assimilated the other completely to native ways, "arraied," as Holland says of his Pliny, "in the . . . habit" of "English weed." If Tudor England was not obsessed with racial purity (at least not as it would be, along with the rest of the West, after, as we have noted, a notion of the *biological* began to emerge in the late eighteenth century), it appears to have been obsessed with linguistic purity; and, indeed, whether implicit or explicit, there appears to have been a close connection between language and racial, or cultural, identity. Arrayed in his English weed, Pliny writes about this connection in the seventh book of his *Natural History,* just after noticing in passing what he finds to be the extravagant blackness of Ethiopians: "Let us come to one only point, which to speake of seemeth but small, but being deeply weighed and considered, is a matter of exceeding great regard, and that is, the varietie of men's speech;

so many tongues and divers languages are amongst them in the world, that one straunger to another seemeth well-neere to be no man at all'' (153). The notion of what is human, this passage suggests, is intimately tied to the perception of linguistic difference. Translation, then, its possibility, we might suppose, is conceived of in early modern Europe as being, quite literally, a humanizing activity, a passport or transport into the fully human of the native speaker's tongue, a tongue that has already been humanized itself by proving its equivalency, or even superiority, to the classical languages.

We must emphasize here that in understanding this ''quest for cultural and national identity'' we are dealing not simply with one group of translators, those working in the domestic sphere, but with two groups, one at home and one far abroad, both, nevertheless, engaged in the activity of translating something designated as ''savagery'' into something designated as ''civility.'' Indeed, it is the figure of translation, in all of its political specificity, that constitutes these two categories; they do not exist prior to or outside of this figure, in some absolute, or natural, or neutral state. We must remember that the activity of intercultural communication, the realm of foreign policy, cannot be separated from the realm of intracultural communication, the realm of domestic policy.

— 6 —

The Empire of Poetics

It has been said that the orators of the Antilles have a gift of
eloquence that would leave any European breathless.

FRANTZ FANON

THE BURDEN OF this book is, of course, that translation was, and
still is, the central act of European colonization amd imperialism in the
Americas. But let us epitomize here. As Stephen Greenblatt puts it, "the
primal crime in the New World [the kidnapping of Native Americans to
serve as interpreters] was committed in the interest of language" (563),
in the interest, precisely, of translation—that is, of *figuring* out the
Indians in the way that we have read the master figuring out the slave in
Douglass's *Narrative*. There is no better paradigm for this process of
translating, or figuring out, the Indians, then the ritual reading of the
Spanish *Requerimiento*, composed in 1513 and put into effect the following year, in which, without regard to problems of translation, the
Indians were informed *in Spanish* of their place in the Catholic/Spanish
imperium. Wilcomb Washburn makes some useful comments on the
importance of this ritual to colonization:

> The status of the American Indian was locked into Catholic doctrine and
> Spanish legalism almost from the moment of discovery. The relationship
> was not to be merely that of conquerer and conquered. The Indian was
> condemned by a preexisting theory to a status by which he served as a
> material resource to be exploited and as a spiritual object to be saved. His
> dependence was fore-ordained by his attacker. His status as a member of an
> independent community or nation could be formally denied even when he
> was able to maintain that independence against his oppressors.
>
> The most direct . . . expression of the Europeans' assumption of
> preexisting status in the New World is contained in the Spanish "Require-
> ment" (*Requerimiento*) which was ordered to be read to the Indians by a

notary before hostilities could be legally commenced. The Requirement was [Washburn quotes from Lewis Hanke in the following] "read to trees and empty huts when no Indians were to be found. Captains muttered its theological phrases into their beards on the edge of sleeping Indian settlements, or even a league away before starting the formal attack, and at times some leatherlunged Spanish notary hurled its sonorous phrases after the Indians as they fled into the mountains. . . . Ship captains would sometimes have the document read from the deck as they approached an island. . . ."[1]

What Washburn's and Hanke's comments suggest is that the conquest of the New World, which is synonymous with the dispossession of the Indians and the institution of slavery, begins with the conversion of the Indians into a religious and legal fiction: "a material resource to be exploited and . . . a spiritual object to be saved." (And material exploitation and spiritual salvation are completely entangled.) In the beginning, then, in the European mind, Indians become a pure figure (the homogenizing of these diverse peoples under the name of "Indians" being the primal act of translation); their independent, or proper, status is "formally denied" in foreign language documents in which this figure is bound to prescribed paths and which, projected on the Indians proper, are then taken for the proper. In the beginning, as preamble to and constitution of the act of dispossession, we find the activity of colonization as translation, both in the sense of conversion from one language into another and in a metaphorical or transferred sense. In this case, however, translation means precisely not to understand others who are the original (inhabitants) or to understand those others all too easily—as if there were no questions of translation—solely in terms of one's own language, where those others become a useable fiction: the fiction of the Other.

In this and parallel cases from the narratives of the voyagers, Stephen Greenblatt and Tzvetan Todorov have deduced a symmetrical figure in regard to the European perception of Native American languages. Writing of Columbus, Todorov provides a summary of this figure:

Columbus's failure to recognize the diversity of languages permits him, when he confronts a foreign tongue, only two possible, and complementary, forms of behavior: to acknowledge it as a language but to refuse to believe it is different [hence Columbus's assertions throughout his *Journal* that he fully understands the Arawaks he meets]; or to acknowledge its difference but to refuse to admit it is a language. . . . This latter reaction is provided by the Indians he encounters at the very beginning, on October

12, 1492; seeing them, he promises himself: "If it please Our Lord, at the moment of my departure I shall take from this place six of them to Your Highness, so that they may learn to speak" (these terms seemed so shocking to Columbus's various French translators that all of them corrected the statement to: "so that they may learn our language"). (30)

While for Todorov this figure of interpretation results from "Columbus's failure to recognize the diversity of languages" because "he is not interested in ['human communications']" (33), for Greenblatt, who tells us in his essay on *The Tempest* that "Indians were frequently either found defective in speech, and hence pushed toward the zone of wild things, or granted essentially the same speech as the Europeans," this figure results not from an individual's failure to recognize the linguistic state of the world after Babel, but from a whole culture's repression of that state because it contradicted "the conviction that reality was one and universal" (572), that all languages were actually the translation of a single universal language.

Although Greenblatt and Todorov acknowledge a third relationship in the European understanding of American languages, one simultaneous with the other two, that Columbus and subsequent voyagers did indeed recognize that they were dealing with different languages that they didn't understand, both writers marginalize this third term in their arguments in order to produce the elegant opposition that we have been reading which, in its claims to comprehend a whole field of complex linguistic relations, takes on the force of a paradigm: the Indians (defined in relation to language) were either absolutely identical to or absolutely different from and inferior to the Europeans (also defined in relation to language). "Though they seem to be opposite extremes," Greenblatt remarks, "both positions reflect a fundamental inability to sustain the simultaneous perception of likeness and difference, the very special perception we give to metaphor" (574–75). For Greenblatt, then, metaphor, defined as "the simultaneous perception of likeness and difference," becomes the positive model for intercultural communication, a model, however, suppressed by or nonoperative in the perceptual apparatus of New-World conquerors.

My own speculations contradict this line of reasoning. I find it more than strange that metaphor, the very engine of Western notions of language, and, in particular, such a powerfully explicit force in the Renaissance, should be absent as a formative agent in European perceptions of the Americas. A theory of Europe's linguistic understanding of the place it named the New World that erases metaphor from the formulation needs querying. Pursuing such a query, we should note that Greenblatt's definition of metaphor is ahistorical; that is, it escapes the burden of violence that otherwise implicates the European translation of Native Americans. Indeed, Greenblatt's conception of metaphor does not simply escape this violence; it transcends it, potentially providing an ideal model of intercultural communication. And if the colonial voyagers, investors, and propagandists did not avail themselves of this model, Shakespeare, according to Greenblatt, did, for

> in *The Tempest* . . . [he] experiments with an extreme version of this problem, placing Caliban at the outer limits of difference only to insist upon a mysterious measure of resemblance. It is as if he were testing our capacity to sustain metaphor. And in this instance only, the audience achieves a fullness of understanding before Prospero does, an understanding that Prospero is only groping toward at the play's close. In the poisoned relationship between master and slave, Caliban can only curse; but we know that Caliban's consciousness is not simply a warped negation of Prospero's:

> > I prithee, let me bring thee where crabs grow;
> > And I with my long nails will dig thee pig-nuts;
> > Show thee a jay's nest, and instruct thee how
> > To snare the nimble marmoset; I'll bring thee
> > To clustering filberts, and sometimes I'll get thee
> > Young scamels from the rock.
> >   (II.ii.167–72)

> The rich, irreducible concreteness of the verse compels us to acknowledge the independence and integrity of Caliban's construction of reality. We do not sentimentalize this construction—indeed the play insists that we judge it and that we prefer another—but we cannot make it vanish into silence. Caliban's world has what we may call *opacity*, and the perfect emblem of that opacity is the fact that we do not to this day know the meaning of the word "scamel." (575)

For Greenblatt, Caliban is the place of metaphor in *The Tempest*, the metaphor of (a notion of) metaphor that figures the possibility of authentic intercultural communication between Europeans and Native Americans, giving to the audience "a fullness of understanding" concerning the cultural "independence and integrity" of those others whom, in the absence of metaphoric understanding, European languages either absolutely absorb or alienate. What Greenblatt performs in this reading of *The Tempest* is the ritual we have examined of saving *Literature* (for Shakespeare is inevitably the figure of great verbal art) from the "merely topical." In this case the play is at once deeply imbued with the historical circumstances that articulate a colonial and imperial politics of language and yet transcends these circumstances through the privileged place of metaphor. For metaphor, like Shakespeare, is inevitably the embodiment of poetic possibility, of plenitude and transcendence in a certain literary tradition.

Clearly, I agree with Greenblatt that Caliban is the place of metaphor, the place of translation, in *The Tempest*. But just as clearly, I do not agree that metaphor is a privileged place, located "outside" of or "beyond" or "above" the colonial and imperial politics of language that we have been reading. Rather, I regard metaphor, in those negotiations between the domestic and the foreign, between one class and another, that we have been exploring and will continue to explore, as the very figure of this politics, as implicated in this politics from the beginning. To define metaphor as simply "the simultaneous perception of likeness and differ-ence" is to repress the metaphors (of the domestic and the foreign) that historically locate the notion of metaphor and that constitute the percep-tion of likeness and difference within the equivocal interplay of domestic and foreign policy. Further, within the field of metaphor, as conven-tionally construed, the perception of likeness and of difference is never simultaneous, but hierarchical. For metaphor, from Aristotle onward, unless we work to deconstruct or, I would say, politicize it in a particular way, is defined by an ideal of self-identity, in which similarity, under-stood as a function of contingency, is subordinate to difference, grounded, as it is, in an idea of essence, or the absolute. We cannot separate metaphor from the idea of self-possession, of having a property in the self, which, as we have read in Locke, cannot be separated from individual ownership of land. In the West, when we recognize in the gnarled limbs of an old person the branches of an ancient tree, the similarities we perceive never, typically, confuse the profound differ-ences between person and tree, what is essential or proper to each, or the fact that a person, by virtue of these differences, has a right under the proper juridical circumstances to claim a property in the tree and the land on which it grows; whereas in Native American cultures, it appears that such a "confusion" of person and tree may be conventional, both prohibiting the relationship of property and stemming from such a prohibition.

I am arguing, then, that far from being absent from the perceptual apparatus of European colonizers in the Americas, metaphor, or translation, was the very motor of this apparatus. Considering metaphor in the ways that I have been and will continue to in the rest of this book, we can replace the figure of Todorov and Greenblatt (the Indians speak no language; the Indians speak our language) with a more accurate figure. In the figure I propose, problems of intercultural communication (of the "foreign") are intimately related to problems of intracultural communication (of the "domestic"); and the linguistic relationship that Todorov and Greenblatt marginalize (the Indians speak a language and it is different from ours) is understood as a crucial part of the figure.

For it is not true that, as Todorov asserts, Columbus was not interested in human communications. He was obsessed with them, which is why, like the Freudian unconscious, where contradictions coexist without the subject's recognizing them as contradictions, his journal fluctuates wildly between assertions that he understands the Indians and admissions that they are speaking a language completely foreign to him and his company. Here power, the dream of absolute power (the conqueror, as conqueror, should comprehend all), refuses to acknowledge, even as it asserts, its own powerlessness (I comprehend virtually nothing, therefore how can I be the conqueror). And, while there was certainly a powerful strain of European thought from the sixteenth through the nineteenth centuries that regarded Indian languages as inherently inferior to European tongues, it cannot be unequivocally assumed that when Columbus wrote that the Indians must "learn to talk" he thought they were without language or, what amounts to the same thing, that they were beasts (although the same strain of European thought running from the sixteenth century, when Las Casas and Sepúlveda debated the humanness of the Indians [1550], through the nineteenth century strives to reduce Native Americans to a lower place on an evolutionary scale).

Cecil Jane, from whose English translation of Columbus's journal I have quoted, was apparently not as shocked at the formulation "learn to talk" as Todorov claims the French translators were; for Jane does not add the culturally relativizing "our language." In interpreting this formulation, we ought first to remember that the original journal is lost to us and that what we are reading today is a transcription of Las Casas's abstract of a copy of the original.[2] This history, at least, problematizes what Columbus may have actually written. But even if we assume that Columbus wrote "learn to talk," rather than "learn to talk our language," what compels us to read this statement literally, particularly when it is juxtaposed with other statements in the journal that recognize language in the Indians? Perhaps what is troubling Columbus throughout his journal is not the question of whether the Indians possess a language, but the question of whether he possesses one, that is, the question of what a language is. For having voyaged from a place of comfortably recognizable languages to a place of radically unrecognizable ones, which, yet, no matter how far-fetched in appearance were still recognizable as language, Columbus's European paradigm of what a language was, and hence of what a human was, must have been challenged. But rather than consciously questioning his culture's centrality, a question that would have threatened terrific anxiety by raising doubts about his grasp of the situation, he represses the question by projecting it onto the Indians; the result is Columbus's hallucinatory attempts to domesticate the far-fetched in his recurring fantasy that he understands the Indians' language. The domestic fantasy, which represses the fear that Columbus himself may not know how to talk (a fear that was quite realistic in the Caribbean context he has invaded), is necessary precisely because Columbus is so sharply struck by the fact of the foreign.

This fact of the foreign was strikingly present to the European colonizers of the Americas. After Columbus, the early expeditions to the New World carried instructions, stressing the problem of translation, for, contrary to Greenblatt's suggestion, the people with power in the Renaissance were acutely aware that they were living in a world after Babel, in a world where there could be no more apostolic preaching in tongues. We have read that Hakluyt, in his *Discourse of Western Planting,* advised prospective voyagers, in the interest of converting the Indians (one form of figuring them out), to "firste learne the language of the people nere adjoyninge (the gifte of tongues beinge nowe taken awaye). . . ." And the opening arguments of *A True Declaration of the Estate of the Colonie in Virginia,* acknowledging that apostolic preaching to the Indians is impossible, "except wee had the gift of tongues, that euerie nation might heare the word of God in their owne language," makes a political virtue out of the fall from language into languages:

> That which *Origen* said of Christs actions in vertues morall, holdeth proportion with Gods actions in gouernment politicall, *Dei facta, sunt*

nostra praecepta, Gods actions, are our instructions: who (in the eleuenth of Genesis) turned the greatest cursing, into the greatest blessing, and by confusion of tongues, kept them from confusion of states; scattering those clouen people, into as many colonies ouer the face of the earth, as there are diuersities of languages in the earth. (4)

According to this argument, the nation-state, with its identity dependent on its distinct language, appears to get its warranty from God at Babel, when he originally created the world in a colonial configuration: "Search the records of diuine truth, and humane monuments of state, you shall find, *Salmanasar* transporting the Babilonians, and other Gentiles, to *Samaria:* and replenishing with the captiues of Israell, the dispeopled confines of *Media"* (4). In the beginning (of history), so this story goes, was the nation-state, and its primal act was to translate itself into colonial forms. The medieval theory of the *translatio imperii et studii,* with its vision of a universal empire with a universal language, putatively Latin, is adapted here to a world after Babel, one of burgeoning and competing nationalisms with their vernaculars, and finds its explicit formulation at the end of *A True Declaration,* where God's promise of English hegemony in North America is invoked: "The same God that hath ioyned three Kingdomes vnder one *Caesar* [a reference to the rule of James I in England, Scotland, and Ireland], wil not be wanting to adde a fourth [in America], if wee would dissolue that frosty Icinesse which chilleth our zeale, and maketh vs so cold in the action" (26). In this call to renew the effort of English colonization at Jamestown, we can locate the beginnings of the translation of the *translatio imperii* into the nineteenth-century idea of Manifest Destiny.

Ernst Robert Curtius provides us with a concise summary of the notion of the *translatio:*

The Bible furnished medieval historical thought with yet another theological substantiation for the replacement of one empire by another: "Regnum a gente in gentem transfertur propter injustitias et injurias et contumelias et diversos dolos" (Ecclesiasticus 10:8). "Because of unrighteous dealings, injuries, and riches got by deceit, the kingdom is transferred from one people to another." The word *transfertur* ("is transferred") gives rise to the concept of *translatio* (transference) which is basic for medieval historical theory. The renewal of the Empire by Charlemagne could be regarded as a transferal of the Roman *imperium* to another people. This is implied in the formula *translatio imperii,* with which the *translatio studii* (transferal of learning from Athens or Rome to Paris) was later coordinated. The medieval Empire took over from Rome the idea of world empire; thus it had a universal, not a national, character.[3]

"The belief that the Empire was universal," Robert Folz tells us,

> was essentially Hellenic in conception and outline. The Greek philosophers, in particular the Stoics, stressed the notion that all mankind formed one community, partaking of universal reason. To them, influenced by Alexander's conquests, it seemed plain that Greek civilisation had a universal mission: they regarded it as human civilisation at its best, dominating the *oikoumene* on the outskirts of which barbarism reigned. It was, indeed, the Greeks who from the second century B.C. had regarded the Roman Empire and the *oikoumene* as one: Panaetius, friend of Scipio Emilianus, considered that the Roman conquest would lead to the realisation of a union of all civilised peoples; its purpose, and at the same time its justification, was to give peace, order and justice to mankind. . . .
>
> This concept of an empire which was the hearth and home of civilisation was reinforced and sublimated by the Christian religion, which had an essentially oecumenical mission. At first there was a conflict between the universalism of Christianity and that of Rome, but by the end of the second century Christians no longer treated the Empire as an object of systematic hostility: on the contrary, they said prayers for it and regarded it as having its place in the design of Providence.[4]

The *translatio,* then, is inseparably connected with a "civilizing" mission, the bearing of Christianity and Western letters to the barbarians, literally, as we have noted, those who do not speak the language of the empire. From its beginnings the imperialist mission is, in short, one of translation: the translation of the "other" into the terms of the empire, the prime term of which is "barbarian," or one of its variations such as "savage," which, ironically, but not without a precise politics, also alienates the other from the empire. Within the dynamics of the *translatio* it is the eloquent orator who is figured as the prime agent of this mission of translation. When Charlemagne begins the translation of empire at the end of the eighth century, he transports Alcuin from England to help "rebuild in the new Carolingian empire the half-obliterated educational system of the earlier imperial epoch." As a principal mark of this effort of translation, Alcuin composed a "thoroughly Ciceronian" rhetoric, which takes the form of a dialogue between himself as teacher and Charlemagne as student, who requests the precepts of rhetoric from Alcuin so that he can rule properly.[5] Alcuin begins the rhetoric, as historically all good classical rhetorics began, by telling Charlemagne the story of the orator who translates a savage humanity into civilization through the power of his eloquence.

The conception of the orator as emperor, conquering men with the weapon of eloquence, is, as we know, a classical and Renaissance commonplace. It is also, as I have been arguing, a commonplace of formal education through at least the middle of the nineteenth century, and persists, in figures such as Tarzan and Ronald Reagan, in our own time. This imperial commonplace finds its place within an equally common classical and Renaissance narrative: the story of the orator as the first settler, that is, as the first civilizer and colonizer of humans. At the very beginning of *De Inventione*, Cicero, that most important influence on the Renaissance idea of eloquence, gives us a version of the story that Alcuin follows to the letter in its crucial details:

> For there was a time when men wandered at large [*passim . . . vagabantur*] in the fields like animals [*bestiarum modo*] and lived on wild fare; they did nothing by the guidance of reason [*ratione*], but relied chiefly on physical strength; there was as yet no ordered system of religious worship nor of social duties; no one had seen legitimate marriage nor had anyone looked upon children whom he knew to be his own; nor had they learned the advantages of an equitable code of law. And so through their ignorance and error blind and unreasoning passion satisfied itself by misuse of bodily strength, which is a very dangerous servant.
>
> At this juncture a man—great and wise I am sure—became aware of the power latent in man and the wide field offered by his mind for great achievements if one could develop [*elicere*] this power and improve it [*meliorem reddere*] by instruction. Men were scattered in the fields and hidden in sylvan retreats when he assembled and gathered them [*compulit unum in locum et congregavit*] in accordance with a plan [*ratione*]; he introduced them to every useful and honourable occupation, though they cried out [*reclamantes*] against it at first because of its novelty [*propter insolentiam*], and then when through reason and eloquence [*propter rationem atque orationem*] they had listened with greater attention, he transformed [*reddidit*] them from wild savages [*ex feris et immanibus*] into a kind [*mites*] and gentle [*mansuetos*] folk. (I.2.2)[6]

We have before us one of the West's most familiar scenes. And, certainly, it is a scene that was familiar to Renaissance schoolboys and to the men they became. This scene of primal colonization is a scene of instruction: first, because it is the narrative that explicitly and implicitly framed the central teaching of rhetoric in Renaissance schools, reminding the pupils that their education would confer on them the very originary power of civilization; and, second, because the scene itself narrates what it posits as *the* original act of instruction, the act whereby savages are converted through the power of eloquence to civility. What we have here, for the Renaissance schoolboys reading it, is a dramatization of the primal schoolroom, where an initially aimless (*passim . . . vagabantur*) and unruly (*reclamantes*) student body is made to cohere by the lessons of a great and wise master. This comparison is not far-fetched. The influential Renaissance scholar Juan Luis Vives constructed a dialogue for schoolboys in which a father tells a schoolmaster that he is bringing his son to school so that the master can transform the boy from a beast into a human being (*Hunc filiolum meum ad te adduco ut ex belua hominem facias*).[7]

We can, then, consider this scene of the primal power of eloquence as one of both intracultural and intercultural colonization, remembering that the two are inseparably related, while not identical in their political impact; for to "colonize" the self, or those of one's own race, gender, or class, is not the same act that colonizing the other is. The schoolboy reading this narrative or listening to his master recite it is taught to identify himself with the wild men in the scene and thus to recognize himself as a kind of foreigner in relation to the orator, as a member of another species, who through the experience of being overpowered by oratory will gain access to oratory's power, the power of speech, and thus become a native of the civil world. We should note here that the translation of *De Inventione*, while stressing the apparently clear frontier between the physical force of the savages and the reason (*ratio*) of the orator mutes the suggestions of the violence of eloquence that the passage contains, and that Cicero himself recognized explicitly when he repeated the scene in the later *De Oratore*. So, for example, while the translation describes the orator's awareness of "the power latent in man" that he "could develop" (*elicere*), the Latin verb *elicio* contains among its meanings notions of *allurement* and *enticement* that suggest the subterfuge of seduction. And when the translation tells us that the orator "assembled and gathered [the wild men]" (*compulit unum in locum et congregavit*), omitting a translation of *"unum in locum"* (in one place) (which I will return to), it erases the notions of force, of *compulsion* and *constraint*, contained in the verb *compello* (*-ere*), even as it fails to take account of the fact that both *compello* and *congrego* can refer to the herding of animals. Finally, there would appear to be an appropriate pun, lost in translation, in the description of the wild men crying out "at first because of [the] novelty [*propter insolentiam*]" of the orator's plan. *Insolentia*, from the root of which, *insolens*, comes the English *insolence*, can mean just that, as well as *arrogant*.

This scene of colonization is also a scene of translation, although the narrative never describes the orator and the savages speaking languages foreign to each other; indeed, it might seem implicit that they speak the same language, for how, speaking a foreign tongue, could the orator persuade these humans into civility? Yet the sense of the scene, I want to argue, points to the primal orator as a translator.

Cicero, who spent his whole life at the center of the civil turmoil that would make his death and that of the Roman Republic virtually conterminous, offers the primal scene of eloquence at the beginning of *De Inventione* as a way of persuading both himself and his readers that eloquence, in spite of so much historical evidence to the contrary, is at its origin an essentially constructive force, and, thus, that its destructiveness is secondary: the result of its misuse by immoral men, subsequent to the founding of civil society, who perverted it to take "the helm of the ship of state" from the truly eloquent, thus bringing on "great and disastrous wrecks [*maxima ac miserrima naufragia*]" (I.3.4), of the kind that *The Tempest* and *A True Declaration* depict. "These events," Cicero continues, "brought eloquence into such odium and unpopularity that men of the greatest talent left a life of strife and tumult for some quiet pursuit [*studium*], as sailors seek refuge in port from a raging storm [*quasi ex aliqua turbida tempestate in portum*]" (I.3.4), thus abandoning eloquence and the ship of state to the worst elements, as Prospero does when he leaves Antonio in charge of Milan to take refuge in his studies. As Cicero brings his comments on the origin of eloquence and its fall to a close, then, he urges men not to abandon its study:

> For from eloquence the state receives many benefits, provided only it is accompanied by wisdom, the guide of all human affairs. . . . Furthermore, I think that men [*homines*], although lower and weaker than animals [*bestiis*] in many respects, excel them most by having the power of speech [*quod loqui possunt*]. Therefore that man appears to me to have won a splendid possession who excels men themselves in that ability by which men excel beasts. (I.4.5)

As Cicero is concluding his remarks on the origin of the civilizing power of eloquence, he presents us, I offer, the analogy that structures the scene of that origin: the ordinary speech of humans is to the eloquence of the orator what the inarticulate cries of beasts are to ordinary human speech. The scene in which the orator organizes savages into civil society through the persuasive powers of eloquence is by analogy a scene in which animals are "transformed" (*reddidit*) into human beings by receiving the power of speech. And this linguistic analogy is strengthened by the fact that one of the meanings of *reddo* is "translate." Within the scope of this analogy, the narrative's description of humans, devoid of reason and thus given over to the dictates of pure physical force and passion, wandering aimlessly in the state of nature, suggests a physical and mental incoherence that could stand as a figure both for the perceived vocal incoherence of animals and for the kind of irresponsible oratory allowed to wander in the purely material entanglements of language unconstrained by wisdom. In *De Oratore,* for example, Cicero compares eloquence ungrounded in wisdom to the speech of a madman (I.12.51).

The sense that this narrative of primal colonization deals with the translation of vocal or verbal incoherency into coherent speech (potential eloquence)—that it is, indeed, a primal scene of translation—is emphasized by the phrase that the translation omits. Thus, the translation tells us: "Men were scattered in the fields and hidden in sylvan retreats when he assembled and gathered them [*compulit unum in locum et congregavit*] in accordance with a plan [*ratione*]." The missing phrase, *"unum in locum"* (in one place), is crucial to understanding the relationship between language and colonization that this primal scene of translation figures forth.

The translator possibly omitted the phrase "in one place" because he felt its sense was implicit in the verbs *compulit* and *congregavit,* though the Loeb translation of *De Oratore* includes the phrase. And yet, clearly, Cicero does not feel that *unum in locum* is a waste of words. The phrase is no waste in this discourse of colonization because, as we read in Chapter 3, in the history of Western colonization and imperialism it is the very sign of civilization, the very sign, that is, of a permanent *settling* of peoples, as opposed to the state, ideologically projected by the colonizer, in which so-called "savage" peoples "wandered aimlessly" (*passim . . . vagabantur*), or were "scattered" (*dispersos*). Being in one place is the ground of that "equitable code of law" (*ius aequabile*) which the narrative of the eloquent orator posits as a key sign of civil society. For, and here let us follow Cicero in his *Topica,* "The civil law is a system of equity [*aequitas*] established between members of the same state [*eiusdem civitatis*] for the purpose of securing to each his property rights [*res suas*]'' (II.9).[8] And without the Western notion of ''place,'' as an objectified space that can be alienated in such hierarchical forms as ''real estate'' and ''the state,'' there could be no civil law in the sense that Cicero's Rome defined it and the West still defines it. ''Over-whelmingly,'' John Crook writes, ''the most important kind of property in the Roman world was land. It was upon the rents of land that a man must live if he was to cut a respectable figure in the community, and those who made money in trade or manufacture hastened to invest it in real estate.''[9]

The scene of colonization in *De Inventione,* in which the legal notion of *place* is so crucial, is also, as we have noted, a scene of translation, put into play by an analogy that dramatizes the scene as one in which animals become human by attaining the power of speech, or humans speaking wildly, that is, without eloquence, attain the ability to speak civilly, that is, with at least a certain degree of eloquence. As we come to recognize that colonization is translation in this scene, so we must come to recognize that the legal notion of place, which defines the idea of civility in the scene, is also the dialectical and rhetorical notion of *place* (*topoi* or *loci*), which defines the scene's idea of eloquence.

''The nature of the *topoi*—or loci or places or commonplaces—is well-known,'' Walter J. Ong tells us in his book on that sixteenth-century apotheosis of topical logic, Peter Ramus.

> They are the headings or key notions to which one turns to find out what is available in one's store of knowledge for discourse on any given subject. . . .
>
> Lists of the topics or places commonly include such things as definition, genus, species, wholes, parts, adjacents (corresponding roughly to what would, in another way, be treated under the various categories of ''accidents''), relatives, comparisons, opposites, and . . . witnesses. These are the headings one is to run through when one has to say something on any subject, to pronounce a eulogy or to plead a case or simply to give a lecture on a question of the day.
>
> The topical tradition is omnivorous in its selection of these headings, and tends to assimilate and adapt any and all sorts of classifications with which its users are likely to be familiar and which thus are likely to be serviceable. Thus, even before Aristotle's *Topics,* and from then on, serviceable bits of the general philosophical apparatus, including the well-known Aristotelian categories or predicaments and the related ''predicables'' (genus, specific difference, species, property, improper accidents)

were more or less incorporated into the classificatory finding-apparatus among the "places."[10]

At the very beginning of the *Topica*, where he acknowledges the authority of Aristotle in the matter, Cicero defines "a topic [*locum*] as the region [*sedem*] of an argument, and an argument as a course of reasoning [*rationem*] which firmly establishes a matter about which there is some doubt" (II.8). Aside from the translation of *locus* as "topic," where I would prefer and will emphasize the less semantically restricted "place," the translation catches the territorial force of topical thinking. A place is the *region* of an argument, its *sedes*, or "seat," in the sense of a place where one sits, "a bench" or "a throne," for example. Or by extension, a seat is a "dwelling place," as in one's home, and then, a "base, ground, [or] foundation." *Sedes* comes from the verb *sedeo*, which means simply "to sit," but can also mean to "be settled," in the sense of "established."

Grounded in the idea of defining ground, topical thinking inevitably declares itself in the prime terms of colonization, the terms not simply of settling and possessing a foreign place (a place in doubt), but, crucially, of converting that place into property. In the West an argument is won (a doubt is transformed into a certainty, or identity), when one combatant is sole possessor of the place of that argument, having driven the other claimant out. It is no accident that in his *Topica* Cicero explains the idea of topical logic in general using examples taken largely from Roman civil law, which, as we have read, is defined in terms of property rights, a concept that historically has been grounded in the right to the ownership of land. And, as Ong remarks, "In Ramus the loci will be pictured as individual structures in real-estate developments, separated from one another . . . by a clear space of so many feet" (121).

Cicero's *De Inventione* holds a crucial place in the history of our mental colonization (the history of settling our doubts) that the "omnivorous" "topical tradition" represents. For Cicero's youthful text, along with the contemporary *Rhetorica ad Herennium*, mark for us the first fully visible formalization, as Howell wrote, "of the dialectical approach to rhetorical invention" (59), an approach that is grounded in the territorial imperatives of topical logic.

It is these territorial imperatives that ground the rhetorical power of the eloquent orator. As we have already noted, the motor of this power is metaphor. Indeed, as its name makes clear, the theory of history figured in the *translatio* is a theory of figuration in which a Christianized Rome becomes both the metaphor for and the proper historical referent of all subsequent imperial power in the West.

In the *Poetics,* Aristotle, discussing style, remarks in passing that "the greatest thing by far is to have a command of metaphor" (XXII.10). And we recall that Quintillian, who, interpreting Cicero in a particular way (VIII.Pr.14–16), elevates the function of style, or *elocutio* (the place of language itself) in the rhetorical machine, calls metaphor "the supreme ornament of oratory [*maximus est orationis ornatus*]" (VIII.2.6). Let me emphasize again that *ornatus* (from *orno -are*) connotes not the superficial but the necessary. In fact, in the history that rhetoric fabricates for itself, metaphor or figurative language (all *translated* words, of which metaphor is the archetype and exemplum) is the necessary origin of language, in that paradox, to which Rousseau was so sensitive, that to imagine the origin of language we must inevitably imagine language as its own origin. Alcuin's *Rhetoric* gives us a concise summary of the history and function of metaphor, or *translatio:*

> Adornment [*ornatus*] is attainable everywhere in the realm of figurative terms [*translatis*], which owe their origin to man's need of a language [*quem genuit necessitas*], and to the sterility and poverty of his early speech. More recently, however, his delight and pleasure in the use of figures have given them prestige. As clothing was first devised to protect him from the cold, and in course of time became an ornament [*ornatum*] of his person and a symbol of his rank [*dignitatem*], so figurative language [*verbis translatio*] was first used to satisfy a need, and later was given new popularity by the pleasure it provided, and by the ornamental effect it produced. . . . Often a figurative term [*translatio*] will on the instant clarify [*inlustratur*] the meaning which a parallel literal term [*verbo proprio*] is powerless to convey. Nevertheless, ideas expressed figuratively [*transferri*] should always be ideas which achieve greater clarity by that means [*quae clariorem faciunt rem*]. . . . Thus in general the greatest virtue of figurative terms [*verbi translati*] is that they lay bare the thought [*ut sensum aperiat*]. (1020–35)

As Alcuin describes the process of *translation* (the movement of metaphor, or figuration) in the preceding passage—and I want to emphasize how commonplace this description is in the history of rhetoric—it is the process of what the West typically calls "civilization"; it is an evolutionary process in which the mute or practically mute (those whose speech is poverty stricken) through the power of translation learn first to speak and then to speak eloquently, that is, ornamentally. And this evolutionary process of translation is translated here by another common-place that I have already remarked upon: that of clothing, the most popular figure in the history of rhetoric for figuration. The movement from muteness to eloquence is translated as the progression from naked-ness, through the bare necessity of clothing as protection, to the pinnacle of clothing as a sumptuous sign of social rank (though we should note a possible paradox in the notion that the function of metaphor is to "lay bare" the thought of the orator). The paradox of the figure of clothing expresses a contradictory movement in the history of eloquence. The desire, indeed the dictum, is always to speak or write clearly, nakedly or properly, yet, ironically, eloquence demands the clothing of metaphor.

Europeans arriving in America projected this evolutionary scenario that structures the *translatio,* of nakedness and clothing, of muteness and speech, on and as the New World. Europeans, typically, perceived the Indians as "naked"; and they equated this nakedness with either the absence of or a deficiency in language (Miranda reminds Caliban that when she and her father arrived on the island the native "wouldst gabble like / A thing most brutish" [I.ii.358–59]), or with a kind of primal or protoeloquence. Puttenham argues for the ultimate superiority of English over classical languages by linking English to this primal poetry or metaphoric speech:

> And the Greeke and Latine Poesie was by verse numerous amd metri-call . . . but without any rime or tunable concord in th'end of their verses, as we and all other nations now vse. But the Hebrues & Chaldees who were more ancient then the Greekes, did not only vse a metricall Poesie, but also with the same a maner of rime, as hath bene of late obserued by learned men. Whereby it appeareth, that our vulgar running Poesie was common to all the nations of the world besides, whom the Latines and Greekes in speciall called barbarous. So as it was notwithstand-ing the first and most ancient Poesie, and the most vniuersall, which two points do otherwise giue to all humane inuentions and affaires no small credit. This is proued by certificate of marchants & trauellers, who by late nauigations haue surueyed the whole world, and discouered large countries and strange peoples wild and sauage, affirming that the American, the Perusine & the very Canniball, do sing and also say, their highest and holiest matters in certaine riming versicles and not in prose, which proues also that our maner of vulgar Poesie is more ancient then the artificiall of the Greeks and Latines, ours coming by instinct of nature, which was before Art or obseruation, and vsed with the sauage and vnciuill, who were before

all science or ciuilitie, even as the naked by prioritie of time is before the clothed, and the ignorant before the learned. The naturall Poesie therefore being aided and amended by Art, and not vtterly altered or obscured, but some signe left of it, (as the Greekes and Latines haue left none) is no lesse to be allowed and commended then theirs. (10)

From this moment on, Europeans will invariably represent Indian speaking in a self-consciously metaphorical way. Caliban, who, unlike the other lower-class characters in *The Tempest,* speaks a poetic speech that, in spite of the rules of decorum, places him in the linguistic territory of Prospero and Miranda, might be understood by the European audience as not violating these rules because his speech is the *natural* speech of New World natives. And yet we are told by Miranda that she taught him this speech to replace the gibberish he spoke when the Europeans arrived. Still, the speech Caliban speaks, in its simple eloquence, appears to have been Shakespeare's attempt to create the kind of "natural" eloquence of which Puttenham writes. In this case, and this case is always true, the logic of ideology overcomes or contradicts narrative logic. Caliban, the beast, the monster, and thereby the naked one, speaks gibberish and a language of protoeloquence, thereby containing in his name the scenario of metaphor that, as just noted, Europeans projected on America. At the same time, and here we turn the ideological screw once more, he has been given, so the story goes, his language by the Europeans.

So in *The Tempest,* as in all New World scenarios of this kind, we have two orators in front of us, two machines of metaphor, the Native American and the European, but inevitably only one has power. Indeed only one of these machines is a machine in this European scenario. For the native's eloquence is always conceptualized as "natural," whereas the European's eloquence is nature "aided and amended by Art." Just as in the ideology of language that maps the world, both Old and New, for Europeans, metaphor occupies the place of both the foreign and the domestic, the savage and the civilized, it occupies the place of both nature and culture; it is, at once, the most natural of languages or language in its natural state and the most cultivated or cultured. Metaphor is nature; metaphor translates nature into culture.

The *translatio imperii et studii* contains, as it is driven by, a theory of metaphor that is in contradiction with itself. As we have read in the case of Tarzan of the Apes or Ronald Reagan, two orators who can figure the historical persistence of the *translatio* for us, the West resolves this contradiction by projecting one language in conflict with itself as two incommensurate languages, the language of the apes and English, for example. In this situation, the translation of the "inferior" by the "superior" language is simultaneously impossible, because of the qualitative discrepancy (conceived as a matter of intellect), and inevitable, because of that same discrepancy (conceived as a matter of power). We should not be surprised at the proliferation of the contradiction. Prospero translates Caliban into the European's language and yet Caliban is effectively barred from this language, in that he cannot speak it with the power of Prospero. In his most expansive vision in *Nature,* Emerson's orator dominates nature with the language of nature acculturated, a language that nature, figured as the "savage" and the "feminine," is barred from speaking with commensurate power because these figures cannot attain culture, or the "father." Tarzan learns English by translating it into the language of the apes; yet the language of the apes is "naturally" incapable of translating the superior English or being translated into it, so that Tarzan, having learned English, must remain virtually isolated in his linguistic imperium, until the arrival of other Westerners. Douglass's *Narrative* denaturalizes these fictions of the *translatio* by suggesting that one language is always two, and that the problem of translation within the confines of the *translatio* is a problem of political power, a struggle between two orators within the dynamics of race, gender, and class for voice.

If we were to trace the history of the *translatio imperii et studii* from the Old World to the New, we would find this struggle for voice at the heart of its manifestations. For in its vision of a universal empire with a universal language, the *translatio* envisions the translation of all languages into one language; it envisions, that is, the end of translation in the obliteration or complete marginalization of difference. Although Sacvan Bercovitch wants to make a distinction between the Old World *translatio,* with its cyclical view of history as decline (a traditional view of the *translatio* that Hans Baron has challenged), and the New World jeremiad, with its messianic vision of unrelenting progress, the force of consensus he attributes to the jeremiad, the melting pot with a vengeance, can be read, for example, as one manifestation of the *translatio's* vision of the end of translation: We, the People, always speaking in one voice or in voices that are always reconcilable into one voice.[11] The doctrine of Manifest Destiny, a phrase coined in the 1840s to justify U.S. expansion across the continent, with its displacement of Indians and Mexicans and its rationalization of slavery, was an explicit translation of the *translatio*. At the end of the eighteenth century, Jedidiah Morris evoked the *translatio* and looked forward to the ubiquitous language of Manifest Destiny when he remarked, "[I]t is well known that empire has been travelling from east to west. Probably her last and broadest seat will be America . . . the largest empire that ever existed . . . we cannot but anticipate the period, as not far distant, when the AMERICAN EMPIRE will comprehend millions of souls, west of the Mississippi." At the beginning of the nineteenth century Thomas Jefferson envisioned a United States that would "cover the whole northern, if not the southern continent, with a people speaking the same language, governed in similar forms, and by similar laws; nor can we contemplate with satisfaction either blot or mixture on that surface."[12] Without a second thought, Manifest Destiny reconciled imperialism and democracy, just as the United States has reflexively reconciled capitalism and democracy. These acts of reconciliation are synonymous. Thomas R. Hietala in his critique of American expansion puts the rationalization succinctly: "Not all empires need be imperial."

> The expansionsists sharply repudiated those who doubted the exceptionalism of American empire. To justify their nation's aggrandizement they argued that their system was superior to all others because it rested on consent rather than coercion; expansion was unimpeachable because the United States acquired and exploited land, not people. . . . expansionsists often perpetuated the myth of an empty continent that had been dormant for centuries, awaiting the energizing presence of Anglo-Americans. Since the principles of this new empire of consent were so different from those of older empires of conquest, comparisons between them had no validity.[13]

The translation of the *translatio* into American space makes the comparison valid even as it is denied. As Reginald Horsman has argued with particular force, the American *translatio* was, and continues to be, violently racist. The American empire was to be an Anglo-Saxon empire with English as the universal language. Despite America's political enmity with Great Britain, "The hope that an Anglo-Saxon union would bring a new Roman age to the world was expressed regularly from the middle of the nineteenth century on" (292). Within this vision of empire, Tarzan of the Apes becomes an appropriate American orator. And the array of Native American languages becomes the language of the apes, or the metaphoric language of Cooper's Indians, or the terminology of property law.

While the *translatio* dreamt and dreams of empire, the struggle for voice, the assertion of the necessity and difficulty of translation, persisted and persists in various forms from Native American resistance to physical and cultural obliteration; to the Afro-American struggle, first against slavery and then against the obdurate forms of social marginalization that white society enforces; to Third World revolutions and liberation movements.

Frantz Fanon, for example, makes this struggle for voice the central force in his understanding of how colonialism and racism work together:

> I ascribe a basic importance to the phenomenon of language [*langage*].
> That is why I find it necessary to begin with this subject, which should provide us with one of the elements in the man of color's comprehension of the dimension of *the other*. For it is implicit that to speak is to exist absolutely for the other [*Étant entendu que parler, c'est exister absolument pour l'autre*].

In the first place, Fanon returns us to a pre-nineteenth-century world, the world before biology; or, more precisely, he refuses the modern myth of biology as the ground of existence; for existence is a matter of a particular cultural relation. It is a matter of speaking, of language, which always implies an other. "To speak means to be in a position to use a certain syntax, to grasp [*posseder*] the morphology of this or that language, but it means above all to assume [*assumer*] a culture, to support the weight [*le poids*] of a civilization" (17–18). Existence is language, and language is always a matter of politics.

In this case the political matter is a matter of colonialism, which historically has never been separable from the problem of racism:

> For the moment I want to show why the Negro of the Antilles . . . has always to face the problem of language. Furthermore, I will broaden the field of this description and through the Negro of the Antilles include every colonized man. (18)

In the paragraph preceding the one just cited, Fanon articulates the particular problem of language the colonized face:

> The Negro of the Antilles will be proportionately whiter—that is, he will come closer to being a real human being—in direct ratio to his mastery [*fait*

sienne] of the French language. I am not unaware that this is one of man's attitudes face to face with Being. A man who has a language consequently possesses the world expressed and implied by that language. What we are getting at becomes plain: Mastery [*possession*] of language affords remarkable power. (18)

The implication here is that the colonized do not possess a language, that they are speechless, like the savages in the classical myth of the eloquent orator. Indeed, Fanon reminds us, "It is said that the Negro loves to jabber [*palabres*]" (26). In the English translation, which stresses the notion of nonsense, and in Fanon's association of *palabres* with the raucous cries of children at play, this recalls Caliban's primal gabbling. Fanon provides the politics that contextualize and thereby demythologize this myth of "savage" speechlessness and "civilized" eloquence:

> Every colonized people—in other words, every people in whose soul an inferiority complex has been created by the death and burial of its local cultural originality—finds itself face to face with the language of the civilizing nation; that is with the culture of the mother country (*métropolitaine*). The colonized is elevated above his jungle status in proportion to his adoption of the mother country's cultural standards. He becomes whiter as he renounces his blackness, his jungle. (18)

Let us emphasize here that just as existence is a product of language, race, a political effect of existence, must also be a matter of language. To become white, that is to become a real human being, is not a physical problem, it is a political problem: the problem of mastering the master's language, of speaking the language of the capital. It is a problem of the difference in power between the center and the periphery. That is, it is a problem of who determines what is proper speech. It is, precisely, a problem of decorum. To begin with, Fanon states the problem in the most alienating of terms—to be human is to be white, or, more precisely, to be human is to speak a European language fluently—for, quite simply, the colonial situation is one of extreme alienation: "I am speaking here," Fanon remarks, "on the one hand, of alienated (duped [*mystifies*]) blacks, and on the other, of no less alienated (duping [*mystificateurs*] and duped) whites" (29). The alienation inheres, we might say, because both colonizer and colonized accept the myth of the eloquent orator as natural. And the point of revolution arrives when the colonized begin to *read* the myth, begin, that is, to understand it as readable, or, to put it another way, as charged with politics.

In the colonial situation, the desire of the colonized to master the master's language is a desire to be white. It is a desire to attain the position of the eloquent orator in the myth, not to explode the myth; quite the contrary, to preserve it. The native speaker who masters the master's language in the colonial situation dreams of assuming a position vis-à-vis the native community that reproduces the position of the eloquent orator vis-à-vis the savages he confronts. Fanon provides us the scenario:

> The Negro who knows the mother country is a demigod. In this connection I offer a fact that must have struck my compatriots. Many of them, after stays of varying length in metropolitan France, go home to be deified. . . . Even before he had gone away, one could tell from the almost aerial manner of his carriage that new forces had been set in motion. . . . The "newcomer" reveals himself at once; he answers only in French, and often he no longer understands Creole. . . . he talks about the Opera, which he may never have seen except from a distance, but above all he adopts a critical attitude toward his compatriots. Confronted with the most trivial occurrence, he becomes an oracle. He is the one who knows. He betrays himself in his speech. (19, 23–24)

In this description of the native speaker translated into the form of the eloquent orator—the demigod of aerial carriage, the oracle, to whom Creole must sound like gabble—Fanon's mode is parodic. Mastery of the master's language does not end alienation; it intensifies it, by alienating the native speaker from his community and hence from himself. Further, mastery of the master's language does not allow the native speaker to assume the position of the eloquent orator; for the rules of decorum that govern the myth forbid such an assumption, even as the myth appears to promise it. That is, the native speaker must speak like a native or, more precisely, like the master's conception of how a native speaks. So, as Fanon points out, the master typically refuses the native's mastery by not recognizing it, by replying to the native, no matter how perfectly the native speaks, in "pidgin-nigger"; or, more "politely," by registering in various forms a kind of surprise, a mode of condescending praise, that a native has achieved this mastery.

In the revolutionary situation, as opposed to the colonial situation, the native speaker masters the master's language not to become white, not to assume the position of the eloquent orator, but to explode, or expose, that position. The native speaker, then, does not so much master the master's language as take possession of it, or, more precisely, take up his rightful place in it. For, in the revolutionary situation, the native speaker makes us understand that the master does not own the language of the capital. This language is not the master's property; it is not simply proper to him. Contradicting the myth of the eloquent orator, which states implicitly that language has its origin in the orator, the revolutionary native speaker demonstrates that the master's language has its origin not in the master but in the political needs of any people who *must* speak it.

The question of the imperative of political needs is paramount here and must be queried in each instance. For Fanon, who is interested in the liberation of colonized countries into their own forms of socialist nationalism, it would appear that the language of the occupying power may be the only language that can provide national unity to peoples who spoke diverse languages before the Europeans' arrival. In some instances, as we know, this is certainly true. European languages have become the official languages of certain emerging African nations. On the other hand, as is the case in Kenya and Ki Swahili, a dominant native language within the territory of colonial rule can become the official language once that rule is overthrown and a nation is formed. What happens to diverse native languages both under colonial regimes and in the process of nationalization, or decolonization, should be of prime interest to us in understanding the historical struggle for voice around the world. Our focus now is concentrated on American space, where, within the context of Fanon's meditation on language (itself contextualized, as I have tried to suggest, within the myth of the eloquent orator), Douglass's *Narrative* is a prime example of this struggle.

From the very beginning of his preface to Douglass's *Narrative,* William Lloyd Garrison introduces Douglass to his largely white, middle-class readership in the prestigious cultural form of the eloquent orator:

In the month of August, 1841, I attended an antislavery convention in Nantucket, at which it was my happiness to become acquainted with FREDERICK DOUGLASS, the writer of the following Narrative. . . . I shall never forget his first speech at the convention—the extraordinary emotion it excited in my own mind—the powerful impression it created upon a crowded auditory, completely taken by surprise—the applause which followed from the beginning to the end of his felicitous remarks. . . . There stood one, in physical proportion and stature commanding and exact—in intellect richly endowed—in natural eloquence a prodigy—in soul manifestly "created but a little lower than the angels"— yet a slave, ay, a fugitive slave. . . . Capable of high attainments as an intellectual and moral being—needing nothing but a comparatively small amount of cultivation to make him an ornament to society and a blessing to his race. . . . (33–34)

Garrison's job in his preface is to authorize or legitimize Douglass's voice for readers of the *Narrative,* to assure these white, middle-class readers, as only a white, middle-class man can assure them, that "Mr. Douglass has very properly chosen to write his own Narrative, in his own style, and according to the best of his ability, rather than to employ some one else. It is, therefore, entirely his own production" (37–38), and the "many passages of great eloquence and power" (39) are his. In 1845, as in 1545, as in 845, as in 45 B.C., the strongest figure for the authorization of voice in the West is the figure of the eloquent orator. And we should note here Garrison's use of the classical opposition between a natural and a cultivated, or ornamental, eloquence that implicitly places Douglass in the position of the savage, no matter what Garrison intends.

But Douglass cannot assume the place of the eloquent orator without the authoritative eloquence of a white man to give his voice legitimacy, to make it audible, or without a white audience. Douglass himself attests to the importance of the audience in the creation of his public voice, when at the end of his narrative he comments on the antislavery meeting at which Garrison first heard him speak. Prompted by the eloquence of Garrison's abolitionist newspaper the "Liberator," Douglass tells his readers, he began attending antislavery meetings:

> I seldom had much to say at the meetings, because what I wanted to say was said so much better by others. But, while attending an anti-slavery convention at Nantucket, on the 11th of August, 1841, I felt strongly moved to speak, and was at the same time much urged to do so by Mr. William C. Coffin, a gentleman who had heard me speak in the colored people's meeting at New Bedford. It was a severe cross, and I took it up reluctantly. The truth was, I felt myself a slave, and the idea of speaking to white people weighed me down. I spoke a few moments, when I felt a degree of freedom, and said what I desired with considerable ease. From that time until now, I have been engaged in pleading the cause of my brethren—with what success, and with what devotion, I leave those acquainted with my labors to decide. (151)

For Douglass, a black man, a fugitive slave, to speak to an audience of white people is a burden, charged with the religious weight of bearing a cross. Yet to refuse the burdensome place of the orator is to lose one's freedom to speak in a way that is powerfully significant to Douglass. For once he assumes the burden it is lifted; he is able to speak "with considerable ease." And from that moment, he is able to undertake the task of the orator, "pleading the cause of [his] brethren." It seems clear from the preceding passage, which ends the *Narrative* proper, that speaking to a meeting of colored people does not carry the same weight for Douglass as addressing a meeting of whites. In the latter case a voice is achieved.

The *Narrative* is the story of Douglass's achievement of this voice, of the politics of achieving it, of the politics, to refer to our earlier discussion of the *Narrative*, of being able to speak literally or properly, like the master. At the end of the *Narrative*, having achieved economic independence in New Bedford, Douglass announces: "I was now my own master" (150), a pronouncement that could also refer to Douglass's voice at narrative's end. It is difficult to read this pronouncement without some irony, whether intended by Douglass or not. For what does it mean to represent one's relation to one's free self in the terms of *master* and *slave*. If one is one's own master, then certainly it follows that one is also one's own slave.

Douglass could have ended his narrative by announcing: I have mastered the master's language. This is the burden of Garrison's preface, as well as of the *Narrative*. It is, to use Fanon's terms, the burden of existing absolutely for the other, the burden of entering existence, of being human—that is, of being white. But having struggled to master the master's language, Douglass is by no means simply alienated like the native speaker in Fanon's colonial situation; nor is he simply liberated like the native speaker in Fanon's revolutionary situation. Douglass neither assumes the myth of the eloquent orator nor explodes it. Rather, he demonstrates its weight in the racial politics of antebellum America, a politics that is still with us today.

Douglass's struggle for voice in the *Narrative* is a struggle for literacy, a struggle to read and write English, practices that were legally forbidden slaves. By 1818, the approximate date of Douglass's birth, we can assume that English, in one form or another, was the native language of most slaves. Torn violently from their own African cultures and languages, mixed together in the slave trade, blacks had no choice but to learn English if they wanted to communicate with each other and with whites. In the *Narrative*, however, Douglass does not represent any of the forms of Black English, that language within a language, that he necessarily must have come into contact with and spoken himself, not only in his life as a slave on the Eastern shore of Maryland and in Baltimore, but in Massachusetts as well. For that matter, Douglass does not represent any of the forms of white English in the regions he inhabited. In the *Narrative,* there is only one form of English, what we recognize as "standard" English, in its nineteenth-century form. Within this form Douglass's prose moves between gothic description (an overseer's whipping of one of his aunts is described as "the blood-stained gate, the entrance to hell of slavery" [51]; and the transformation of his mistress in Baltimore is figured as an "angelic face [which] gave place to that of a demon" [78]) and a powerful plain style, as when he describes his mother's visits to him as a child: "I do not recollect of ever seeing my mother by the light of day. She was with me in the night. She would lie down with me and get me to sleep, but long before I waked she was gone" (48).

If Douglass does not represent any of the forms of Black English that gave voice to himself and the members of the black communities where he lived, he does allude to one such form (of which he quotes only two lines), the slave songs, which we discussed in Chapter 2 as an "alternative eloquence": "I have sometimes thought that the mere hearing of those songs," Douglass remarks, "would do more to impress some minds with the horrible character of slavery, than the reading of whole volumes of philosophy on the subject could do" (57). "To those songs," which "still follow me," we remember Douglass writing, "I trace my first glimmering conception of the dehumanizing character of slavery" (58). Yet, he remarks a moment earlier, "I did not, when a slave, understand the deep meaning of those rude and apparently incoherent songs. I was myself within the circle; so that I neither saw nor heard as those without might see and hear" (57).

> If any one wishes to be impressed with the soul-killing effects of slavery, let him go to Colonel Lloyd's plantation, and, on allowance-day, place himself in the deep pine woods, and there let him, in silence, analyze the sounds that shall pass through the chambers of his soul,—and if he is not thus impressed, it will only be because "there is no flesh in his obdurate heart." (58)

For Douglass, political consciousness of slavery began with the slave songs' eloquent effects on him. But it was only a "glimmering" of consciousness; for Douglass remained "within the circle" of that eloquence, an intimate part of the community that produced the songs. In order "to understand the deep meaning" of those songs, Douglass suggests, the slave must stand outside the circle, like the putative listener who lies alone "in the deep pine woods . . . in silence, [and] analyze[s] the sounds" of the songs as they "pass through the chamber of his soul."

There is something troubling in the way that Douglass describes his relation to the slave songs. For he implies in his remarks that the singers of these songs, the orators of this eloquence, do not themselves understand the deep meaning of their own production, are not themselves fully conscious of the political conditions of their enslavement; and that, perhaps, this "rude" eloquence does not itself possess the analytic ability necessary to achieve such consciousness. Full political consciousness, Douglass suggests, must come from a certain kind of alienation, represented by the distance from the community of the solitary listener in the woods who analyzes what passes through his soul.

We are quite aware as we read Douglass's narrative of his life as a slave that he is writing it from a point of alienation. He makes his alienation in the North, his necessary mistrust, as a fugitive slave, of both blacks and whites quite clear. And he is clear as well about how much he misses the black community in which he grew up: "It is my opinion that thousands would escape from slavery, who now remain, but for the strong cords of affection that bind them to friends. The thought of leaving my friends was decidedly the most painful thought with which I had to contend" (142). The narrator of the *Narrative* is a solitary figure. Franklin's and Emerson's self-reliance is ironized by the notion of the fugitive slave's self-mastery, and the political price paid for such autonomy.

We are also aware that this point of alienation from which Douglass writes is very much a point of linguistic alienation: that the eloquence with which Douglass writes about the slave songs is not the eloquence of the songs; that there are two orators facing each other here, the "rude" orator of the songs and the cultivated orator of the narrative, just as there are two languages in communication with each other, Black and white English, and that these orators and these languages translate each other, as do the literal and the metaphoric, the proper and the figurative. Yet we are also aware at this moment that the cultivated orator, while acknowledging the power of "rude" eloquence, is also repressing that eloquence to achieve political ends bound up with Douglass's estimation of what it takes to achieve black liberation in an America where whites of all political persuasions control the power.

Douglass recounts his linguistic alienation, his acquiring of literacy (though he does not recount it as alienation from another language, as, that is, an act of translation) in a section of the *Narrative* that we have read in part: the section where the young Douglass "got hold of a book entitled 'The Columbian Orator,'" and found in it a dialogue between a master and a slave, in which the slave through the power of his eloquence convinces the master to emancipate him. Unable to receive an education from his at first willing mistress, Sophia Auld, Douglass "was compelled to resort to various stratagems" (81) to learn to read and write. Exchanging bread for the "bread of knowledge" from "the poor white children in our neighborhood" (83) is the principal stratagem he describes having used to learn how to read; it is a moment in the narrative where we understand how class solidarity can overcome racial alienation and are reminded how such solidarity remains to be achieved in America. Having learned how to read in such exchanges, Douglass, at age twelve, gets hold of "The Columbian Orator" and reads not only the dialogue between the master and the slave, but "one of Sheridan's mighty speeches on and in behalf of Catholic emancipation." These "documents," Douglass tells his readers, "gave tongue to interesting thoughts of my own soul, which had frequently flashed through my mind, and died away for want of utterance." They "enabled me to utter my thoughts, and to meet the arguments brought forward to sustain slavery." But the price of this newfound political consciousness was, just as his master "had predicted," a tormenting "discontentment" with his condition, so that at times Douglas felt that

> learning to read had been a curse rather than a blessing. It had given me a view of my wretched condition, without the remedy. It opened my eyes to the horrible pit, but to no ladder upon which to get out. In moments of agony, I envied my fellow-slaves for their stupidity. I have often wished myself a beast. I preferred the condition of the meanest reptile to my own. Any thing, no matter what, to get rid of thinking! It was this everlasting thinking of my condition that tormented me. It was pressed upon me by every object within sight or hearing, animate or inanimate. The silver trump of freedom had roused my soul to eternal wakefulness. Freedom now appeared, to disappear no more forever. (83–85)

This moment that Douglass describes is pristine, in that he seems to have had no political consciousness of his condition before it. The eloquence of the slave songs does not even glimmer here. Political consciousness is brought to the politically speechless black youth by the eloquent orator of the Western rhetorical tradition, by the figure of the *translatio imperii et studii* itself, in this case, "The Columbian Orator." This scene follows precisely the figure of the eloquent orator bringing language to the savages, and it echoes the representation of this figure in *The Tempest*. Douglass's description of what he feels is *the* language of political consciousness does not represent it as a particular form of language, but as language itself. The "stupidity" of Douglass's "fellow-slaves" becomes a figure for Douglass's own stupidity before he acquired this language, and juxtaposed, as it is, with figures of primal nature, the "beast" and the "reptile," this figure becomes a figure for the savage, or mute, state from which "The Columbian Orator" delivered Douglass. The cursing that this acquisition of language initially provokes in Douglass intensifies the scene of primal language-giving and recalls Caliban's complaint that his acquisition of the Europeans' language only enabled him to curse his own lack of power, even though he had apparently acquired the terms of power.

While it is true that in a political situation dominated by literacy, the acquisition of literacy is a crucial tool of liberation, as Douglass's *Narrative* attests (gathering crucial information, forging documents, etc., are impossible without being able to read and write), it is also true that political consciousness, the critical awareness of one's condition, is not the sole or necessary province of the literate, as Douglass's narrative also attests with its evocation of the slave songs. Indeed, literacy can be used to repress political consciousness, as anyone who has gone through our educational system knows. And, in fact, in the scene we are reading from Douglass's *Narrative,* literacy is at once enabling political consciouness and repressing it. For as Douglass is becoming conscious of the political condition of slavery by translating himself into the language of the eloquent orator, and thus is making a commitment to free himself and his "fellow-slaves" from the imperial power of this orator, by distributing this power in the form of literacy to the enslaved, he is simultaneously taking up the position of this orator in relation to his "fellow-slaves" by at this moment denying them the eloquence of their own language. Betrayed by Douglass's increasing grandiloquence, the increasing inflation of his language in the passage under consideration, this moment is one of exemplary alienation. For in it, not only can we read Douglass's own alienation from himself, the repression of one orator by another through the naturalization of the former, but our culture's profound alienation from itself through the repression of languages within the language that are still struggling in the margins for voice.

Yet the passage in Douglass's *Narrative* that we have been considering, between the eloquence of the slaves' songs and the eloquence of the master's language, suggests another form of alienation, a productive or liberatory form, although this form goes unrealized in the *Narrative,* as it does in Western history. In this form, translation would not be a mode of repression of languages (within a language) by a master language. There would be no master language. There would be no native speakers. Rather, all speakers would exist in translation between languages, which is where we all exist. Our refusal to recognize this existence constitutes our repression of its realization. Walter Benjamin expresses this existence when he writes: "Translation thus ultimately serves the purpose of expressing the central reciprocal relationship between languages [*des innersten Verhaltnisses der Sprachen zueinander*]." But this "reciprocal relationship," or "kinship [*Verwandtschaft*] of languages. . . . does not necessarily involve likeness [*Ahnlichkeit*]." Rather, as I read Benjamin's essay somewhat against what may appear to be its idealistic strain, this kinship of languages is constituted by an inevitable tension between conflict and complementarity:

> While all individual elements of foreign languages—words, sentences, structure—are mutually exclusive [*sich ausschließen*], these languages supplement [*erganzen*] one another in their intentions [*Intentionen*]. Without distinguishing the intended object [*Intention vom Gemeinten*] from the mode of intention [*die Art des Meinens*], no firm grasp of this basic law of a philosophy of language can be achieved. The words *Brot* and *pain* "intend" the same object [*das Gemeinte*], but the modes of this intention are not the same. It is owing to these modes that the word *Brot* means something different to a German than the word *pain* to a Frenchman, that these words are not interchangeable for them, that, in fact, they strive to exclude [*aussuchließen*] each other. As to the intended object [*Gemeinten*], however, the two words mean the very same thing [*das Selbe und Identische bedeuten*].[14]

For Benjamin, "these languages supplement one another in their intentions" in the sense that "no single language can attain [its intention] by itself" but "only by the totality [*der Allheit*] of their intentions supplementing each other: pure [*reine*] language" (74). Ideally, then, on the "suprahistorical [*uberhistorische*]" (74) plain, translation envisions the totalization of all languages in a pure language. Benjamin seems to project in the aesthetic realm what we have read the *translatio imperii et studii* projecting in the historical realm: the homogenization of all languages in a universal language. Ideally, translation leads to the end of translation. The vision may appear totalitarian from a certain angle, though Benjamin's totalizing vision is not based, as is the *translatio,* on a hierarchical division of languages—quite the contrary. He envisions no master language translating all the others; rather, for him each language is incomplete and thus dependent on its translation by all the others for its completeness. Yet in the ideal realm, all roads seem to lead to Rome: pure language, the end of translation.

What democratizes Benjamin's vision of translation, however, is that in it translation can never reach its end. History must translate suprahistory; mode of intention, intention. The possibility of translating *Brot* into *pain* is its impossibility. The harmony of translation is its conflict. Benjamin's notion of supplementarity, with its suggestion of a community of languages with mutual needs, resists the mastery of one language by another. His situating of this supplementarity in history, where it cannot reach an end, resists the mastery of these languages by a final supplement, a pure language, keeps the democratic interplay of voices alive in a vision that has a profound respect for the foreign:

> Our translations, even the best ones, proceed from a wrong premise. They want to turn Hindi, Greek, English into German instead of turning German into Hindi, Greek, English. Our translators have a far greater reverence for the usage of their own language than for the spirit of the foreign works. . . . The basic error of the translator is that he preserves the state in which his own language happens to be instead of allowing his language to be powerfully affected [*gewaltig bewegen*] by the foreign tongue. (80–81)

Quoting Pannwitz, Benjamin gives us a concise history of the ideology of translation in the West: each language's refusal to embrace its own alienation, each language's drive to master the foreign. Political consciousness, Douglass's *Narrative* suggests, resides in a counter movement *between* languages, between the slaves' songs and the master's language, where we understand each only in its moment of translation, its moment of alienation, by the other. In this moment, the eloquent orator relinquishes the illusion of mastery that comprises his imperial foreign policy. Prospero arrives at such a moment in a passage that we have explored in part for what it could tell us about the illusion of absolute, or immediate, power: about power's need, in order to achieve its immediacy, for mediation by the very "objects" it would rule. This is the passage in which Prospero halts the betrothal masque of Miranda and Ferdinand when he recalls the rebellion-in-process of his slave Caliban. Both daughter and future son-in-law are amazed at how agitated the duke becomes at the recollection. And Prospero, responding to what he sees as Ferdinand's "dismay[. . .]," urges him to "be cheerful." But the speech that follows hardly seems intended to cheer, for it is filled with despair:

> Our revels now are ended. These our actors,
> As I foretold you, were all spirits, and
> Are melted into air, into thin air;
> And, like the baseless fabric of this vision,
> The cloud-capp'd towers, the gorgeous palaces,
> The solemn temples, the great globe itself,
> Yea, all which it inherit, shall dissolve,
> And, like this insubstantial pageant faded,
> Leave not a rack behind. We are such stuff
> As dreams are made on; and our little life
> Is rounded with a sleep. Sir, I am vex'd;
> Bear with my weakness; my old brain is troubled:
> Be not distur'd with my infirmity:
> If you be pleased, retire into my cell,
> And there repose: a turn or two I'll walk,
> To still my beating mind.
>
> (IV.i.147–63)

Power confronting its own powerlessness in the other despairs, sees the baselessness of its empire, feels its own mortality. Don Cameron Allen, commenting on this passage, remarks: "When Prospero talks about ruined towers, temples, and palaces, he may be speaking in general terms, but a travelled Jacobean . . . would certainly think of the waste of Imperial Rome. No dream was ever greater than this imperial one; no dream ever passed more sadly and left grander evidence of its passing."[15] Confronted with the name *Caliban,* the slave's song, an alternative eloquence, with that resistance to translation that alienates the master in his mastery ("this thing of darkness I / Acknowledge mine"), the eloquent orator momentarily gives up the vision of the *translatio imperii et studii,* sees it as the illusion it is, yet has nothing to put in its place but despair. This, quite literally, is how *The Tempest* ends: "And my ending is despair'' (Epilogue, 15), unless, Prospero suggests, Christian forgiveness takes the place of temporal power, a suggestion that is pure romance.

The despair in which Shakespeare's romance ends is the despair in which Anglo-American foreign policy in the New World begins. The Jamestown colony, as we have read, was continually on the brink of failure. For the Indians, we can say succinctly, resisted translation. This resistance persists today and can mark for us the clearest horizon of the failure of the *translatio:*

> For the most part, Indians have not accepted the mythology of the American past which interprets American history as a sanitized merging of diverse peoples to form a homogenous union. The ties to tribal heritage are too strong, the abuses of the past and present too vivid, and the memory of freedom too lasting for many Indians. A substantial number of reservation Indians see the white man as little more than a passing episode in a tribal history which spans millennia. The white man may be the most destructive influence which the tribe has encountered, but he is still not regarded as a permanent fixture on the continent.[16]

An American Indian tribalism that persists is the present and powerful force that resists the *translatio.* In the words of William Bevis, this tribalism ''constitute[s] a profound and articulate continuing critique of modern European culture, combined with a persistent refusal to let go of tribal identity; a refusal to regard the past as inferior; a refusal—no matter how futile—of even the wish to assimilate. . . . Indian students right now have relatives who heard from the lips of the living what it was like to ride a horse, belly deep in grass, across unfenced plains dark with buffalo. Several of my Crow students speak English as a second language; many members of all tribes have relatives who tell the old stories.''[17]

The two central and interlocking forces of the *translatio* that tribalism resists are those of the proper and property. These forces work to destroy the tribe by individualizing its members. In her novel *Ceremony,* a story that should be most urgent for us in its improvised retelling of the old stories, Leslie Marmon Silko suggests how the proper and property act together within the *translatio* to force individualism on the tribe. In the beginning, ''the people shared a single clan name. . . .''

> But the fifth world had become entangled with European names: the names of the rivers, the hills, the names of the animals and plants—all of creation

suddenly had two names: an Indian name and a white name. Christianity
separated the people from themselves; it tried to crush the single clan name,
encouraging each person to stand alone, because Jesus Christ would save
only the individual soul; Jesus Christ was not like the Mother who loved
and cared for them as her children, as her family. . . . the old instinct had
always been to gather the feelings and opinions that were scattered through
the village, to gather them like willow twigs and tie them into a single
prayer bundle that would bring peace to all of them. But now the feelings
were twisted, tangled roots, and all the names for the source of this growth
were buried under English words, out of reach. And there would be no
peace and the people would have no rest until the entanglement had been
unwound to the source.[18]

In the preceding passages, Silko gives us her Laguna version of Babel.
For the Indians, however, the fall is not from a single language into
languages, but from a world in which there were only Indian languages,
or "names," into a world in which "all of creation suddenly had two
names: an Indian name and a white name." European languages, specifically English in this case, "entangle[. . .]" this world—perhaps
appearing to translate Indian names into gabble—and finally bury the
Indian words for tribal feelings. Resistance to this linguistic violence—
the assertion of English as the master language—does not reside in any
form of mastering the master's language, although we might understand
Native American writers like Silko to be engaged in the Benjaminian
project of trying to alienate English from itself by immersing it in a tribal
context. In Indian–white conflict in North America, there are no masters,
no slaves. There are only cultures in conflict, with the Indians struggling
to maintain the integrity of cultural bases that, like all such bases, cannot
be separated from the languages that articulate them. So "there would be
no peace and the people would have no rest" until, to follow Silko's
figure of burial, they tunneled through the English words to unearth the
Indian names. For Indians, resistance to the *translatio* resides, in central
ways, in speaking their own languages. Keith Basso chronicles an
eloquent example of this resistance among the Cibecue Apaches:

> In the opinion of Apaches . . . Cibecue's conservative character is most
> clearly reflected in the fact that everyone continues to learn and to speak
> Western Apache. This is regarded as an achievement of substantial
> proportions because ever since 1904, when a Lutheran missionary opened a
> one-room schoolhouse on the bank of Cibecue Creek, Anglo-Americans

have made systematic attempts to eliminate the native language and replace it with standard English. The Bureau of Indian Affairs (BIA) established a school at Cibecue in 1933; the Lutherans opened another in 1947; and in 1968, by which time the old Bureau facility had become overcrowded and obsolete, the government constructed yet another. Plainly, it was not from lack of exposure that the people of Cibecue refrained from speaking English.

Right from the start, most Apache parents sent their children to school. After all, hot meals were served in the late fall and winter, clothing was sometimes given away, and healthy pupils who failed to attend class were hunted down by truant officers and punished. But right from the start, Apache parents also instructed their children not to behave like Whitemen, and, more than anything else, this injunction applied to the speaking of English. (27–28)

But the struggle for voice that the Cibecue Apache represent, their resistance to being translated, results, as N. Scott Momaday writes, in the ironic silencing of Indians:

One of the most perplexing ironies of American history is the fact that the Indian has been effectively silenced by the intricacies of his own speech, as it were. Linguistic diversity has been a formidable barrier to Indian-white diplomacy. And underlying this diversity is again the central dichotomy, the matter of a difference in ways of seeing and making sense of the world around us. [19]

Central to this "difference" in worldview, for Momaday, is the difference between the Indian oral tradition, which fosters a "respect for words . . . an inherent morality in man's understanding and use of language," and the European written tradition, which "tends to encourage an indifference to language" (160). The difference between the oral and the written traditions comes into conflict most sharply for Momaday in "the language of diplomacy," a conflict that "constitute[s] the most important issue in Indian–white relations in the past five hundred years." Historically, the written tradition has developed a

legal diction of a special parlance, one that is far removed from our general experience of language. Its meaning is obscure; the words themselves seem to stand in the way of meaning. [The oral tradition] is in the plain style, a style that preserves, in its way, the power and beauty of language. In the historical relationship in question, the language of diplomacy has been determined by the considerations that have evolved into the style of [the written tradition]. It is far removed from American Indian oral tradition, far from the rhythms of oratory and storytelling and song. (161)

We have before us, in Momaday's description, two forms of eloquence in conflict, two forms of eloquence that do not supplement each other, that share no common intention, but exclude each other, two forms of eloquence, neither of which can translate the other. The development of the language of diplomacy in the written tradition is part of the history of class in the West, wherein languages become alienated from themselves in various specialized jargons, forms of power of the upper classes over the lower; whereas in the American Indian oral tradition, which developed in societies with rank but without class, this kind of alienation cannot take place. The translation of these two languages into each other is impossible because one of these forms of eloquence, the written, is based on the proper and property—on, that is, a system of decorum (which, as we have read, is inseparable from a class system) and on the alienation of land in individual title that is also inseparable from that system. The oral form of eloquence, however, is based on an inalienable notion of land grounded in a kinship economy. Each one of these languages utterly rejects the other.

In the passage we have been reading from *Ceremony,* Silko represents this rejection by juxtaposing white names and the solitary figure of Jesus Christ, who represents "the individual soul," with Indian names and the Mother, who represents the community in its inalienable relation to the land. In European languages, each Christian must stand, singly, in *his* proper relation to property. This dictum becomes increasingly stringent with the rise of Protestantism in the sixteenth and seventeenth centuries. Look, for example, at the beginning of John Winthrop's *A Model of Christian Charity* (1630), which helps inaugurate the Massachusetts Bay Colony: "God Almighty in His most holy and wise providence, hath so disposed of the condition of mankind, as in all times some must be rich, some poor, some high and eminent in power and dignity, others mean and in subjection."[20] But look as well at James Madison's *Federalist* 10 (1787), which translates Winthrop's belief into secular terms that govern us today:

> The diversity in the faculties of men, from which the rights of property originate is not less an insuperable obstacle to a uniformity of interests. The protection of these faculties is the first object of government. From the protection of different and unequal faculties of acquiring property, the

possession of different degrees and kinds of property immediately results; and from the influence of these on the sentiments and views of the respective proprietors ensues a division of the society into different interests and parties. . . . Those who hold and those who are without property have ever formed distinct interests in society.[21]

Winthrop grounds property relations, which are always radically unequal because of their inseparability from a class system, in the sacred, which in the secular *Federalist* becomes translated into the "natural," the West's modern version of the sacred. In this way property relations are made absolutely proper, or transcendent. How, then, could we translate either of these documents into Native American languages, where there are no Christians in proper relation to property, where there are, that is, no individuals, but only persons whose identity is conceptualized not as apart from the community but as stemming from it in its sacred, or inalienable, relation to the land?

How, then, could we translate Native American languages into these documents without exceptional violence? It is such violence, as we discussed in Chapter 1, that constitutes the history of Anglo-American foreign policy in the New World, and beyond that, in the Third World as well, where our insistence on the primacy of property relations, where our power operates, insures poverty its hold. It is such violence that continues to ground Anglo-American foreign policy in despair. In *Ceremony*, Silko sounds the note of this despair:

[T]he lies devoured white hearts, and for more than two hundred years white people had worked to fill their emptiness; they tried to glut the hollowness with patriotic wars and with great technology and the wealth it brought. And always they had been fooling themselves, and they knew it. (191)

But white people have not taken the knowledge of their foolishness to heart. Continually resublimating their despair in hallucinations of immediate power, instead of learning an alternative eloquence, they still believe that they can translate *Caliban*.

─── 7 ───

Eloquent Cannibals

EUROPEANS ARRIVING in the New World had, even before they arrived, mapped it according to the trajectory of metaphor. The agent of this mapping is the eloquent orator. The political context of this agent, and there is nothing beyond a political context, is the *translatio imperii et studii*. To think metaphorically within the confines of the *translatio* is to think imperialistically: to appropriate the other in the name of a national propriety that conceives of itself as universal, as absolutely proper. This does not mean that we cannot change our thinking. But this would mean to ironize, or denaturalize, the proper, to see it for what it is, as a figure itself, the way Montaigne does in his essay "Of the Caniballes," when, in the Florio translation, he writes: "[M]en call that barbarisme [*barbarie*] which is not common to them" (162).

For Europeans the New World is inevitably about the translation of eloquence from the Old. The passage from Montaigne/Florio that Shakespeare used in *The Tempest* has Gonzalo projecting the Golden Age on Prospero's New World, an age of innocent nakedness without property or class, in which Montaigne imagined South American Indians, the Tupi-Kawahib, to be living. The English colonists held this dream even as they began to translate America into property and to found a class system, tied to the exclusivity of race and gender, on this property. Within this dream, I want to argue in this concluding chapter, the Indians figure the promise and the threat of a democratic eloquence for Europeans. Montaigne's essay explores the promise; Shakespeare's play, the threat. Both promise and threat are contained conflictually and conspiratorially in the translations of that unknown Arawak word that Columbus heard and that we now read as *cannibal/Caliban*. Both the promise and threat appropriate the Indians to figure European visions about the politics of language. Whatever its intentions or pretensions, anthropology winds up being hopelessly about the desires of the culture from which it springs.

142

In his address to the reader that prefaces his essays, Montaigne makes plain the kind of eloquence to which he aspires in his writing:

> Had my intention beene to forestal and purchase the worlds opinion and favor, I would surely have adorned my selfe more quaintly, or kept a more grave and solemne march. I desire therein to be delineated in mine owne genuine, simple and ordinarie fashion, without contention, art or study; for it is my selfe I pourtray. . . . For if my fortune had beene to have lived among those nations, which yet are said to live under the sweet liberty of Natures first and uncorrupted lawes, I assure thee, I would most willingly have pourtrayed my selfe fully [*tout entier*] and naked [*tout nud*].

These introductory remarks should serve first to remind us of the paradox that structures the history of eloquence in the West: the purpose of the clothing of speech, of which metaphor is the foundation garment, is to lay bare the thought of the orator, a paradox, as we have read, that is at the heart of metaphor itself, which is at once nature and culture. Montaigne, however, expresses the paradox as an opposition. There are two kinds of eloquence, he suggests, the clothed and the naked, the civilized and the savage. The former is bent on courting the world's favor, on affecting a certain kind of appearance, on following the rules of decorum that establish and are based on a hierarchical system. The latter, in contrast, is devoted to full, or open, self-expression. It seeks to express the self stripped down to essentials, the self without the accoutrements of hierarchy. It is a prototype of what we might imagine today constitutes the ideal of democratic speech, the ideal of full disclosure among equals. Montaigne tells his readers that he aspires to this democratic, or natural, eloquence without being able to fully attain it; for its location is elsewhere, in the New World to be precise, and Montaigne is an inhabitant of the Old.

Montaigne's remarks to the reader, in which he appropriates the figure of the Native American to figure the kind of eloquence that inspires him, transports us immediately to "Of the Caniballes," and alerts us to the fact that what the West terms cannibalism (or in today's parlance terrorism) may only be a projection of a Western poetics that we could term "the writing of savagery."

In Chapter 3 we noted that, beginning with Columbus, the idea of cannibalism developed not as an anthropological fact but as a political fiction that the West employed to justify its exploitation of Native Americans. W. Arens puts the basis of this fiction succinctly: "Resistance [to Spanish invasion] and cannibalism became synonymous and also legitimized the barbaric Spanish reaction."[1] While Montaigne appears to accept the "fact" of cannibalism reported by the Europeans, he subverts this fact by transporting it from its "proper," or New World, context and making it a figure for Old World politics:

> I am not sorie we note the barbarous horror [*l'horreur barbaresque*] of such an action [the putative eating of the enemy dead by native Brazilians], but grieved, that prying [*jugeans*] so narrowly into their faults [*fautes*] we are so blinded [*aveuglez*] in ours. I thinke there is more barbarisme [*barbarie*] in eating men alive, than to feed upon them, being dead; to mangle by tortures and torments a body full of lively sense, to roast him in peeces, to make dogges and swine to gnaw and teare him in mammockes (as wee have not only read, but seene very lately, yea and our own memorie, not amongst ancient enemies, but our neighbors and fellow-citizens; and which is worse, under pretence of pietie and religion) than to roast and eat him after he is dead. (166–67)

"Fact" becomes figure becomes a new fact, the effect of which is to relativize, or make equivocal, as opposed to univocal, the term *cannibal*.

It is, indeed, one of Montaigne's strategies, as we noted in his reading of "barbarous," to democratize terms by making them relational or equivocal. Thus: "They are even savage [*sauvages*], as we call those fruits wilde [*sauvages*], which nature of her selfe, and of her ordinarie progresse hath produced: whereas indeed they are those which our selves have altered by our artificiall devices, and diverted from their common order, we should rather terme savage [*sauvages*]" (163). Civility becomes savagery here; savagery, civility. The force of this kind of reading is to loosen the absolute hold of a term over a particular referent by playing with its propriety. Montaigne attacks the decorum of a particular political vocabulary, the vocabulary of what today we call "ethnology." At the heart of this vocabulary is the classical opposition *physis*/*nomos* (nature/nurture, or nature/culture, or nature/art). And as the pressure of the passage just cited suggests, Montaigne is out to complicate this opposition. So while "Of the Caniballes" is typically read as a key document in that Western history that fabricates the "noble savage," or natural man, it seems to me more to the point to read Montaigne's "nature" not as a precursor of Rousseau's "state of nature" but as a fully formed counterculture. For Montaigne's cannibals do not utter the cry of nature or speak some primitive poetry. Rather, as Montaigne dramatizes them, they have achieved the kind of eloquence to which

Europeans should aspire: one grounded in a certain moral economy of language.

This economy begins in the morning:

> Some of their old men, in the morning before they goe to eating, preach in common to all the household, walking from one end of the house to the other, repeating one selfe-same sentence many times, till he have ended his turne (for their buildings are a hundred paces in length) he commends but two things unto his auditorie, *First, valour against their enemies, then lovingnesse unto their wives.* (165)

This sermon, the precepts of which Montaigne greatly admires, is repeated by the Indians' prophets:

> The Prophet speakes to the people in publike, exhorting them to embrace vertue, and follow their dutie. All their morall discipline [*science éthique*] containeth but these two articles; first an undismaied resolution to warre, then an inviolable affection to their wives. Hee doth also Prognosticate of things to come, and what successe they shall hope for in their enterprises: he either perswadeth or disswadeth them from warre; but if he chance to misse of his divination, and that it succeed other wise than he foretold them, if hee be taken, hee is hewen in a thousand peeces, and condemned for a false Prophet. And therefore he that hath once misreckoned himselfe is never seene againe. Divination is the gift of God; the abusing wherof should be a punishable imposture. (165–66)

As the fate of false prophets in this interpretation of Tupi culture instructs Montaigne's readers, these Indians take language seriously. They actually require that their eloquence be grounded in wisdom. In fact, "All their morall discipline," which is focused in the twin poles of love of wives and war ("Their men have many wives, and by how much more they are reputed valiant, so much the greater is their number" [170]), is grounded in eloquence. Witnessing the power of their polygamous love, which, Montaigne tells his readers, "is [not] done by a simple [*simple*], and servile [*servile*], or awefull dutie unto their custome [*ancienne coustume*]," but with "discourse [*discurs*]" and "judgment [*jugement*]," Montaigne offers his readers the translation of the beginning of an "amorous canzonet," which, he comments, "hath no barbarisme [*barbarie*] at all in it, but is altogether Anacreontike. Their language," he continues, "is a kinde of pleasant speech, and hath a pleasing sound, and some affinitie with Greeke terminations." "Adder stay," the translation of the Tupi song begins,

> Stay good adder, that my sister may by the patterne of thy partie-coloured coat drawe the fashion and worke of a rich lace, for me to give unto my love; so may thy beautie, thy nimblenesse or disposition be ever preferred before all other serpents. (170)

Who knows how far this translation is from the original. I imagine quite far. At best Montaigne, who has never been to the New World, is working through interpreters. He mentions two in his essay whom he knew personally. The first had acted as translator between the essayist and one of three Tupi Indians who were presented to Charles IX in 1562 at Rouen; Montaigne tells us he was exceptionally "bad [*si mal*]" (171). The other, who had lived in South America, for "ten or twelve years" (160), was a servant of Montaigne's,

> a simple [*simple*] and rough-hewen [*grossier*] fellow: a condition fit to yield a true testimonie [*propre a rendre véritable tésmoignage*]. For, subtile people [*fines gens*] may indeed marke more curiously, and observe things more exactly, but they amplifie and glose them: and the better to perswade, and make their interpretations of more validitie, they cannot chuse but somewhat alter the storie [*l'histoire*]. They never represent things truly [*pures*], but fashion and maske them according to the visage they saw them in; and to purchase credit to their judgment, and draw you on to beleeve them, they commonly adorne, enlarge, yea, and Hyperbolize the matter. Wherein is required either a most sincere [*très-fidelle*] Reporter, or a man so simple [*si simple*], that he may have no invention to build upon, and to give a true liklihood unto false devices, and be not wedded to his owne will. Such a one was my man; who besides his own report, hath many times shewed me divers Mariners, and Merchants, whom hee had knowne in that voyage. So I am pleased with his information, that I never enquire what Cosmographers say of it. (162–63)

This translator's veracity does not depend on his proper relation to the New World, which neither we nor Montaigne can verify, but on his figurative force in "Of the Caniballes," where, like the cannibals themselves, he is a figure of democratic eloquence. Here, in a way that opposes their representation in *The Tempest*, Native Americans and the lower classes figure the integrity, or power, of language. Our question *must* be, then, not how close are Montaigne's translations of the Tupis to the original, but what is the figurative force of the Tupis in Montaigne's writing. Curiously, I will want to suggest, this figurative force will return Montaigne's readers in certain significant ways to the force of the Tupis proper. For if in the passages we are reading Montaigne appears to be putting the words of the "master" into the mouths of the Indians by assimilating them to a classical model of language, a practice that, well into the nineteenth century, one line of scholarly endeavor will follow in an attempt to legitimize the Indians, he is performing this act of translation, as we will read, in order to translate the idea of mastery into what he can make of the Tupis' language, where it will necessarily be obliterated.

At the center of Montaigne's essay is his implicit interest in the way that eloquence functions to define his Indians' notion of valor:

> If their neighbours chance to come over the mountains to assaille or invade them, and that they get the victorie over them, the Victors conquest is glorie, and the advantage to be and remaine superior in valour and vertue: else have they nothing to doe with the goods and spoyles of the vanquished, and so returne into their countrie, where they neither want any necessarie thing, nor lacke this great portion, to know how to enjoy their condition happily, and are contented with what nature affoordeth them. So doe these when their turne commeth. They require no other ransome of their prisoners, but an acknowledgment and confession that they are vanquished. And in a whole age, a man shall not finde one, that doth not rather embrace death, than either by word or countenance remissely to yeeld one jot of an invincible courage. There is none seene that would not rather be slaine and devoured, than sue for life, or shew any feare: They use their prisoners with all libertie, that they may so much the more hold their lives deare and precious, and commonly entertaine them with threats of future death, with the torments they shall endure, with the preparations intended for that purpose, with mangling and slicing of their members, and with the feast that shall be kept at their charge. All which is done, to wrest some remisse, and exact some faint-yeelding speech of submission from them, or to possesse them with a desire to escape or run away; that so they may have the advantage to have danted and made them afraid, and to have forced their constancie. For certainly the victorie consisteth in that only point. . . . Wee get many advantages of our enemies, that are but borrowed and not ours. . . . Constancie is valour, not of armes and legs, but of minde and courage: it consisteth not in the spirit and courage of our horse, nor of our armes, but in ours. . . . He that in danger of imminent death, is no whit danted in his assurednesse; he that in yeelding up his ghost beholding his enemie with a scornefull and fierce looke, he is vanquished, not by us, but by fortune: he is slaine, but not conquered. The most valiant, are often the most unfortunate. So are there triumphant losses in envie of victories. (167–68)

The purpose of war among the Indians, according to Montaigne—and he is essentially accurate in this assumption—is not to gain either territory or material possessions, because "they neither want any necessarie thing, nor lacke this great portion, to know how to enjoy their condition happily, and are contented with what nature affordeth them." It is, simply, to display their valor, which, as we can read in the preceding passage, can be done more powerfully in losing than in winning. For in losing, that is in being taken captive and facing the inevitable torture, death, and devouring, the Indian tests his "constancie," the very essence of valor, what is purely "ours" after all war's accoutrements from physical strength to weaponry have been stripped away. Just as the finest eloquence is naked speech, so true constancy is naked valor. In the face of fear, one displays no fear, either in word or deed. Words or their witholding are particularly important in this ritual. The victors make speeches to the captives, eloquently summoning up the torture, death and devouring to come, in an attempt to "exact some faint-yeelding speech of submission from them." The captives, in their turn, display their constancy, either by resisting the desire to make such speeches, that is, by an eloquent silence, we assume, or by making a speech in return that articulates their naked valor. Montaigne gives his readers the translation of an example of the Native American eloquence of constancy:

> I have a song made by a prisoner, wherein is this clause, Let them boldly come together, and flocke in multitudes, to feed [*disner*] on him; for with him they shall feed upon [*mangeront*] their fathers, and grandfathers, that heretofore have served his body for food and nourishment: These muscles, (saith he) this flesh, and these veines, are your owne [*les vostres*]; fond men as you are, know you not that the substance of your forefathers limbes is yet tied unto ours? Taste them well, for in them shall you finde the relish of your owne flesh [*propre chair*]: An invention, that hath no shew of barbarisme [*barbarie*]. (169)

The function of the cannibals' song about the theoretics of cannibalism is to counter the terrorizing eloquence of the captor with the fearless eloquence of the captive. But the content of the song should interest us as well; for through it Montaigne makes of the cannibalism practiced by the cannibals, as opposed to that practiced by the Europeans, an activity "that hath no shew of barbarisme" in it, an activity, it is suggested, that is quite civil.

Cannibalism is literally civil in this formulation, for its basis, or what it expresses so eloquently, is the basis of most Native American civilization: kinship. Cannibalism expresses, or figures forth, a radical idea of kinship that cuts across the frontiers of hostile groups. To eat the other is to eat the self, for the other is quite literally composed of the selves of one's kin, who compose oneself, just as the self, it follows, is composed of the others one has eaten. Cannibalism, like kinship, expresses forthrightly the essentially equivocal relationship that obtains between self and other. It expresses, if you will, a radical theory of relativity, at a time, as we have read, when the West was in various stages (most advanced in England) of repressing its own versions of this theory in the name of an emergent individualism.

Montaigne's essay has been criticized for representing Native American societies merely as negatives of European society. In adducing this critique, critics cite the passage that Shakespeare used in *The Tempest:*

> It is a nation . . . that hath no kinde of traffike, no knowledge of Letters, no intelligence of numbers, no name of magistrate, nor of politike superioritie; no use of service, of riches or of povertie; no contracts, no successions, no partitions, no occupation but idle; no respect of kindred, but common, no apparell but naturall, no manuring of lands, no use of wine, corne, or mettle. The very words that import lying, falshood, treason, dissimulations, covetousnes, envie, detraction, and pardon, were never heard of amongst them. (164)

Taking this passage alone, we cannot counter the critique. But, as I am arguing, there is a positive content to Montaigne's depiction of Native American societies, which is his representation of the moral economy of kinship.

Before arriving at the cannibal's song of cannibalism as kinship, Montaigne presents, in passing, the economy of kinship for his readers:

> Those that are much about one age, doe generally enter-call one another brethren [*frères*], and such as are younger, they call children [*enfans*], and the aged are esteemed as fathers [*pères*] to all the rest. These leave this full possession [*possession*] of goods in common [*in commun*], and without division to their heirs [*héritiers*], without other claime or title [*titres*], but that which nature doth plainly impart unto all creatures, even as shee brings them into the world. (167)

Given what we know today about the intricacies of kinship terminologies in the Americas, Montaigne's description of Tupi kinship nomenclature is crudely general, as is his description of how this nomenclature relates to this Native American economy. As we have read in Chapter 3 terms like *brother, father,* and *child* do not translate with ease between Native American and European languages. And, of course, there are no female terms for relation in Montaigne's description, not to mention the absence of relational terms beyond the nuclear family. In addition, the terms Montaigne uses to describe an essentially communal economy are the terms of property, terms such as *possession, title,* and *heir,* which, as we have also read, cannot translate this economy without destroying it.

Yet for all the problems of translation that we can be aware of today, Montaigne is attempting to present to his readers a positive idea of what a kinship economy is: the social group as extended family holding wealth in common. In fact, the logic of Montaigne's description, if not the description itself, figures the proper force of kinship economies, if not their proper content. For in not making a clear distinction between the proper and the figurative family, the passage tends to render obsolete terms like *heir, title,* and *possession,* which depend on such a clear distinction. Following the logic of Montaigne's description, we can say with some ethnographic accuracy that the force of kinship systems is that they do blur or, more precisely, make equivocal, the frontier between the proper, or what the West would term "biological," and the figurative family. And it is such equivocation that allows the moral economy of kinship, based as it is on the communal, to operate. The incest taboo in kinship economies, summed up in the following passage by Lévi-Strauss, gives us a prime example of such equivocation:

> Even if the incest prohibition has its roots in nature it is only in the way it affects us as a social rule that it can be fully grasped. In form and in field of application it varies greatly from group to group. While highly limited in our society, in certain North American tribes it is extended to the most distant degrees of kinship. In this case there is no need to add that the prohibition is less concerned with true consanguinity, which is often impossible to establish, if at all, than with the purely social phenomenon by which two unrelated individuals are classed as "brothers" or "sisters," "parents" or "children." [2]

Once again, referring to our discussion in Chapter 3, we can say that the drive in capitalist economies as they have developed in the West (and with particular virulence in the United States) has been increasingly to naturalize cultural places, that is, to naturalize the literal or proper by placing these cultural forces in the realm of the absolute or the natural. In

Western cultures, the incest taboo articulates itself today in terms of a biological notion of the family that not incidentally tends to isolate the nuclear family in its social and economic relations with the rest of the community, fostering competition rather than cooperation by emphasizing the "natural" over the social. When, beginning at the end of the eighteenth century, biology assumed the function of metaphysics in the West, the natural became implicitly equated with the individual, with the single, irreducible, self-contained entity—that is, with *essence*. This quite clearly is a particular cultural, or political, view of nature that serves to emphasize the sheer opposition, or conflict, or competitiveness of components rather than their cooperation. We might term this political view the "naturalization of nature," a process that took place with increasing force between the sixteenth and the nineteenth century, so that while for Montaigne, as we have noted, nature is a particular kind of counterculture, for Rousseau it is almost if not quite a part of the pre-social, and for twentieth-century Western cultures, it appears as the most radical of others: that which we are not, Emerson's "not me."

In contrast, kinship economies socialize nature. Bevis puts it this way:

> Native American nature is urban. The connotation to us of "urban," suggesting a dense complex of human variety, is closer to Native American "nature" than is our word "natural." The woods, birds, animals, and humans are all "downtown," meaning at the center of action and power, in complex and unpredictable and various relationships. . . .
>
> The reasons for the reversible connotations of "urban" and "natural" are not difficult to unravel. Europeans have long assumed a serious split between man and nature, and after 1800, they have often preferred nature to man's works. Lacking respect for their own civilization, when European whites have imagined a beatific union of "man and nature" they have assumed that the union would look not "human" but "natural"; therefore, they perceived the Indians as living in a "primitive" union of man and nature that was the antithesis of civilization. However, respecting civilization as they knew it, when Native Americans imagined man and nature joined, they assumed the combination would be "human," "civilized." Thus, the variety of personality, motivation, purpose, politics, and conversation familiar to human civilization is found throughout Indian nature. "Mother Earth" is not wild. Nature is part of tribe. (601–602)

In "Of the Caniballes," Montaigne works, against the extreme difficulties of translation, to represent the way that Native American kinship economies socialize nature. But because in Montaigne's time nature was still a part of the cultural (still, as we noted in Chapter 2, within the territory of the book), we might more accurately say in the language of the Renaissance that Montaigne works, against the extreme difficulties of translation, to represent the way that American kinship economies figure the proper, or to show how the proper is merely a figure itself, or, to put it another way, to show how the terms of a system are inevitably in translation between each other. Nowhere does Montaigne do this work more forcefully than at the end of his essay, where he articulates a scene of translation that can figure for us the strategy of writing, the kind of New World eloquence that Montaigne attempts in the essay itself.

I have already briefly alluded to the scene I have in mind, which takes place in Rouen in 1562:

> Three of that nation [Tupi-Kawahib], ignorant of how deare the knowledge of our corruptions will one day cost their repose, securitie, and happinesse, and how their ruine shall proceed from this commerce, which I imagine is already well advanced, (miserable as they are to have suffered themselves to be so cosoned by a desire of new-fangled novelties, and to have quit the calmness of their climate, to come and see ours) were at *Roane* in the time of our late King *Charles* the ninth, who talked with them a great while. (170)

The scene begins with a lamentation of the loss of innocence to come. The Indians, lured to France by the dazzle of European technology, aren't aware of what their implication in this trade will cost them in terms of "ruine" to the good life they lead at home. Historical violence is sublimated in this opening. These Indians are not captives, as was typically the case, of Europeans who abducted them to bring them home as evidence of the voyage and train them as translators. Rather, they are held captive in this story by their own innocence, which falls prey to the exotic objects of Europe and blinds them to the politics of trade. Under the spell of this sublimation, both Europeans and Indians become passive participants in a drama of fatal attraction. Metaphysics displaces and mystifies politics for a moment. This is atypical of the essay, which moves in the opposite direction; yet it recalls the apocalyptic opening of the piece, where, trying to imagine the origin of the New World, Montaigne gives us the figure of the whole world that, like Atlantis, will eventually be devoured by the sea. There is an air of despair that envelops all of anthropology from its beginnings, the despair of the cannibal who gains no nourishment, no kinship, from his meat.

The opening of this scene of translation ends with an innocent statement that is at once characteristic of all the travel narratives of the time and yet so inevitably complicated by them, as we have read in the case of John Smith and Columbus, that its innocence can only appear as utter violence. King Charles, Montaigne tells his readers, "talked with [the Tupis] a great while." This statement is a fiction. We know this, for only a few sentences later Montaigne admits it, however inadvertently: "I talked a good while with one of them, but I had so bad an interpreter [*truchement*], and who did so ill apprehend my meaning, and who through his foolishness was so troubled to conceive my imaginations, that I could draw no great matter from him" (171).

The Tupis, it appears, do not speak French, and Montaigne does not speak their language. We can assume that King Charles is not a Tupi speaker. So, in the first instance, it is safe to say, King Charles cannot talk with the Indians. Rather, he, like Montaigne, can only talk with them *through a translator*. Further, the only translator mentioned in the text is a bad one, so bad that Montaigne cannot communicate with the Tupis in any significant way. But it is not only the Tupi with whom Montaigne has difficulty speaking. He has trouble, in the first place, communicating with the translator, who "ill apprehend[s]" his meaning. Montaigne, it would seem, needs a translator to translate between himself and the translator. It makes us wonder, indeed, what the native language of the translator is.

In the scene of translation that ends "Of the Caniballes," a scene, surely, of verbal slapstick, translation, whether inter- or intracultural (the bad interpreter may, ironically, be a native French speaker), is virtually impossible. If we are tempted to write this scene off as a comedy of linguistic errors that will be corrected in time with better translators, we might recall the case of the Cibecue Apaches, who, four hundred years after this scene, dramatize what appears to be the impossibility of translation between whites and Indians through a system of jokes, acted out in English, in which the Indians portray the whites as hopeless intercultural bumblers. We might recall as well twentieth-century U.S. foreign policy toward Third World nations in which, despite the sophisticated array of translators at its disposal, the United States might as well be talking to itself. Or we could recall that Montaigne's scene of translation is representative of those that appear in the voyagers' narratives and that constitute the formative beginnings of European foreign policy in the Americas.

This scene, then, is no abberation. Montaigne makes it the culmination of an essay that begins by foregrounding the problem of ethnographic knowledge. Having decided that there is no authoritative—that is, textual—link that can locate the New World in relation to the Old (the figure of Atlantis in the *Timaeus* would not appear to find its proper place in the Americas), Montaigne, in that movement that makes the Renaissance the opening moment of modernity, places the basis of knowledge in experience:

> We had need of Topographers [*topographes*] to make us particular narrations of the places they have beene in. For some of them, if they have the advantage of us, that they have seene *Palestine*, will challenge a privilege to tell us the newes of all the world besides. I would have every man write what he knowes, and no more: not only in that, but in all other subjects. For one may have particular knowledge of the nature of one river, and experience of the qualitie of one fountaine, that in other things knowes no more than another man. (163)

In the preceding passage the practice of topography becomes a figure for all modes of knowing. And topography within the context of Montaigne's essay is the equivalent of ethnography: the description or, literally, the writing of a foreign place. And to be a proper topographer, Montaigne tells his readers, one must have been in a place; that is, to translate the figure, knowledge is experience. The notion that one must have been in a place to know it seems particularly, not to say self-consciously, ironic in an essay whose writer admits that he is not a proper topographer by announcing to his readers that he has not been in the place that he is writing about. Yet even when the topography is proper, the essay suggests, the necessity of translation complicates the notion of knowing as simply having been in a place by always locating it equivocally between at least two places, two languages, the domestic and the foreign. Montaigne bases his argument not in knowing a place by being there, but in the translated knowledge of those who were there and who themselves faced the problem of translation that Montaigne dramatizes at the end of his essay. Montaigne's argument has no proper place then. In this sense, it is utopian, and as such violates the epistemological dictates that ground proper topography and the dialectical dictates that underlie proper eloquence. Yet what the strategy of Montaigne's essay implies is that any argument about the other, that is any topographical, or ethnographic argument, has no proper place, for it must be based in translation. And I would emphasize here that insofar as topography is a figure for all knowing in "Of the Caniballes" (and an appropriate figure it is too, given the importance of "place" in Western ideas of knowing), all arguments are inevitably about the other. Rhetorically and geographically speaking, then, Montaigne establishes himself in his essay as the topographer of no place, and suggests this figure as the figure of all topographers. He is, to put it another way, like the cannibals about whom he writes, as opposed to the Tupis proper, propertyless. The actual Indians cannot be propertyless because, as I have ventured throughout, they do not have property in the first place.

The scene of translation that ends "Of the Caniballes" calls into radical question Western modes of knowing that are grounded in ideas of "place" as "property." In previous chapters, we have considered the importance of these ideas to the force of eloquence, and we have understood eloquence as the primary expression of these modes of knowing, as their primary form. The eloquent orator grounds his civilizing mission, his very language, in these ideas, which, as we have read, are inextricably tied to the idea of *identity*, of the univocal, the individual, in the West. In Montaigne's essay we have noted how the figure of cannibalism as kinship offers the equivocal as an alternative, a challenge, to the univocal, and how Montaigne himself, like a true cannibal, writes to equivocate: to blur the frontier between the proper and figurative meanings of an essential ethnological vocabulary, itself grounded in the word *cannibal*. Following this thrust of Montaigne's essay, we might say that the force of Montaigne's cannibalism is to rework, like Lévi-Strauss's savage *bricoleur,* the traditional technology of metaphor, the very motor of eloquence; to displace the univocal opposition between the proper and the figurative with an equivocal, or kin-based, relationship, where mastery is impossible in as much as, as we noted in Chapter 2, it is based in such an opposition. In doing this work, the cannibal, we might expect, could use the force of metaphor against itself; for, as we have also noted, metaphor is always a double agent, at once the upholder of domestic authority and the foreign subverter of it. In the scene of translation that ends Montaigne's essay, the figure of cannibalism as kinship that we will turn to now returns to call into question the entire ideology that drives and is driven by the figure of figures, *translatio.*

After being shown the culture of Rouen, the Indians, Montaigne comments, were asked by their European hosts to comment on what was most striking in French culture. Among their translated comments,

Montaigne centers on the following: "they have a manner of phrase [*leur langage*] whereby they call men but a moytie [*moitié*] one of another."

> *They had perceived, there were men amongst us full gorged with all sortes of commodities, and others which hunger-starved, and bare [décharné] with need and povertie, begged at their gates: and found it strange, these moyties so needy could endure such an injustice, and that they tooke not the others by the throte, or set fire on their houses.* (171)

For Montaigne, as we read, true eloquence must be naked; the sumptuary laws of speech must be outlawed. Here at the end of his essay, at the center of his scene of translation, the naked cannibals give revolutionary voice to the naked poor of Europe, who are "bare with need." The fully clothed rich cannot speak here; they are too busy devouring the poor. The ground of the nakedness that grounds true eloquence is a theory of identity that figures Native American kinship economies. In Native American languages, Montaigne suggests in an uncanny moment of understanding what he can't understand because of the problems of translation, there are no individuals; for all persons are articulated as halves of one another (*moytié* meant two *equal* parts in sixteenth-century legal terminology). True eloquence, it follows, cannot be achieved in a language that expresses the hierarchical relationships contained in the notion of mastery, the notion that one person or class has the right to exist at the expense of another. This will become the language of individualism that, developing along with capitalism, will rationalize or naturalize capitalism's cannibalizing of the poor. It is a language the ideal of which is univocality: the assertion of a single voice over others, the mastery of one voice by another. It is a language whose emphasis is on monologue rather than dialogue, on semantics rather than syntax (on identity rather than relation). Doubt, or equivocality, is a wilderness to this language, the terms of which strive to drive doubt out and clear places in the name of the proper. The terms of this language are fences against the encroachment of other terms. And what of a language so desperately in need of surety? The revolutionary vision of Montaigne's Indians suggests that this language betrays its radical doubt through the act of repressing it. The language of reaction is primed to become the language of revolution, if it can find eloquent orators, who, exploding its univocality, release the power of equivocality, the power of voices in translation that possessing no proper places must share a common place equally. Montaigne's Indians are such orators. Filling the silent spaces of his text with their doubly translated speech (from Tupi to French and French to Florio's English), they prophetically tell his English readers, on the brink of the New World and an emerging capitalist economy, that the language of capitalism and the language of democracy cannot translate each other. "[B]ut what of that?", Montaigne ends his essay, "They weare no kinde of breeches nor hosen [*haut de chausses*]" (171).

Whereas Montaigne writes to translate *cannibal* equivocally, Shakespeare writes to translate it univocally. There may be moments of cannibalistic equivocality in *The Tempest,* such as we have examined in the lines "this thing of darkness I / Acknowledge mine," but they occur only against the massive force of repression that the univocal, in the imperial figure of Prospero, exerts in the play. Montaigne's cannibals are revolutionary. Caliban's rebellion is played for comedy and fails. Even as he fears for their ultimate corruption in European trade, Montaigne's cannibals remain resolutely naked at the end of his essay. In the penultimate act of *The Tempest,* Stephano and Trinculo are distracted from Caliban's planned assassination of Prospero by the lure of royal garments. Caliban resists this lure. But in the final act, his repentance dresses him in proper Christian clothing and puts into his mouth a speech that is the precursor of a speech from *Tarzan of the Apes* that we have understood as a figure of U.S. foreign policy in the twentieth century: "I have come across the ages out of the dim and distant past from the lair of the primeval man to claim you—for your sake I have become a civilized man—for your sake I have crossed oceans and continents—for your sake I will be whatever you will me to be." *The Tempest* ends in the despair of an exhausted imperial oration that cannot imagine an alternative. Montaigne's essay ends with a liberating irony that recognizes the need for an alternative eloquence.

Montaigne's essay grounds itself in the excruciating problem of translation, taking a barely veiled pleasure in the movement of displacement, the inevitable groundlessness of topography. Shakespeare's play, even as it articulates the New World as no place, struggles against the play of this utopianism in the figure of Prospero, who, like the eloquent orator of the *translatio imperii et studii,* gathers the figures of the drama *in one place* in order to restore the decorum of an Old World, where, before the act of usurpation, everyone, it would seem, knew his or her place. *The Tempest,* we might say, and I want to argue this explicitly now, dramatizes the struggle to master the problem of translation. And nowhere is this struggle more evident or more representative than in that section of the drama, which we have looked at in part and to which I promised to return, when Prospero orders Caliban to speak.

This order to speak opens an exchange between Caliban, Prospero, and Miranda that figures the imperialist rationale for the colonization of the New World and the subjugation or attemped subjugation of its native inhabitants. This rationale begins with Caliban's claim that

> This islands mine, by Sycorax my mother,
> Which thou tak'st from me. When thou cam'st first,
> Thou strok'st me, and made much of me; wouldst give me
> Water with berries in't; and teach me how
> To name the bigger light, and how the less,
> That burn by day and night: and then I lov'd thee,
> And show'd thee all the qualities o'th'isle,
> The fresh springs, brine-pits, barren place and fertile:
> Curs'd be I that did so! All the charms
> Of Sycorax, toads, beetles, bats, light on you!
> For I am all the subjects that you have,
> Which first was mine own King: and here you sty me
> In this hard rock, whiles you do keep from me
> The rest o'th'island.
>
> (I.ii.333–46)

As we have already noted, Caliban is the only figure in the play who tells, even in part, his or her own history. Prospero tells everyone else's. (That, is he tells the history of the nobility; the lower class, from the perspective of the upper, have no history to speak of, with the exception of Caliban and Ariel, who escape any simple hierarchical placement because of their topographical position between the Old World and the New.) "You have often / Begun to tell me what I am" (I.ii.33–34), Miranda reminds her father as he begins to narrate the history of the usurpation and their transportation to the island. At this moment in the play, Prospero is, necessarily, the one voice that can speak her history; for, as he tells her, she "wast not / Out three years old" (I.ii.40–41) at the time of their exile. Yet Prospero's relationship to Miranda at this moment is emblematic of the univocality he asserts throughout the drama. For we never hear another account of this crucial history than the one he authors at this early moment in the play. And in the last act of the play, Antonio's silence in the face of Prospero's simultaneous condemnation and forgiveness of his brother is emblematic of this univocal history as well. The play proper ends in fact with Prospero "invit[ing]" Alonso and his retinue

> To my poor cell, where you shall take your rest
> For this one night; which, part of it, I'll waste
> With such discourse as, I not doubt, shall make it
> Go quick away: the story of my life,
> And the particular accidents gone by
> Since I came to this isle.
>
> (V.i.301–306)

"I long / To hear the story of your life, which must / Take the ear strangely" (V.i.310–13), Alonso replies, apparently rapt as the duke speaks. From the beginning of *The Tempest* to the end, it is Prospero's eloquent voice that will articulate history. There is virtually no alternative eloquence. Prospero's subjects speak only when spoken to. The duke discourages independent speech. When Ariel reminds Prospero that the duke "hast promis'd" him his "liberty" for the "worthy service" (I.ii.243,245,247) that the slave has performed for the master, the master, with a growing anger, reminds the slave that "I must / Once in a month recount what thou hast been, / Which thou forget'st" (I.ii.261– 63), and proceeds to recount the slave's history—his liberation by Prospero from the spell of Sycorax—silencing the slave. The ending of Act I emphasizes the control that Prospero asserts over the speech of others, when, in the last two lines, Ariel, ever the faithful translator, promises his master that he will carry out his orders "[t]o th'syllable," and Prospero repeats an order forbidding Miranda to intercede on Ferdinand's behalf: "Speak not for him."

When Caliban speaks his history it is not the sign of an authentic equivocality. The savage makes his claim of property in the island and recounts his enslavement by Prospero, as we will read in a moment, only so that Prospero can justify his usurpation of this claim by recounting the "true" history of their encounter. The dialogue between Caliban and Prospero/Miranda is not a dialogue, but a monologue, an ideological set piece that will be used again and again to rationalize, in one form or another, European imperialism in the New World. As we proceed in our reading of this monologue, we should recall that the name *Caliban* is the sign of a violent history of translation that robs the name of its integrity. The scene we are reading is a figure of and a figure in this history.

According to Caliban's narrative, the first contact between the Old World and New was one of tender trade. The Europeans exchanged wine and language for lessons in the topography of the island. Caliban speaks here in certain metaphoric circumlocutions that will become characteristic of European representations of Native American speech habits. I take it, then, that the phrase "Water with berries in't" refers in the first place to wine. One of the immediate meanings of berries in the sixteenth century was grapes; and the Europeans brought wine with them to the New World. In Act II, Scene ii, Stephano gets Caliban drunk with wine (thus giving Anglo-American literature an enduring stereotype, the drunken Indian); and the giving of wine is juxtaposed, as it is in the scene that we have in front of us, with the giving of language: "[H]ere is that which will give language to you" (84–85), the Old World servant tells the New World slave, who, finding the drink heavenly, vows to Stephano: "I'll show thee every fertile inch o'th' island; and I will kiss thy foot: I prithee, be my god" (148–49). Thus the tender trade that Caliban narrates in Act I finds its parody in this comic business in Act II. There is, however, an ironic condensation in the reference to water with berries, for if it can figuratively (and most logically in the context) refer to an Old World concoction, it can literally refer to a New World concoction as well. In Hakluyt's collection of voyages, we find an account of a shipwreck in the New World, during the Humphrey Gilbert expedition in 1583, that recounts how "those which were the strongest holpe their fellowes unto a fresh brooke, where we satisfied our selves with water and berries very well."[3]

When Caliban speaks of being taught "how / To name the bigger light, and how the less," he is employing, as Kermode has pointed out, figures for the sun and moon taken from the English translation of the Bible. This is the first moment in the play where its dominant figure, the figure of the eloquent orator as language-giver to the savages, explicitly emerges, though this figure is always being prepared for, and subsequently elaborated, in the sense we have that Prospero is the origin of language, not in the absolute sense of *origin* but in its political sense, in that Prospero determines decorum through his control of the flow of speech. Yet imperialism always justifies, or mystifies, the political in the name of the absolute or the natural, and so it is difficult to tell here whether Caliban is learning new or first names for the sun and the moon. This ambiguity is the sign of a conflict within the ideology of imperialism, between what this ideology represses (that imperialism is always acting in the interests of its own power) and what it admits (that imperialism is acting in the interest of enlightening the other).

Caliban's narration of the tender trade ends abruptly in self-recrimination for engaging in the trade. After cursing himself, he curses Prospero for usurping and enslaving him. But the savage offers no explanation for what appears in his narrative as a sudden and arbitrary shift from loving reciprocity to brutal hierarchy. It is Prospero, the historian, who immediately fills in the logical gap in Caliban's narrative:

> Thou most lying slave,
> Whom stripes may move, not kindness! I have us'd thee,
> Filth as thou art, with human care; and lodg'd thee
> In mine own cell, till thou didst seek to violate
> The honour of my child.
>
> (I.ii.346–50)

The savage's fall from reciprocity into hierarchy, Prospero announces angrily, is the savage's fault, the result of the savage's attempt to rape the duke's daughter. An ironic political fable is being elaborated here, one that rationalizes a class system and its colonial ventures by locating the origin of that system in the very people it oppresses, in their need for oppression. Along with the stereotype of the drunken Indian, we have here the stereotype of the Indian who rapes, the precursor of Cooper's Magua in *The Last of the Mohicans*. That Native American cultures typically have powerful taboos against rape would not have been known by Shakespeare, but such knowledge has never prevented the promulgation of stereotypes anyway. Quite the contrary. Stereotypes function to repress such knowledge, so that the other can become a screen for the repressed and projected crimes of the self. It is the master who rapes the slave woman at will, not the male slave who rapes the master's wife or daughter. All of this is a historical fact of corrupt power relationships, not of metaphysics. Fanon reminds us not to idealize the native:

> The look that the native turns on the settler's town is a look of lust, a look of envy; it expresses his dreams of possession—all manner of possession: to sit at the settler's table, to sleep in the settler's bed, with his wife if possible. The colonized man is an envious man. And this the settler knows very well; when their glances meet he ascertains bitterly, always on the defensive, "They want to take our place." It is true, for there is no native who does not dream at least once a day of setting himself up in the settler's place.[4]

But it is the settler, we remember, who institutes the violence that triggers this dream of counterviolence. Revolution, whether it is Tayo's return in *Ceremony* to the communal world of the pueblo, or the Sandinista's communism, becomes the possibility of replacing this dream with a social reality that is independent of the settler's institutions.

Caliban does not deny Prospero's charge (for that would indeed introduce a strain of equivocality), but he does give it a political twist. It is not lust that prompts rape but the need for power:

> O ho, O ho!would't had been done!
> Thou didst prevent me; I had peopled else
> The isle with Calibans.
>
> (I.ii.350–53)

Like Caliban, Miranda is Prospero's property. Both Caliban and Miranda, as we have noted, are identified with the land. In line with the politics of culture and class, Prospero cannot afford Caliban's appropriation of Miranda because the father needs the daughter to secure a political alliance with Naples that will restore his Old World power. To this end, Prospero appears to cast a spell on Miranda and Ferdinand so that they will fall in love (I.ii.422–23). Both Caliban and Prospero, then, are crucially related to Miranda through the activity of appropriation for the purposes of gaining power. And as Caliban defines it in the preceding lines, rape is the sexual appropriation of women for political purposes. We could say that if Caliban attempts this appropriation, Prospero succeeds in it, by giving Miranda, without regard for her will (under *his* spell), to Ferdinand. So Prospero's accusation of Caliban is no more than a repressed self-accusation. What forbids this identity between Prospero and Caliban is that European culture recognizes Miranda as Prospero's property, and so relations of sexual appropriation, as Caliban defines them, are translated as relations of love. Caliban, on the other hand, does not have title to Miranda, and so he is not entitled to her, unless Prospero consents. To possess her, then, he must steal her from Prospero. The question of the relation between rape and property law opens here.

Juxtaposed to the accusation of rape as the rationale for subjugating Caliban is a charge made by Miranda that concerns Caliban's relation to language:

> Abhorrèd slave,
> Which any print of goodness wilt not take,

Being capable of all ill! I pitied thee,
Took pains to make thee speak, taught thee each hour
One thing or other: when thou didst not, savage,
Know thine own meaning, but wouldst gabble like
A thing most brutish, I endow'd thy purposes
With words that made them known. But thy vile race,
Though thou didst learn, had that in't which good natures
Could not abide to be with; therefore wast thou
Deservedly confin'd into this rock,
Who hadst deserv'd more than a prison.

(I.ii.353–64)

Miranda's speech transports Caliban's subjugation by Prospero out of the realm of politics and places it in the realm of metaphysics. It is not that Caliban has lost a power struggle with Prospero to control a crucial piece of property. Rather, his fall, as Miranda rationalizes it, is the result of the essentially evil nature of his ''vile race.'' Miranda's use of the term ''vile,'' as with her use of ''villain'' earlier in the scene, which we discussed in Chapter 2, suggests the class basis of her metaphysics; but class is so naturalized in her world, as is gender, that the identity of *vile* and *evil* remains undisturbed. Thinking of the way that Montaigne dislocated the ''proper'' meaning of the word *cannibal* by translating it as a figure both of the civility of New World kinship and the savagery of Old World politics, we can understand that Miranda is moving in the opposite direction with *Caliban,* locating the word in a ''proper'' place that will uphold the Old World hierarchy of the savage and the civilized. Miranda, in the name of Prospero, speaks to master the equivocal figural power of *cannibal/Caliban* that Montaigne writes to release. From Benjamin's perspective, which we reviewed in Chapter 6, Miranda commits ''the basic error of the translator [in that she] preserves the state in which [her] own language happens to be instead of allowing [her] language to be powerfully affected by the foreign tongue.'' Whereas Montaigne uncannily imagines the language of the cannibals so he can alienate his own language in it, Miranda images Caliban as speaking no language (he can only ''gabble like / A thing most brutish''). The translation in this case can only go one way. Miranda's language cannot be alienated in Caliban's if Caliban possesses none. So it is only Caliban who is left to be alienated, or translated (thus imperialism fantasizes the univocality of its power):

> You taught me language; and my profit on't
> Is, I know how to curse. The red plague rid you
> For learning me your language!
>
> (I.ii.365–67)

We have here at the end of this "exchange" on language and rape the same ambiguity that the exchange began with: it is not clear whether Caliban is learning language for the first time (as the first line of this speech suggests) or a new language (as the last line suggests). Whatever Caliban uttered, however, before Miranda taught him (her) language, was, from the perspective of the Europeans, gibberish, as Miranda's speech makes clear. Within the historical context that I am elaborating, Caliban's relationship to his own language or his lack of language becomes a figure for the Europeans' need to feel that the Old World languages were superior to those of the New. Europeans needed to feel, that is, that New World languages were virtually a lack of language. How else justify the *mission civilatrice* that rationalized and still rationalizes Western imperialism?

The ironic figure of language as a lack of language that emerges from the scene of Western imperialism finds its place in the scene that structures this scene, the scene that, as I have been arguing, is at the very heart of the poetics of imperialism. This is the scene of translation, which in Chapter 6 we quoted from Cicero, where the orator through the power of eloquence transports a savage, or wandering, humanity into the place of civility. As noted, this primal scene is structured by an analogy that posits that ordinary human speech is to eloquence what the cries of beasts are to ordinary speech. That is, in relation to eloquence, ordinary language is a lack of language. And this analogy in turn interprets the scene as one of primal instruction, in which beasts are transformed into humans through the gift of language that the Promethean orator bestows on them. Caliban's instruction in language repeats this scene in two salient ways: the Promethean Prospero, through Miranda, bestows language on Caliban, Caliban's brutish utterance having been to ordinary speech what ordinary speech is to Prospero's eloquence. This analogy is confirmed by the fact, remarked on in Chapter 2, that when Caliban does acquire ordinary speech his curses cannot literalize themselves in power the way Prospero's curses can. In *The Tempest,* no one's word has the transforming power of Prospero's.

Inherent in the ideology of race, gender, and class that informs the primal scene of translation is the notion that full humanity is not attainable without eloquence. To speak ordinarily is to remain part beast, to be a kind of monster. Only eloquence can produce a purely human form, a fully human speech, that is, the form and speech of a European male aristocracy that struggles to circulate eloquence only within its own race, gender, and class. Caliban can acquire language yet still remain brutish, as Miranda makes clear in his scene of instruction; for, if we follow the analogy that structures the scene, the language he acquires, in relation to Prospero's eloquence, is the most ordinary language. If Caliban is given a few eloquent speeches in the play, the audience, as I speculated in Chapter 6, is to understand this as a natural or naked, eloquence, a primitive poetry of the kind that Puttenham associated with New World natives, not the eloquence refined by art that Prospero practices so powerfully. Through enforcing such distinctions, which Montaigne so radically blurs, the European upper-class male protects the frontier of decorum.

Yet if in the course of the drama Prospero is finally able to keep Caliban in his place, in its ideological course *Caliban,* functioning as a name that names the place of translation in the play, articulates the equivocality of this frontier. The word most often used to describe Caliban in the play is *monster,* which is a sign of *Caliban*'s ambiguous place between human and beast, between language and gabble, or, properly (that is, politically), between eloquence and ordinary language. In *The Tempest, Caliban* is always in translation, a figure for the equivocal processes of usurpation and transportation that Prospero struggles to surpress. Trinculo articulates both the ambiguous place of Caliban and the ideological force of *Caliban,* when, wandering lost on the island, he first encounters the savage:

> What have we here? a man or a fish? dead or alive? . . . Were I in England now, as once I was, and had but this fish painted, not a holiday fool there but would give a piece of silver: there would this monster make a man; any strange beast there makes a man: when they will not give a doit to relieve a lame beggar, they will lay out ten to see a dead Indian. (II.ii. 24–34)

If Trinculo almost immediately discovers that Caliban "is no fish, but an islander" (36–37), this does not lessen Caliban's ambiguity. He remains a monster, that is, an equivocal figure, throughout the play. The question remains, however: what is the ideological force of this equivocality, for its dramatic force is continually repressed by the univocal? The answer offers itself in a pun on the phrase "monster make a man." In the immediate context of profiteering from foreign voyages, the phrase means that a man can make money by placing a "monster" on display in England (the characters are Italian voyagers; the inadvertent reference to England gives the topographical game away). The term "monster" here measures what Europeans perceived as the outer limits of the alien, the far-fetched, we might say, employing the classical term for metaphor that means the point at which it disturbs decorum. But if the phrase "monster make a man" refers immediately to profiting from human difference, read literally it says that the basis of such difference is cultural, not natural: if one transports a "monster" from its native place to England, then this "monster" becomes a man.

Trinculo's pun on "monster make a man" finds a useful historical precedent in one of the early accounts of voyaging to the New World in Hakluyt:

> This yeere also [1502] were brought unto the King [Henry VII] three men taken in the New Found Island [Micmac or other mainland Algonquians]. . . . These were clothed in beasts skins, and did eate raw flesh, and spake such speache that no man could understand them, and in their demeanour like to bruite beastes, whom the King kept a time after. Of the which upon two yeeres after, I saw two apparelled after the maner of Englishmen in Westminster pallace, which that time I could not discerne from Englishmen, til I was learned what they were, but as for speach, I heard none of them utter one word. (32)

The place of these Native Americans as Native Americans is their clothing, eating habits, and speech, with, as the end of the anecdote emphasizes, particular stress on clothing and speech. Although Robert Fabian, who narrates, initially nominates these Indians as "men," he appears to qualify their human identity when he notes that *"no man* could understand" their language, thereby suggesting that this language articulates itself beyond the frontier of the human, implicitly defined here as the languages that the Europeans present could understand. This qualification of Indians' human identity is intensifed when the clothes they are wearing, beasts' skins, become a figure of their own bestiality. Like Caliban, in translation between the human and the bestial, these Native Americans are monsters. Two years after this initial encounter, Fabian finds the Indians in a different place (of clothing and speech). Dressed like Englishmen and remaining silent (one presumes that if they had opened their mouths and spoken the King's English the effect would have been the same), these monsters make men.

Embedded in Trinculo's pun and Fabian's anecdote, we have a theory of translation, which is dependent, as all theories of translation must be, on a notion of place. This theory of translation constitutes a theory of what is human. Put another way, we could say that in the Renaissance and until the founding of biology in the nineteenth century, theories of what is human are theories of translation, theories of culture rather than of nature. In *Tarzan of the Apes,* we read how a theory of evolution, a theory of nature, is the repressed form of a theory of translation that blurs the boundary between "human" and "ape" by articulating the boundary as literal, that is, scriptural, rather than natural. In other words, we speculated that theories of evolution are always theories of translation. Montaigne, we can say, endorses this speculation and in doing so relativizes, or politicizes, the notion of the human. Trinculo's pun and Fabian's anecdote make the process of becoming human a process of translation as well; and this makes sense, for, as we have noted, in the Renaissance nature was part of a process of inscription. Yet there is a crucial difference between Montaigne's theory of translation and Shakespeare's. For in Trinculo's pun, as in Fabian's description, the translation from "monster" to human only moves in the direction of Europe (although the possibility of irony is there, however muted). England is *the* place of humanness. A theory of cultural absolutism, which forms the basis for the imperial rationale, is implicit here. When the notion of the biological develops in the nineteenth century and is used to ground this theory of cultural absolutism, the last vestiges of its irony, of its doubt, are repressed. The very surface of *The Tempest* ripples with repressed irony, whereas *Tarzan of the Apes* is a smooth imperial sea.

Trinculo's pun, and the figure of *Caliban* that informs it, cannot help but raise the question: what is the frontier of the human? Europeans' confrontation with the radically different cultures of the Americas brought this question in whatever its guises to the forefront of Western cultural consciousness, as Fabian's anecdote suggests. The debate, which we have noted in passing, over the humanness of the Indians between Las Casas and Sepúlveda in 1550 at Valladolid is one example of the question's cultural/political force. Independent of its outcome, the fact of the debate is scandalous and tells us all we need to know about the virulent cultural narcissism of the West. Central to this narcissism, which posits an identity between language and the human, was the West's fantasy that the languages of Europe were superior to those of the Americas. In Chapter 1, we have read how this fantasy persists in the twentieth century, informing U.S. foreign policy, just as Columbus defended his own cultural narcissism by projecting doubts about his own language, his own humanness, onto the Indians. Fabian's anecdote represents the same kind of defense. The Indians function as a screen on which cultural self-doubt can be projected and thus repressed in order to buttress Eurocentrism against the shock of its own potential marginality. There is of course the dissenting tradition that we have read in Montaigne, where the Indians function no less as a screen perhaps, but in order to end this repression. The dissenting tradition, however, has never, to this day, determined official policy. And we have virtually no tradition in the West, at least in terms of political practice, that can deal with the cultural/political integrity of the peoples of what we term the Third World.

In *The Tempest,* Caliban functions as a screen that represses Prospero's doubts about the power of his word, about his own univocality. Prospero's ordering Caliban to speak figures the politics of this univocality, the politics of decorum that we studied in Chapter 5. For decorum is defined by the power of speech: who can order whom to speak; that is, who is the source of language. Prospero offers himself in this scene as the source of language, the language-giver; or, rather, Shakespeare has Caliban, however ambiguously, nominate him as such. But what we already understand is that *Caliban,* as the place of *translatio* in *The Tempest,* is also the source of language. That is, the ideology contained within the primal scene of translation in the West contradicts itself (and this contradiction, I must keep insisting, is the sign of a repressed politics); for it at once offers the eloquent orator as the source of language, the very sign of decorum, and as dependent on a source, that of metaphor, which, as we have read, is at once the basis of decorum, the very sign of civility, and decorum's antithesis, the savage. When Prospero orders Caliban to speak he is expressing this double ideology; for the order is not only an assertion of the orator's primacy, but a denial of his own dependency on Caliban for eloquent speech, just as we have understood Columbus and Fabian in their assertions about Indian languages to be expressing repressed doubts about the power of their own.

If Caliban is Prospero's screen, the mode of translating extreme self-doubt into violent power, *Caliban* is the West's screen, or, rather, the screen of patriarchal power in the West: the way this power projects its own ambivalent relation to language, and thus identity, onto a foreign scene, repressing this ambivalence through an imperial rationale. In *The Tempest*, Caliban figures, or performs, *Caliban*. The savage slave, like the apes in *Tarzan*, is the place where Prospero projects, as a foreign language, the lack of language, the failure of imperial power or the sign that no power is immediate, already inscribed in his language. The opposition of Tarzan and the apes, which within Burrough's narrative is given an apparent priority through the biological rationale of Greystoke's birth, is in political fact (and what other kind of fact is there?) the projection of a prior division within Greystoke (and his class) figured by the title *Tarzan of the Apes:* "this thing of darkness I / Acknowledge mine." Prospero struggles not to acknowledge this thing of darkness, this problem of translation that he struggles to master so that he can dream undisturbed the dream of imperial power, the dream of an eloquence that literalizes itself immediately in the world.

Caliban performs this problem of translation, the drama of *translatio*'s double agency. The perfect servant of Prospero's eloquence, in the sense that he is the sign of the power of Prospero's word to literalize itself, to escape its own figuration or translation, Caliban also attempts to usurp this eloquence, in the sense that his rebellion aims at destroying its source: Prospero's books. Performing the problem of translation as usurpation, Caliban points to the motor of the play where usurpation is precisely equated with translation: "The government I cast upon my brother, / And to my state grew stranger, being transported / And rapt in secret studies" (I.ii.75–77), Prospero tells Miranda as he narrates to her the history that brought father and daughter to the island.

Among the definitions that the OED gives for "translate" we find the following: "To transport with the strength of some feeling; to enrapture, entrance." The earliest use of this definition that the OED gives is from Browne's *Religio Medici* (1643): "That elegant Apostle, which seemed to have a glimpse of heaven, . . . was translated out of himself to behold it." The example itself points to another definition of translation that would have been common enough in England from at least the end of the fourteenth century: "To carry or convey to heaven without death. . . ." And this definition was, as well, a primary definition of the word "rapt," which could also have precisely the opposite meaning, that is, "raped." "Transport" too, in its most literal sense of carrying from one place to another, would have been understood by a contemporary

English audience as a synonym for "translate," which the literate would have known came from the past participle of the Latin verb *transfero*, itself a translation of the Greek *metaphero*. We can find in Hakluyt's *Navigations*, for example, *translation* used in the literal sense of *transfero* and *metaphero* to mean to carry something from one place to another (130). My point is that when Prospero describes himself at the end of the passage we are considering as "being transported / And rapt in secret studies" and thus becoming a "stranger" to his "state," the description that he offers of his alienation is grounded in the figure of translation. The idea of Prospero as a "stranger" could only have served to emphasize for the audience this figure, which is evoked by the words "transported" and "rapt." Prospero then prepares the way for his usurpation by Antonio, who as the acting duke becomes Prospero's unfaithful translator, translating himself into a province where he is a stranger to his state: the province of his "library" which, as he tells Miranda, "Was dukedom large enough" (I.ii.109–110). And the transportation of Prospero and Miranda to their exile on Caliban's island literalizes in the dramatic terms of the play this initial act of translation. For what does the island become to Prospero but an expanded library, a library transformed into a state, a state into a library, where the scholar, who in the Renaissance must always be a translator, literally rules his subjects by the book.

On the island, as if to compensate for his loss of power through translation in Milan, Prospero plays the part of the potent translator. His account of releasing Ariel from Sycorax's spell stresses the bestial sounds Ariel made in prison:

> thy groans
> Did make wolves howl, and penetrate the breasts
> Of ever-angry bears: it was a torment
> To lay upon the damn'd, which Sycorax
> Could not again undo: it was mine Art,
> When I arriv'd and heard thee, that made gape
> The pine, and let thee out.
>
> (I.ii.287–93)

Within the context of the primal scene of translation, Ariel's release from prison is his translation by the eloquent orator, Prospero, from the inarticulate cries of beasts into language, where, as we have noted, he becomes Prospero's faithful translator. But it is on Caliban's translation, through the agency of Miranda, that Prospero lavishes the most care, a care that Caliban repays by attempting to rape Miranda.

We have read Caliban's rape attempt as a question of property relations. I want to read it here, at the end of this book, as a problem of the proper, as a question of decorum as it relates to the problem of translation. Within this problem, I want to argue, the attempted rape of Miranda by Caliban figures the translation of *Miranda* by *monster*.

At their roots, before the word *monster* takes on the notion of deformity, both of these words signify something *marvelous* (OED). In this sense, it is not only *monster* that can translate *Miranda*, but *Miranda* that can translate *monster*. The translation process works both ways. What appears most univocal in the play, what guarantees the frontier of decorum, the opposition between the innocent, upper-class, European female and the vile savage, is most equivocal. Critics have noted this equivocality on the structural level of the play, where, for example, Caliban can function as the figurative child of Prospero, thus forging a bond of kinship between the monster and Miranda. Both children are also types of New World innocence. One critic has offered Miranda as the figure of the noble savage;[5] and Caliban refers to her as "nonpareil" (III.ii.99), a figure that John Smith uses in his *True Relation* to describe Pocahontas. If Caliban falls from his innocence, his position in the tender trade, to become the ignoble savage, we can read the opposition *noble/ignoble* as a way of repressing the structural affinities between these two marvelous creatures of the island.

Prospero's struggle to keep Caliban and Miranda as far apart as possible figures a cultural struggle to repress the ideological kinship that these structural affinities are a part of and that are contained in the translation of *Miranda* by *monster* or *monster* by *Miranda*. Prospero's struggle to master Caliban figures a cultural struggle to master the ideological equivocalities of this translation by translating these equivocalities of race, gender, and class into the word *cannibal*, of which *Caliban* is a translation. Working within the figurative dynamics of the drama, which cannot be separated from its literal action, we can say that to master Caliban is to master speech, to be the perfectly eloquent orator. Caliban's attempted rape of Miranda contradicts this mastery, which would be the perfect assertion of decorum (the marking of a clear frontier between the domestic and the foreign, the upper and the lower class, the civilized and the savage, the male and the female), because this attempted rape figures as it conceals the kinship of *monster/Miranda*, the kind of kinship between the self and the other that Montaigne's cannibalism asserts openly, and that Shakespeare's *Caliban* denies. Caliban's attempt to rape Miranda is literally an attempt to translate *Miranda* into *monster*: to people the island with Calibans, to give Miranda the name of *monster* by making her the mother of monsters, in order to usurp Prospero. As we noted, Prospero justifies his mastery of Caliban by referring to this attempted violent translation. And Miranda explains it by noting a primal, or racial, character flaw in the savage. She finds proof of this flaw in the fact that, while the savage can learn the master's language, he apparently cannot learn the morals embedded in that language. This discourse of morals, which juxtaposes language and rape without ever drawing a precise connection between the two, conceals a discourse of power in which, as we have read in Douglass and Fanon, the master struggles to deny the slave access to the full potency of language, that is, eloquence, by asserting the frontier of decorum as an absolute, or natural, frontier. In the discourse of power, we can read the precise connection between language and rape. For the master uses the charge of rape to rationalize the frontier of decorum by concealing the power politics of language that establishes this frontier. This politics, we can say now, as opposed to the fantasized rape that masks it, is based on a violent act of translation: the translation of the lost Arawak word into *cannibal*, of which the translation *monster/Miranda* is a particular derivative. This violent translation is figured in *The Tempest* by the scene that commands our concentration, in which Prospero, through his pupil Miranda, gives language to Caliban. But this scene is figured, of course, not as a scene of violence, but as a scene of failed education, in which the savage, naturally enough, cannot cross the frontier of translation to attain the eloquence of the imperial orator.

Afterword

Repetition and
Resistance in the
Representation
of Roanoke

Translation in a Colonial Context

THE COVER FOR THIS NEW EDITION of *The Poetics of Imperialism* reproduces an engraving of a John White watercolor drawing, circa 1585, of a Native American from one of the coastal communities of what is today North Carolina, but was at the time named Virginia by the English. Such naming, the first colonizing acts of translation, constituted those grandiose linguistic gestures that marked the beginning of imperial ventures in America (itself a name derived from one of those gestures) by projecting an alien unity of place on a native plurality of places, corresponding to the diverse languages of the peoples who had lived there for centuries when the European invaders arrived. The engraving, which was done by Gysbert van Veen, an assistant to the master engraver Theodor de Bry, first appeared under the title of "The Coniuerer" in 1590 in De Bry's *America,* part 1. This book (hereafter referred to simply as *America*), which was the first part of an ambitious venture by De Bry to publish certain European chronicles of the "New World," concerned itself with "the first serious English efforts to examine and settle North America":[1] the voyages sponsored by Sir Walter Raleigh that took place between 1584 and 1590 under a patent from the queen and whose principal base of operations in America was established in coastal North Carolina on Roanoke Island.

De Bry's *America*, which is divided into three sections, each with a distinct title page, focuses in its first two sections[2] on the settlement at Roanoke that persisted from June 1585 to June 1586 under the overall authority of Sir Richard Grenville, acting for Raleigh (who never visited Virginia throughout his six-year sponsorship of the voyages), and the governorship of Ralph Lane. The first section is composed of a reprint of *A briefe and true report of the new found land of Virginia* (1588), the narrative of Thomas Hariot. According to the official English record, Hariot was the principal ethnographer, along with White, and translator, of English origin, for the expedition. There were two Indian translators as well, Manteo and Wanchese, who journeyed to England with the first voyage (with what degree of willingness is never stated in the English narratives)—that of Philip Amadas and Arthur Barlowe in the spring and summer of 1584—and then returned to Roanoke with the Grenville voyage in the spring of the following year. There is also an unofficial record —the testimony, taken by the Spanish in Jamaica, of an English castaway from the 1585 voyage—of two unnamed Englishmen who were left with the Indians as hostages for Manteo and Wanchese, and who thus could have potentially acted as translators for the subsequent settlements. But apparently no record, beyond this mention of them as hostages in 1584, exists.[3]

Along with another Indian, Towaye (of whom virtually nothing is known [*RV*, vol. 2, 502]), Manteo is also listed among the colonists who accompanied John White,[4] acting as governor, to Roanoke in the late spring of 1587 in order to establish what was to be the second and last colony of the Raleigh venture.[5] If the list is accurate, we understand that Manteo had returned to England with the first colonists, all of whom abandoned the colony in 1586, and had spent almost a year abroad before returning home with the White expedition. In sum, according to the information we have, Manteo spent almost a year and a half in England between 1584 and 1587, when he returned home for good. Wanchese, it would appear from the official record, upon his return to Roanoke in 1585, joined Indians who actively opposed the English settlement (*VV*, 37). These included Wingina, whom the English had identified in 1584 as the principal leader in the area of Roanoke. Wingina apparently received the English cordially in 1584 and 1585 (*VV*, 4–11; 71–72); after hostilities developed between his community and the English, they killed him in a subterfuge in June of 1586 (*VV*, 41–42).[6] Manteo remained an English ally, who, according to the official record, "behaved himselfe toward us [the colonists] as a most faithfull English man" and on August 13, 1587, "by the commandment of Sir Walter Ralegh, was christened in Roanoak, and called Lord thereof, and of Dasamongueponke, in reward of his faithfull service" (*VV*, 101, 102). We have no record of what Manteo's motives might have been in the political complexities that developed with the English invasion or what he made of these official ceremonies.[7] Of all the visible principals in this drama, though, he was in the best position, in terms of length of time and continuity of contact, to have learned the language of the other, if we except the two English hostages whose history is lost to us.

Barlowe, Lane, and White, in addition to Hariot, all produced narratives of the Roanoke voyages that were published, along with the Hariot, in 1589 in *The principall navigations, voiages and discoveries of the English nation*, compiled by the younger Richard Hakluyt, the prime propagandist and eminent translator for the English colonial venture in America. White in fact produced three narratives that we have: one of his 1587 voyage to plant a colony on Roanoke after the failure of the 1585–1586 venture; one of a 1588 voyage to resupply that colony, a voyage that had to return to England before reaching America due to damage sustained in privateering; and, the last, of his 1590 voyage, again to resupply the settlement on Roanoke, which the voyagers found abandoned.[8] Forced to return to England by bad weather, the White expedition never was able to search for the colonists, the so-called "Lost Colony," whose fate remains a mystery to this day, though the White narrative reports clues that suggest a migration of the colony to the birthplace of Manteo on Croatoan island (*VV*, 125–27).

These narratives of Barlowe, Hariot, Lane, and White, along with White's drawings and De Bry's *America*, constitute virtually all of what we know of these Carolina Algonquians whose populations dwindled radically over the next century, due to disease and warfare brought about by the English presence. According to an essay by Christian F. Feest in the *Handbook of North American Indians:* "By 1709 North Carolina Algonquian population was down to some 600, and by the end of the century only a handful were still being regarded as Indians [though the question of exactly who is doing the regarding is masked by the passive construction]. . . . [N]ative languages were being replaced by English during the eighteenth century [the *Handbook* lists these languages as "extinct" (71) in that century]. . . . Around 1915, about 100 persons of suspected Indian descent were found living on Roanoke island, some of the adjacent sand islands, and on the mainland in Dare and Hyde counties."[9] The *Handbook* reports no oral traditions, either from these "suspects" or others. Perhaps, like the Native languages, no such traditions survive. What we must rely on to construct a history, then, are the English narratives, which, along with the White drawings and the De Bry, constitute what I have referred to as "the official record."

The title page that precedes Hariot's narrative in De Bry's *America* (Figure 1) is a somewhat shortened version of the title page from the first edition of *A briefe and true report,* which, among other things, mentions "the government of Rafe Lane Esquier" (*VV,* 150) by name. It is the first title page that the reader encounters in *America;* followed, as it is immediately, by the dedication "TO THE RIGHT WORTHIE AND HONOVRABLE, SIR WALTER RALEGH," it may have been considered by Renaissance readers as the title for the whole volume, though it does note that the Hariot narrative now constitutes a "fore booke" to the volume of which it is a part.[10] The title reads in its English version (De Bry published simultaneous Latin, French, and German versions of *America* as well):

> A briefe and true report of the new found land of Virginia. *of the commodities and of the nature and manners of the naturall inhabitants. Discouered by the English Colony there seated by* Sir Richard Greinuile Knight *In the yeere 1585. Which Remained Vnder the gouernement of twelue monethes, At the speciall charge and direction of the Honourable* SIR WALTER RALEIGH *Knight lord Warden of the stanneries Who therein hath beene fauoured and authorised by her* MAIESTIE *and her letters patents: This fore booke Is made in English By Thomas Hariot seruant to the abouenamed Sir* WALTER, *a member of the Colony, and there imployed in discouering.* . . . (See Figure 1)[11]

This typically descriptive Renaissance title highlights, with the exception of White and Lane, (the latter's name, as noted, appears in the 1588 version), the principal actors and the pertinent information of the 1585–1586 Roanoke venture, but with a decided race and class bias (women did not venture to Roanoke until the 1587 voyage). From the queen through Hariot, the names listed are of the English upper classes and possess various interlinked forms of authority—financial, political, and

A briefe and true report
of the new found land of Virginia.
of the commodities and of the nature and man
ners of the naturall inhabitants. Discouered by
the English Colony there seated by Sir Richard
Greinuile Knight In the yeere 1585. Which Rema
:ined Vnder the gouernement of twelue monethes,
At the speciall charge and direction of the Honou=
rable SIR WALTER RALEIGH Knight lord Warden
of the stanneries Who therein hath beene fauoured
and authorized by her MAIESTIE
:and her letters patents:
This fore booke Is made in English
BY Thomas Hariot seruant to the abouenamed
Sir WALTER, a member of the Colony, and there
imployed in discouering

CVM GRATIA ET PRIVILEGIO CÆS.MA.TIS SPECIA.LD

FRANCOFORTI AD MOENVM
TYPIS IOANNIS WECHELI, SVMTIBVS VERO THEODORI
DE BRY ANNO CIƆ IƆ XC.
VENALES REPERIVNTVR IN OFFICINA SIGISMVNDI FEIRABENDII

Figure 1. Title page preceding Thomas Hariot's *A briefe and true report of the new found land of Virginia* in the English edition of Theodor de Bry's *America*, part 1 (Frankfurt, 1590).

rhetorical: the authority to author a *written* narrative, which in this case is synonymous with the authority to translate. No Indians are named in the title; they are referred to en masse as "naturall inhabitants," not actors in their own right, but the "discovered" and "patented" subjects, like "the commodities," of a certain authoritative knowledge. Further, none of the approximately six hundred men, "including more than 100 would-be colonists," who sailed on the seven ships in various laboring capacities are mentioned either individually or en masse (*VV,* xxi).

If White's name is not explicit on the first title page, it is implicit in the engravings of five of the figures from his drawings that frame the page, including a version of the figure titled "The Coniuerer" (see Figure 6, below [*America 1585,* figure 15, 117; engraving XI in *America*]) but that White had named "The flyer" (see Figure 5, below [*America 1585,* plate 49, 79]). White's name itself appears on the title page to the second section (Figure 2), which reads:

THE TRVE PICTVRES AND FASHIONS OF THE PEOPLE IN THAT PARTE OF AMERICA NOVV CALLED VIRGINIA, DISCOWRED BY ENGLISMEN sent thither in the years of our Lorde 1585. att the speciall charge and direction of the Honourable SIR WALTER RALEGH Knigt Lord Warden of the stannaries in the duchies of Corenwal and Oxford who therin hath bynne fauored and auctorised by her MAAIESTIE and her letters patents. *Translated out of Latin into English by RICHARD HACKLVIT.* DILIGENTLYE COLLECTED AND DRAOWne by IHON WHITE *who was sent thiter speciallye and for the same purpose by the said SIR WALTER RALEGH the year abouesaid 1585. and also the year 1588. now cutt in copper and first published by THEODORE de BRY att his wone chardges.* (America 1585, figure 3, 105)

This title page maintains the authoritative hierarchy of the first title and adds to that hierarchy, in addition to White, the crucial name of Richard Hakluyt, who was instrumental in brokering both the Roanoke voyages and the De Bry book (*ADJW,* vol. 1, 3, 26). The date "1588" suggests itself as a misprint for "1587," because, presumably, De Bry would have known that White's 1588 voyage of resupply never reached its destination. The second section itself consists of two maps of Virginia and twenty-one engravings of North Carolina Indian life taken from White's drawings. However, for three of the engravings of Indian life, no drawings exist. These are the engravings titled "The manner of makinge their boates" (*America 1585,* figure 16, 118; engraving XII in *America*), "Ther Idol Kiwasa" (*America 1585,* figure 25, 127; engraving XXI in *America*),

THE TRVE PICTVRES
AND FASHIONS OF
THE PEOPLE IN THAT PAR-
TE OF AMERICA NOVV CAL-
LED VIRGINIA, DISCOWRED BY ENGLISMEN

fent thither in the years of our Lorde 1585. att the fpeciall charge and direction of
the Honourable SIR WALTER RALEGH Knigt Lord Warden
of the ftannaries in the duchies of Corenwal and Oxford who
therin hath bynne fauored and auctorifed by her
MAAIESTIE and her let-
ters patents.

Tranflated out of Latin into English by
RICHARD HACKLVIT.

DILIGENTLYE COLLECTED AND DRAOW-
ne by IHON WHITE who was fent thiter fpeciallye and for the fame pur-
pofe by the faid SIR WALTER RALEGH the year abouefaid
1585. and alfo the year 1588. now cutt in copper and firft
publifhed by THEODORE de BRY att
his wone chardges.

Figure 2. Title page to the second section of Theodor de Bry's *America*, part 1.

and "The Marckes of sundrye of the Cheif mene of Virginia (*America 1585,* figure 27, 129; engraving XXIII in *America*). The figure in "Ther Idol Kiwasa" appears almost Asian in its stylization and besides is wearing "a Timucuan headdress, exactly as seen in Le Moyne's *Florida* illustrations" (*America 1585,* 17). De Bry published *Florida* in 1591 as the second part of the *America* venture. It is "Jacques Le Moyne's illustrated account of Laudoniere's ill-fated Huguenot colony in Florida, 1564–5," which De Bry intended to publish first, because of the temporal priority of the Florida colony, until, as is "likely," Hakluyt "persuaded" him to publish the Virginia volume before it (*America 1585,* 17). Raleigh was the patron of both White and Le Moyne; and among White's watercolors, we find a drawing of an "Indian Man of Florida, after Jacques Le Moyne de Morgues" (*America 1585,* plate 61, 87), who is wearing the same headdress as De Bry's "Kiwasa." This figure is represented on a much smaller scale (and off to one side) in engraving XXII in *America,* "The Tombe of their Werowans or Cheiff Lordes" (*America 1585,* figure 26, 128), for which there is a corresponding, though not identical, watercolor, with a longer, more descriptive title (*America 1585,* plate 38, 68). Nevertheless, in both this engraving and this watercolor the figure of the "idol" is wearing Le Moyne's Timucuan headdress. This visual conflation of Timucua and Southeastern Algonquian Indians, which is repeated in the text that accompanies "Ther Idol Kiwasa," raises questions of representation that I will take up in the following section.

According to Paul Hulton and David Beers Quinn, "De Bry himself engraved the majority of White's drawings, a few being the work of his assistant, Gysbert van Veen" (*ADJW,* vol. 1, 26). Each engraving is accompanied by a title above it and a short explanatory text below. Hariot composed the texts or "notes" in Latin; and as the title page to this section tells us, Hakluyt then translated the Latin for the English edition of *America.* David Beers Quinn understands the text as very much the collaborative effort, with not particularly happy results, of De Bry, Hariot, and Hakluyt: "Though Harriot wrote the notes in Latin it is likely that he did them in a hurry and it is likely that De Bry changed them about somewhat as he made his final selection of drawings from which to engrave the plates once he got back to his Frankfurt workshop. (The crude versions of the captions in English were attributed by De Bry to Hakluyt, but some are so garbled it would seem that De Bry himself may have been responsible for them . . .)."[12]

Quinn's sense of dissatisfaction with this project may come from his belief in a kind of ur-text of the Roanoke voyages, a happy collaboration between Hariot and White that never reached fruition and that in comparison to which (a comparison that seems to gain power from the fact that it must remain imaginary) all other works are a fall—fragmentary translations of a transcendent original:

> In 1587 Thomas Hariot was preparing to publish a report of what had been observed in America in 1585–86. It is evident that he contemplated an elaborate illustrated record which would include engravings after White's drawings of fauna and flora as well as Indian scenes, and it is not unlikely that he discussed the technical aspects of this scheme with the engraver, Theodor de Bry. . . . The decision to postpone the publication and to concentrate instead on a brief propaganda pamphlet [*A briefe and true report* of 1588] may have resulted from Raleigh's desire for such a publication, but it was probably influenced by the fact that the collection of natural history drawings was incomplete. This is not necessarily a reflection on the thoroughness of the survey made in America but resulted rather from the loss or damage of much of the written and drawn material when the settlers were leaving Roanoke Island in June 1586. (*ADJW*, vol. 1, 25–26)

Political exigencies and natural disasters conspire to deprive posterity of a grand ethnography. Raleigh needs propaganda to attract capital for further voyages; and in June of 1586 a tempest on the Outer Banks of North Carolina devils departure: ". . . the weather was so boysterous, and the pinnaces so often on ground, that the most of all wee had, with all our Cardes, Bookes and writings, were by the Saylers cast over boord" (*VV*, 44). This scene of chaos aboard ship in the New World recalls the first scene of Shakespeare's *The Tempest*, written twenty-five years later.

In line with imagining what might have been in all its putative plenitude—a New Book to equal the New World—Quinn has also engaged in the imaginative reconstruction of a "lost archetype" of White sketches made in the field from which, he argues, the surviving watercolors as well as putative drawings made by White for De Bry and Hariot, and their copies, ultimately derive (*RV*, vol. 1, 392–98; *ADJW*, vol. 1, 24–29). Quinn's purpose in proposing this reconstruction is to argue that whereas "[it] was formerly thought that the elaborations and variations [of the White watercolors] were wholly the work of De Bry and his fellow engravers . . . a closer study shows that White was responsible for a considerable number of the variations from corresponding items in the British Museum set, and makes it quite clear that both derive from the lost archetype" (*RV*, vol. 1, 394).

I have chosen in what follows, however, to compare the extant Whites and the De Bry engravings as if the latter were direct translations of the former. If this is not literally true, then it has a figurative force borne out for me in the historical record of the fundamental stylistic variation between the De Bry engravings and the White drawings, the material record of *what we have,* not what we would like to have or what we imagine to have been there. Quinn, in his praise of those White water-colors "done from the life . . . [as] more spontaneously naturalistic than anything known by an English artist at this period or for the next half century at least" (*ADJW*, vol. 1, 10), would seem to concur.

But historians do not love lacunae, which is another way of saying they do not love the figurative. In this antagonism, ironically, they risk missing the very materiality, that is, the historicity of the figurative. But I must admit that this antagonism to absences has its powerfully pro-ductive side. In its material reconstruction and imaginative speculation, Quinn's work on Roanoke, which is preeminent, clearly provides the material on which cultural critics like myself depend. But cultural crit-ics do or should love (in the sense of *cultivate*) lacunae, and historians might do well to at least develop a liking for them. My sense of the Roanoke materials that we have in hand—the texts of Hariot, Barlowe, White, and Lane; the drawings of White; the engravings of De Bry—is not that they represent the fragments of some ethnographic ur-text but that these fragments are that ur-text, with all its ideological distortions, its contradictions, its problems of translation, to which we ought to pay close attention.

What this complex of textual production can figure is the centrality of translation to the European imperial enterprise in America. To begin with, we might note a central irony of this translation process: "After the appearance of *America,* pt. I, De Bry, its publisher and principal en-graver, came to be regarded as the originator of the Indian plates while their creator was virtually forgotten by succeeding generations" (*ADJW*, vol. 1, 6–7). William Strachey used the De Bry engravings to illustrate his own ethnography of early seventeenth-century Virginia, "ignoring the differences in time and distance which separated the Carolina Algon-kians of the 1580's from the Powhatan Indians of Virginia of a quarter of a century later." And Robert Beverley, almost a century after Strachey, used De Bry again to represent the Indians of Virginia. In effect, the De Bry engravings of the White drawings "conventionalized an image of the American Indian of the Atlantic seaboard that has persisted to the present day, when differences of tribes and periods have ceased to have much relevance for the perpetuators of the legend" (*ADJW,* vol. 1, 58). Ironically, Hulton, who along with Quinn has made the White drawings available to a wide audience, remarks in his introductory material to *America 1585* that due to De Bry's modification of and addition to the watercolors his "plates give us greater insight into the culture of these South-eastern Algonquians than do the drawings themselves" (18). Ironically or contradictorily enough, as well, while Hulton accepts unquestioningly Quinn's hypothesis that "De Bry was working from different versions [of the watercolors we have] with added landscapes and other additional detail" (18), he also assumes that De Bry's engravings are innovations and additions to the extant watercolors.

The irony of translation occluding original that is so central to the focus of *The Poetics of Imperialism* is not a metaphysical irony—one that inevitably points to a pristine point of origin—but a political one—one that points to a usurpation. The process of stylization by which De Bry conventionalized the White drawings, a process I discuss in the section that follows, is also the process by which the White watercolors, which only come to light again beginning in the late nineteenth century,[13] translated the Carolina Algonquians. The process is ideological and is perhaps best figured by the imperial gesture par excellence: Columbus's translation of the indigenous peoples of *America* into *Indians.* This is not to say that through some reductive political calculus we can simply equate all of these processes of translation, but that we cannot separate them from the contexts that render them political and thus imbricate them with one another. (Indeed, to use the notion of "context" in any conventional sense is to give the field a stability, a sense of boundary between text and context, it does not possess.) So, for example, while I consider the White drawings progressive in relation to the De Bry engravings for reasons that I will elaborate, I also consider that the drawings cannot be separated from the regressive project of imperialism that enabled them in the first place.[14]

Translation of various kinds structured this project, from the need for intercultural communication to the desire to transfigure Indian communal lands into property. Hariot's texts along with the other Roanoke narratives, White's watercolors, and De Bry's engravings all lay claim to being the result of accurate processes of intercultural communication. To a significant extent twentieth-century historiography of Euramerican-Native American contact has validated and continues to validate these claims, even as it recognizes the problematic construction of the documents, perhaps because in the absence of other decisive records (archaeological or oral), these early modern texts constitute the only readable record. Crucially, though, much of this historiography, locked in an outmoded positivism that lacks a destabilizing sense of irony (what deconstruction refers to as the "undecidable"), can only read coherencies, even, perhaps especially, where the signs of incoherency abound. Such historiography shares this mode of reading with the early modern "travel narratives" themselves—narratives of conquest and settlement—which sutured the wounds in narratives proclaiming European invulnerability with fictions of translation.

In her "History of Research" on northeastern Indians in the *Handbook of North American Indians,* Elisabeth Tooker notes what we have noted: that "the drawings of John White (Hulton and Quinn 1964) and the other records of Sir Walter Raleigh's expeditions (Quinn 1955) including the descriptions accompanying Theodor De Bry's engravings (Hariot 1588) of John White's drawings . . . constitute [. . .] much of what is known about some North Carolina Algonquians" (vol. 15, 4). The introduction to *The American Drawings of John White* makes the value of these documents even more explicit: ". . . the White drawings, with Hariot's texts, are the sole literate records of a group of tribes which disappeared before being studied further and whose material culture was unsuited to extensive preservation for archaeological study" (vol. 1, 36). (Quinn's use of "literate" here suggests, perhaps, the survival of some oral tradition; but in the scholarship I have surveyed, including Quinn's, I have found no mention of such a tradition. His use of "disappeared" is disingenuous; one reads the word now with the ironies it has taken on in the context of contemporary Latin American state terrorism.) Quinn appears to be epitomizing all the Roanoke narratives in the Hariot-White collaboration of 1585–1586, which certainly yielded the most ethnographic "knowledge." The question is, however: What passes for knowledge in this instance?

Feest notes that in these documents that circumscribe our knowledge "[n]o data has been preserved on kinship, form of family, marriage, de-

scent, residence, and kin groups among sixteenth-century North Carolina Algonquians" (*HNAI*, vol. 15, 277). Quinn, noting that "[v]ery little
is known about the social and political organization of these tribes, especially the Carolina ones," remarks on the English adventurers' habit of
translating their apparent lack of knowledge in these areas into a pleni-
tude of English terms: ". . . the English described them [those apparently
'leading men' designated as *werowans*, for which there also appeared to
be 'a feminine equivalent'] according to preconceptions based on their
own European experience, and it is uncertain how much political authority these men had, how they obtained their status, whether there
were subcategories of *werowans*, whether the political structure was
hierarchical within or among villages, and even whether authority within
the village was vested in a council of some sort" (*ADJW*, vol. 1, 38).

Acknowledging the absence of information about the social organization of these Carolina Indians, but ignoring what we do know about other
kinship-based cultures of this kind—that, based in an equable distribu-
tion of resources, where the source of the common wealth (land) could
not be commodified, these communities did not possess class structures
—Feest proceeds to assert that "social stratification was pronounced in
coastal North Carolina" (*HNAI*, 15, 278), translating the Indians, following the Roanoke narratives, into the terms of the English class system. Quinn, who has the sophistication to be more skeptical than Feest,
can nevertheless extrapolate from the White drawings to the "marked
[. . .] . . . differences in sex and social status" (*ADJW*, vol. 1, 39) of the
Indians, though the titles that White put on his watercolors, as we will
read, in contradistinction to those of De Bry on his engravings, do not by
and large point to such differences. And Quinn, in passing, as we have
read, can suggest that there were female as well as male *werowans*, a
suggestion that is strengthened by the knowledge we have of the female
leadership roles among both the seventeenth-century Iroquois and the
Algonquian-speaking tribes of New England.[15]

Following Hariot and White, buttressed by "[m]odern authorities"
(who, like Feest presumably, read Hariot et al. without a requisite skepti-
cism), Karen Kupperman reads sixteenth-century Carolina Algonquian-
speaking communities as "moving in the direction of true statehood"
(*Roanoke*, 50) with highly stratified social structures. Yet at the same
time, she understands these incipient states as based in the egalitarian,
or "redistributive," economic and political structures of kinship-based
communities. She never explores this contradiction; clearly, she does

not understand it as such, coining such paradoxical phrases as "redistributive kingship" (51) to describe her construct. In Chapter 3 of this book, following Eric Wolf, I discuss the difference between *rank,* which is a social designation in kinship-based communities, and *class,* which is not. With the exception of Montaigne, who increasingly seems remarkable in this area, the sixteenth- and early seventeenth-century travelers did not have the analytical tools for or the interest in making such a distinction. Or, perhaps, in view of Montaigne's achievement (see Chapter 7), it would be more accurate to say that the ideological interests of the travelers overrode their analytical tools. The twentieth-century historians I am discussing possess the tools (from anthropology), however flawed, and should possess the interest. But these tools and this interest are not as much in evidence as they should be in contemporary historiography. Kupperman herself, in the passages cited, seems to be conflating rank-inflected kinship societies, which decidedly did not possess state structures, with class-based state structures.

If the drive for intercultural communication powers the imperial enterprise and is the very motif of the graphics, both text and pictures, that represent it, then a prior or constitutive act of translation drives this drive: the granting of patents from sovereign to subject that forms an essential part of the content of the titles of the first book of De Bry's *America.* The titles of this book about founding, we can say, are themselves founded on the granting of title, specifically title to Indian lands. One of the terms English common law uses to articulate the power that title confers, the power of *alienating* that constitutes land as *property,* is *translation* (see Chapter 3).

Because *The Poetics of Imperialism* focuses on the Anglo-American aspect of this enterprise, its classical origins and its ongoing consequences, it seemed useful, not to mention tempting, in writing this Afterword to begin with the first concerted, though failed, attempt at colonization by the English; to return, that is, to a certain primal scene of translation.

The Example of De Bry and White

De Bry has translated the White drawings in several respects: the color drawings have been transformed into black and white engravings that are stylized in a traditional European mode. This changes White's reddish-brown Indians into De Bry's strangely decontextualized or familiar figures, a decontextualization or familiarization that is intensified by the European features of the De Bry figures, though I want to emphasize here that the question of European versus Indian features, of the familiar versus the alien, of contexts, is not a question of reality but of representation. We have no way of knowing what these Indians "looked" like other than the White watercolors, so we begin not with any originals but with translations. Some comments from the introduction to *The American Drawings of John White* specify my point:

> The deliberate portrayal of racial types . . . had hardly begun to be undertaken in England before the voyages of exploration. . . . In Europe the tradition is older and can be traced back at least as far as Pisanello's studies of Moors and Mongols of the earlier fifteenth century. . . . By White's time this interest in the documentation of races and their clothing had resulted in a considerable production of illustrated costume and travel books. . . .
>
> White's surviving work consists of carefully finished water-colour drawings. Those done from the life are more spontaneously naturalistic than anything known by an English artist at this period or for the next half century at least. This quality is so marked as to seem revolutionary. . . . Yet even in his portrayal of the Algonkian Indians White does not quite discard the Mannerist imagery of Europe, in several of the attitudes they strike. . . . Sometimes he seems to have slightly Europeanized the faces of his Indians, the women more than the men, but less than . . . his engraver De Bry. . . . (8–9; 10–11)

Citing Jean de Lery's *Histoire d'un voyage fait en la terre du Bresil* (1578), the "Introduction" emphasizes this problem of representation even more forcefully: "Jean de Lery himself was very conscious of the difficulties of observing and drawing the Indians. He comments, 'Although I diligently perused and marked those barbarian people, for a whole year together, wherein I lived amongst them, so as I might conceive in my mind a certain idea or proportion of them, yet I say, by reason of their diverse gestures and behaviours, utterly different from ours, it is a very difficult matter to express their true proportions, either in writing or in painting . . .'" (32–33).

As if to compensate for his Europeanization of White's "naturalistic" Indians, De Bry has supplied for his figures backgrounds that are representations of local scenes: Natives shooting bows and arrows, for example, or spear fishing, or paddling canoes (see Figures 3 and 6, below), whereas the White drawings are presented for the most part against blank backgrounds (see Figures 4 and 5, below).[16] But this contrast of Native locale with the Europeanized figures has a way of heightening their decontextualization rather than compensating for it. It is possible, if we follow Quinn's conjectures about missing watercolors, that De Bry was working from White drawings that contained these backgrounds. Whatever the case, however, the effect of the contrast between Europeanized figure and Native ground would still differentiate the De Bry from the White in the way I am suggesting.

De Bry has with few embellishments translated faithfully the White representations of Native dress and other material artifacts of these Algonquian-speaking cultures. But at the same time a certain formalism has subverted White's "naturalism," or perhaps it would be more accurate to say that a certain familiarization has subverted White's representation of cultural alienation, by the doubling of White's single figures. In a number of the engravings we are presented with both front and rear views of the figure represented (see Figure 3, below), whereas in the White drawings we have only single figures in front view (see Figure 4, below). Again, following Quinn, we can imagine that De Bry is working from a now lost set of White watercolors that contain this double vision (*RV,* vol. 1, 420). We can also imagine that White made separate drawings for front and rear views, which De Bry then represented in single plates. But whatever the case, the dynamic between familiarization and alienation would hold.

De Bry (and I use his name here to represent the collaboration of himself, Hariot, and Hakluyt) has also translated the titles of White's drawings in a more Europeanized language, adopting, it would appear, such translations from the notes. So, for example, the first engraving of a figure in the De Bry book, a figure of a Native man, both front and back, posed with a long bow resting on the ground in a vertical position, is titled "A weroan or great Lorde of Virginia" (Figure 3 [*America 1585,* figure 7, 109; engraving III in *America*]), whereas the White drawing from which it is translated is titled "The manner of their attire and painting them selues when they goe to their generall huntings or at theire Solemne feasts" (Figure 4 [*America 1585,* plate 48, 78]). De Bry familiarizes the figure by imposing a European hierarchical distinction

Figure 3. "A weroan or great Lorde of Virginia," from De Bry.

("Lorde of Virginia") on a figure that White does not distinguish in this way. While some of White's titles do take note of the rank of his subjects, this rank is transliterated in Native terms, not translated into European terms of class, as in De Bry's. So, for example, White's drawing "A chiefe Herowans wyfe of Pomeoc. and her daughter of the age of .8 or .10 yeares" (*America 1585*, plate 33, 63) is transformed by De Bry to "A cheiff Ladye of Pomeiooc" (*America 1585*, figure 12, 114; engraving VIII in *America*). Of course, we can imagine that the set of White drawings from which De Bry was working contained the same titles as the engravings, in which case we must also imagine a John White whose cultural understanding of his subjects is highly unstable, indeed, at odds with itself. But we can also imagine that the putative lost set of drawings contained no titles. None of these cases, however—including, as I am, imagining that De Bry was working from the Whites we have—alters the contrast I am suggesting between ideological distortion and relative ethnographic accuracy.

This translation of titles is particularly striking in the case of the figure that De Bry titled "The Coniuerer," but that White, as noted, had

Figure 4. "The manner of their attire and painting them selues when they goe to their generall huntings, or at theire Solemne feasts," by John White.

named "The flyer" (see Figures 5 and 6). The White title is obscure. According to Quinn, it "is probably descriptive of his [the Indian's] ceremonial dancing abilities" (*RV*, vol. 1, 442). Julie R. Solomon (see note 13) connects the title to the Native shaman, as well as to the European figure of Mercury (534, 546), both of whom make flights between the spiritual and the earthly realms. In authorizing the connection to shamanism, however, Solomon cites Robert Beverley's description of "The Conjurer," which is not derived from independent observation, as Solomon appears to believe (534–35), but from De Bry. As we have noted, Beverley reproduces versions of the De Bry engravings as though they were representations of the Virginia Indians about whom he believes he is writing. In fact Beverley tells us that he could "learn little" from Indians about their spiritual beliefs, "it being reckon'd Sacriledge, to divulge the Principles of their Religion," [17] a caveat we ought to keep in mind when Hariot tells us that he gained his knowledge of Native religion through a "special familiaritie with some of their priestes" (*VV*, 70). Solomon, then, distinguishes "The flyer" from "The Coniuerer" — the putative ethnographic accuracy of the former from the anthropological projections of the latter — by unwittingly confusing the latter with the former. She repeats, that is, the closed circuit of translation from De Bry to Beverley to De Bry, which excludes the putative subject of translation: the actual Native "shaman," if shamanism is indeed the cultural complex that accurately describes the practice being represented. But then she repeats without comment the fiction of translation that grounds the process: "Harriot's learning of Algonquin facilitated relations with the Roanoke Indians" (529).

The pose of "The flyer" certainly suggests flight, of the airborne not the fugitive kind, though, curiously, one of the Renaissance definitions of *flyer* is "fugitive" (OED). In the Renaissance context, *flyer* can also mean a great personage as in "high flyer" or a "volatile spirit" (OED). These latter two meanings bring the title closer to that of De Bry's "Coniuerer," which is elaborated by the text that comments on the figure:

> They haue comonlye coniurers or iuglers which vse strange gestures, and often contrarie to nature in their enchantments: For they be verye familiar with deuils, of whome they enquier what their enemys doe, or other suche thinges. They shaue all their heads sauinge their creste which they weare as other doe, and fasten a small black birde aboue one of their ears as a badge of their office. They weare nothinge but a skinne which hangeth

The flyer.

Figure 5. "The flyer," by John White.

Figure 6. "The Coniuerer," from De Bry.

downe from their gyrdle, and couereth their priuityes. They weare a bagg by their side as is expressed in the figure. The Inhabitants giue great credit vnto their speeche, which oftentymes they finde to bee true.

The central figure of *The Poetics of Imperialism* is Shakespeare's Prospero, who with his latter-day apotheosis, Tarzan, represents Western imperialism's dream of achieving absolute power in the world through the projective technology of *eloquence*. The imperialist believes that, literally, everything can be translated into *his* terms; indeed, that everything always already exists in these terms and is only waiting to be liberated, like Ariel from the tree. In 1997, as it has historically, this belief characterizes the foreign policy of the United States, with its dream of a universal "free" market, a freedom that capitalist power solipsistically equates with the democracy of a "free" society. The De Bry project bears witness to this belief in the power of translation at the beginning of the Anglo-American imperial project. In *A briefe and true report,* Hariot describes Indian "religion" in a way that suggests an unwitting parody of Christianity with its heaven and hell (a duality that does not appear to be a part of Native North American religions), all the while believing, apparently, that he is describing something *other* than his own religion. The Indian religion he describes is, not surprisingly, in awe of his own, as if it intrinsically comprehended Protestant Christianity: "through conversing with us they were brought into great doubts of their owne, and no small admiration of ours, with earnest desire in many, to learne more than wee had meanes for want of perfect utterance in their language to expresse" (*VV*, 70). In this fiction of translation, the English may not be perfectly fluent in the language of Wingina's people, but they are eloquent enough in it to tempt the Indians to Christianity through dialogue.

At the end of *The Tempest*, Shakespeare, who, we can imagine, knew the Roanoke narratives as well as he did the Jamestown documents, represents Caliban, promising to "seek for grace," as repentant for his idol worship of Stephano and Trinculo (V.i.294–97), a relationship that throughout the play seems intended to parody the relationship between Caliban and Prospero. Reading Hariot's narrative, we can understand that the Caliban-Prospero relationship is itself a parody—whether witting or unwitting it is difficult to say—of European dreams of absolute, that is, imperial, power achieved through the eloquence of translation. We know that historically Native American resistance to Christianity has been strong in various forms. Witness, for example, the Pueblo revolt of 1680, or the lack of Puritan success in converting the Indians. Where, after long struggle against Christianity, Indians have adopted it, initially under terms of force, the meaning of such adoption often remains ambiguously embedded in complex forms of syncretism. It is this history of resistance, coupled with what we know of the rigors of intercultural communication, that allows us to read the narratives of imperialism, like those of Shakespeare and Hariot, as fictions of translation. How long would it have taken sophisticated dialogue in fundamentally incommensurate languages to develop where no technical tools of language acquisition existed?

Prospero is himself, of course, a "conjurer" or "juggler": "One who works marvels by the aid of magic or witchcraft, a magician, wizard, sorcerer . . . ; one who plays tricks by sleight of hand; a performer of legerdemain . . ." (OED). In the sixteenth century, *conjuration* could also mean "conspiracy," a designation that from Caliban's point of view characterizes Prospero's reign accurately. Like De Bry's conjurer, Prospero works his magic through the word. Though, in contradistinction to the Native tradition De Bry believes he is representing, Prospero's words come from books, which Caliban reveres. Indeed, Hariot, who devotedly elaborates his fiction of translation as if it were simple fact, reports the awe with which the Roanoke Indians viewed the English books, particularly the Bible (*VV*, 70–71). He also reports the European diseases to which the English had developed resistance but that devastated the Indians, including Wingina, who "was so grievously sicke that hee was like to die" (*VV*, 71). Wingina recovered, only to be killed by the English. In Hariot's narrative, this near fatal bout with what must have been a terrifying because unknown illness converts Wingina to Christianity, though this conversion apparently was not strong enough to keep Wingina from ultimately resisting the English. This resistance is central to the Lane narrative but is passed over hurriedly by Hariot, who, diplomatically, both condemns and approves, though without naming names, the murder of Wingina (*VV*, 74). Whatever may have activated what the English perceived, entirely in their terms, as the Indian interest in Christianity, terror of these unknown diseases cannot be discounted as one of the motives. For this alone the Indians would have had reason to develop an interest in English conjuring, both as conspiracy and cure.

Until quite recently, the Western critical tradition of reading *The Tempest*, as opposed to the Caribbean tradition of Fanon, Césaire, and Retamar, has been at pains to distinguish the "white" magic of Prospero from the "black" magic of Sycorax, Caliban's mother, who, like De Bry's conjurer, is reported in Prospero's narrative to consort with "devils." The text of Shakespeare's play, however, blurs the boundary of this distinction, when in his speech "abjur[ing]" his magic Prospero admits, and admits proudly, to having raised the dead, a practice traditionally confined to black magic (V.i.33–57). Prospero not only possesses Caliban but is possessed by him: ". . . this thing of darkness I / Acknowledge mine" (V.i.275–76). This double process of possession is also a process of projection. Hariot's narrative might be said to conjure Wingina as the devoted convert for the English audience, just as Lane's narrative conjures him as the arch-apostate for that same audience. These narratives should remind us not of the Indians' belief in magic, which is a separate and complex cultural matter beyond the authority of Renaissance ethnography (and dependent in the first place on knowing the translations of the term *magic* in Native languages), but of the importance of magic to Western science and religion, both in the Renaissance and beyond. Reading De Bry's "Coniuerer," which is both derived from and opposed to White's "flyer," we are reading the place where the frontier between Caliban and Prospero blurs.

Fictions of Translation

The coherence of the reports of the Roanoke voyages is dependent on a fiction of translation. This fiction, subscribed to by a range of scholars, essentially argues, explicitly or implicitly, for the fluency of Thomas Hariot in the Algonquian language of the Roanoke community of the two Indians, Manteo and Wanchese, who returned to England with the 1584 voyage in September of that year. Quinn gives us a particularly elaborate version of this fiction:

> Hitherto it has been supposed that Harriot became involved with North America directly only after the return of the ships to England in September; that it was then he learnt to understand something of what the two Indians brought home had to say and was able to teach them some English. The narrative of Arthur Barlowe, as we have it in the form in which it was first published in 1589, was almost certainly prepared for circulation as promotional material for the 1585 venture as early as November or the beginning of December 1584. It contains geographical information which would seem to have required some linguistic bridge to be established before it could become intelligible. Since the Indians brought back were reported on 18 October to be still unable to make themselves understood in English, but were referred to in mid-December as sources of information on the new land discovered by Amadas and Barlowe, it is clear that remarkable advances in contact with them were made during a very short period, so short as to raise serious doubts on whether it was possible in the time available. Nonetheless it was Harriot who was credited with making the bridge; it was he who by July 1585 had a working knowledge of Carolina Algonquian; and who was sent out then to take special note of everything concerning the Indians which was relevant to the English plans for settlement. . . . Thus, though there is no direct evidence that Harriot was in Virginia in 1584, if we accept him as the main (or sole) linguistic link between the Algonquian-speaking Indians brought to England and the English public, his employment on the 1584 voyage would appear to be a necessary concomitant. (*EC*, 242–43)

The issue that Quinn wants to explain is the construction of the Barlowe narrative in November–December 1584 and, beyond that, English communication with the North Carolina Indians on subsequent voyages, particularly the 1585–1586 voyage, which resulted in Hariot's narrative and John White's drawings. Quinn knows, and in this he is representative of his professional cohort of historians, that if proof of such communication cannot be established or assumed, then the basis of historical knowledge in these travel narratives, which are themselves based on assumptions about the coherency of Indian-white communication, is called into question. And, as we have noted, these travel narratives, in the absence of any significant archaeological record of Native culture or survival of Native oral tradition, are virtually all we have with which to construct the historical record of Euramerican–Native American contact at the first colonies in Virginia, at both Roanoke and Jamestown.

If, according to Quinn, the Indians weren't communicating as late as the middle of October, then where did Barlowe get his information—the information that is not simply a "description" of what Barlowe reports he saw but what he implicitly and explicitly claims to be derived from communications with the Indians. As Quinn acknowledges, it is problematic to suppose that Manteo and Wanchese suddenly started speaking fluent English in the month or so between mid-October when they were "still unable to make themselves understood" and the putative date for the compilation of the narrative. The English landed on the Outer Banks on July 4 by Barlowe's account and returned to England by mid-September. That is a little less than two and a half months. The homeward voyage must have departed America for England near the beginning of August (the trans-Atlantic voyage back to England taking approximately five or six weeks), which means the expedition was barely on the Banks for a month. Quinn's estimate of six weeks would seem to be taken from Hariot's *A briefe and true report* (*VV*, 47). If we use Barlowe's dates, Quinn's estimate stretches the duration of the stay considerably. Barlowe himself writes of "the shortnes of the time we there continued" (*VV*, 11).

Even supposing steady contact with the Indians on the Banks, which by Barlowe's account did not begin until mid-July when the first Indians were encountered, and then given the continued contact, though out of the American context, with Manteo and Wanchese, by mid-October there would have only been a three-month period for the English and the Indians to learn an utterly foreign language of which neither group had any prior knowledge. Imagine trying to learn a language that has no linguistic relation to one's own, without the aid of either grammar or vocabularies. How does one begin this process of translation? How fraught with misunderstanding and how painstakingly slow must such a process be? How much of either language could either group, English or Indians, have learned at that point? Even if, as Quinn speculates, Hariot was along on this voyage, for which there is absolutely no evidence, as Quinn admits, how much of this particular Algonquian language could he have learned by November of 1584, particularly considering the fact that for most of the time he was not in the environment where the language functioned? Manteo and Wanchese were in fact in a much better contextual position to learn English and, no doubt, under much more pressure to do so. But they also had strategic motives for dissembling their knowledge in various ways. As noted, we surmise from Lane's narrative of the 1585–1586 expedition that while Manteo remained an ally of the English and translated for them (*VV,* 32), Wanchese was one "of our great enemies" (*VV,* 37). But if, speculating that the two Indians had more of an opportunity to gain linguistic competence in English than Hariot did in their language, we shift the burden of translation from Hariot to Manteo and Wanchese, then we also must be willing to accept that the linguistic power, the control over information, lay with the Indians at this stage of operations. In this case the European narratives we are reading, which stage the drama of European control (through fictions of translation), are not in the control of the Europeans. The power of the Indians in the linguistic balance that these narratives pretend is articulated in what I discuss farther on as the incoherencies or contradictions of the narratives.

Hariot's *A briefe and true report* contains only one explicit mention of Hariot's linguistic competence, though in ways that we have considered it is assumed throughout. The Indians, he tells us in a passage I have cited, were desirous of learning "more" about the religion of the English "then wee had meanes for want of perfect utterance in their language to expresse" (*VV,* 70). If we follow Quinn's narrative, we can note that, at the time to which this comment refers, Hariot would have had contact with the Indians anywhere from approximately one to two years, depending on whether or not one accepts his presence on the 1584 voyage. Appearing first in 1955 as a footnote to this section of text (*RV,* vol. 1, 375), Quinn's comment is that this passage is "Harriot's only specific admission that he could speak (however imperfectly) the Algonquian tongues" (*VV,* 156).

In order to give credence to the Barlowe narrative, Quinn must give credence not only to Hariot's presence on the 1584 voyage but also to his incredible linguistic skills. By 1990 Quinn has dropped the open question, implied in "however imperfectly," about Hariot's fluency in this Algonquian language, and we find the following formulation: ". . . there would then be a good possibility that, with his rapid capacity for learning new techniques, he had himself established some command over the language by the time of their return in the middle of September 1584. Even if the Indians were not able to make themselves understood by the middle of October, their English was probably sufficient, and Harriot's Algonquian adequate, for a good deal of information to be incorporated rapidly in the version of Barlowe's narrative . . ." (*EC,* 242). Under the circumstances I am outlining, what can terms like "sufficient" and "adequate" possibly mean? How can Quinn call the Indians' English "sufficient," while simultaneously admitting the possibility that they "were not able to make themselves understood"? If Hariot's command of the language was imperfect in 1585–1586, then what was it like in 1584, whether one believes that Hariot sailed with Amadas and Barlowe or not? We should remember that Hariot did not simply encounter a single language in North Carolina, but as he notes: "The language of every government [community] is different from any other, and the further they are distant, the greater is the difference" (*VV,* 67). What Hariot is perhaps noting here is not simply the modulation as different dialects of the same language become different languages, but the difficulty of mastering or even getting to know in any sufficient way this complex range of linguistic differences. In this situation we can imagine that Manteo and Wanchese, who only had to learn one language (English), and who had several months to do it in place while at the same time being native to the complex linguistic matrix of coastal North Carolina, would have been in a better situation to translate than Hariot.

According to the *Handbook of North American Indians,* "Carolina Algonquian [which, we remember, became 'extinct' in the eighteenth century] . . . is known only from two short collections of words: some miscellaneous natural history terms, and a few others, recorded at the Roanoke Colony in the 1580s . . . and a 37-word general vocabulary obtained from the Pamlico remnant in the early eighteenth century . . ." (vol. 15, 74). European conquest, as we know, diminished considerably a rich diversity of American languages and their dialectical variants. In the case of what the *Handbook* "conveniently call[s]" "Carolina Algonquian," synthesizing from a diversity an imagined linguistic unity, bare fragments remain, and a significant number of these fragments come from Hariot's *A briefe and true report*. As Quinn points out: "Of their language [Carolina Algonquian] the only remnants, apart from those enshrined in modern place-names, are those preserved by the Roanoke voyages," principally the narratives of Hariot and Lane, along with "[n]ames found on White's drawings, but probably recorded by Hariot" (*RV*, vol. 2, 884).

> The result is that 82 distinct words have been recovered of those gathered between 1584 and 1590; in addition there are 56 distinct place- or tribal-names (plus 2 doubtful), as well as 19 personal names. All but about 20 of this total of 155–60 words belong to the Algonkian tribes of the Carolina group, and, unless Hariot's detailed word-lists come to light [alluded to in *A briefe and true report*], represent all that is likely to be found. (*RV*, vol. 2, 884)

Hariot's *A briefe and true report* "contains 33 Indian words (excluding place- and personal names) . . ." (*RV*, vol. 2, 877). It is fair to say that composing word lists is not the same as learning a language. Grammar, syntax, systems of logic and rhetoric, all of which were of profound interest to the Renaissance, as *The Poetics of Imperialism* details, go unmentioned in Hariot. This lack of detailed linguistic knowledge is characteristic of all the early travel narratives, with the notable exception of Montaigne, who of course only traveled figuratively to the Americas but, as I argue in Chapter 7, had the most acute, if figurative, insights into its languages. Perhaps a lost remnant of Hariot's writing contains such commentary (*VV*, 76). Or perhaps he did not know enough of the Native languages to undertake it. One of the things we learn from the travel narratives is the way projection, in a massive form, fills the gaps of knowledge.

But even assessing the accuracy of the words collected by the early adventurers presents its problems to modern scholarship, as James A. Geary's essay "The Language of the Carolina Algonkian Tribes," which forms an appendix to *The Roanoke Voyages*, attests:

> Part of the difficulty in explaining the forms as Algonquian arises from the irregularities of English spelling at this period, and from imperfect interpretation of the handwriting of the original authors by their earlier printers and editors. Photographic reproductions of the original manuscripts where

they exist would provide a more solid basis for the study of the linguistic forms of the words cited, but many are available only in printed forms [as is the case with the narratives of the Roanoke voyages (*RV*, vol. 1, 10)] or in manuscript copies, while, even when we have what the recorder wrote down, we still have to contend with the possibility of his mis-hearings and mis-writings, not to mention the problems created by our imperfect knowledge of Elizabethan and Jacobean pronunciation. (*RV*, vol. 2, 873)

In the face of these difficulties, coupled with the extreme fragmentary condition of what has been considered an extinct body of languages since the eighteenth century, the professional linguist must use a speculative system of analogy to determine if "the words cited really belong to the Algonquian family"; that is, their validity "is shown by their resemblance to forms found in dictionaries or word-lists of other languages, or discovered to be in actual use at the present time in living languages of that family" (*RV*, vol. 2, 874). In sum, then, we have no effective way of gauging Hariot's competency in North Carolina Algonquian (to use a linguistic fiction for the sake of convenience) other than Hariot's narrative, which is complicated not only by the absence of any coherent linguistic display but by its ideological distortions. This narrative represents the situation in the long run. In the short run (1584), we are left with Quinn's speculation that Hariot was on the Barlowe expedition and his belief in Hariot's "rapid capacity for learning new techniques," which would have allowed him to become the virtual author of the Barlowe narrative.

But a language is not simply a *technique*. Rather, it is a whole cultural system. Anyone reading the Barlowe narrative today can understand how little of Southeastern Algonquian culture has been understood by the way the narrative translates that culture immediately in English terms. Thus, for example, Indian polity is explained in the language of the English class system, as—and we have read this in the De Bry—was typical of the early European travel narratives. So Wingina, who, under the systems that North American kinship cultures had of following "leaders," would have been the *consensual* and thus *provisional* leader of this particular community (and we must be wary of understanding the notion of *leadership* in Western terms), is termed the "King"; and the narrative asserts of the Indians that "no people in the worlde carry more respect to their King, Nobilitie, and Gouvernours, then these doe" (*VV*, 6). To the readers of the narrative, who are, not incidentally, prospective investors in future ventures, the Indians become perfect examples of Western political subjects, just as in Hariot's narrative they become perfect examples of Western religious subjects.

The narrative refers to the country, presumably following the custom of the Indians but in effect suggesting the European custom of naming as a mark of ownership, as "Wingandacoa," until the English within a short time rename it "Virginia" as a mark of the transfer of possession from Wingina to the Crown in the person of Elizabeth, the Virgin Queen (*VV*, 4). If, indeed, the Indians that Barlowe encountered did call the country "Wingandacoa" or something that sounded to English ears like that, and if this name bore some connection to the name *Wingina,* what is likely to be the case is not that the country was named after Wingina, but that Wingina was named after the country or some aspect of it, not as a mark of possession, for no single person or group of persons in kinship cultures could possess the land, but as a mark of connection. To complicate matters, we learn from Lane's narrative that "upon the death of his brother Granganimo" Wingina "changed his name" to "Pemisapan" (*VV*, 29), for which we are given no translation in English.[18]

According to Raleigh in his *History of the world* (1614), the notion that the country was named *Wingandacon* was the result of the fact that the English colonists, like the Spaniards who "first discovered" Peru, were "vtterly ignorant of that language" spoken by the Carolina Algonquians. The word, according to Raleigh, who may have gotten the translation from Hariot, meant "you weare good clothes, or gay clothes" (*RV*, vol. 1, 116–17). Using his comparative method, Geary corrects Raleigh's correction, speculating that the word is more accurately translated as "fine evergreens" (*RV*, vol. 2, 853). Whatever the case of this Indian's name or names, and we know that for Native Americans naming was (and is) a complex of intimate relations with the social and natural environment, let this problem of translation or mistranslation figure the issues that provoked *The Poetics of Imperialism.*

A central argument of *The Poetics of Imperialism* is that while the language of land as *property,* with its companion vocabulary of *identity* (*I* versus *you*) and *hierarchy* (*governor/governed* or *owner/worker*), was at the time of the conquest of the Americas (and today) fundamental to the cultures of the West, it was at the same time utterly foreign to Native cultures. It remains in crucial respects antagonistic to them, even as these cultures have had to operate within this language increasingly over the last five hundred years as subjects of colonialism. What remains remarkable to me, as I have been suggesting, is that Western scholars writing today about Native American–Euramerican contact issues practice the same kind of translation that animates the early European travel narratives, and in doing so repeat the same kind of linguistic gestures that constitute the poetics of imperialism. The Barlowe narrative is exemplary of this poetics:

> The first [river flowing into the sea] that appeared unto us, we entred, though not without some difficultie, and cast anker about three harquebushot within the havens mouth, on the left hande of the same: and after thankes given to God for our safe arrival thither, we manned our boates, and went to viewe the lande next adjoyning, and to "[*sic*] take possession of the same, in the right of the Queenes most excellent Majestie, as rightfull Queene, and Princesse of the same, and after delivered the same over to your [Walter Raleigh] use, according to her Majesties grant, and letters patents, under her Highnes great Seale. Which being performed, according to the ceremonies used in such enterprises, wee viewed the lande about us, being whereas we first landed, very sandie, and lowe towards the water side, but so full of grapes, as the very beating, and surge of the Sea overflowed them, of which we found such plentie, as well there, as in all places else, both on the sande, and on the greene soile on the hills, as in the plaines, as well on every little shrubbe, as also climing towardes the toppes of the high Cedars, that I thinke in all the world the like aboundance is not to be founde: and my selfe having seene those partes of Europe that most abound, finde such difference, as were incredible to be written. (*VV,* 2)

The early travel narrative is not constituted by accuracy or even adequacy of translation but by a congeries of contradictions that attempt to parade as linguistic coherence by constructing a fiction of translation, which is, however, itself contradictory. This kind of contradictory dynamic is one definition of *ideology*. It should be plain enough from the above passage, with its representation of the ceremony of possession and its lyrical evocation of material abundance, that the primary purpose of the Barlowe narrative is to enact rhetorically what the English hope will come to pass historically: the political and economic domination of America. The travel narrative establishes the verbal *forms* of conquest in their social, cultural, political, and economic aspects. These are the forms that power requires in order to take shape effectively. As we know, increasing colonial power will activate these forms. To take only one example of such activation, we can note that the "doctrine of discovery," which will become the *legal* basis for the Anglo-American claim to the title of all Indian lands, finds its original form in the routine ceremonies of possession that marked the European conquest of America and were first instituted by the Spanish in the form of the *Requerimiento* (1513). We should note that Barlowe's narrative, characteristically, begins with a declaration that is a *claim* of discovery, and that a claim of discovery was, in European terms, a claim of possession:

> The first voyage made to the coastes of America, with two barkes, wherein were Captaines Master Philip Amadas, and Master Arthur Barlowe, who discovered part of the Countrey, now called Virginia, Anno 1584: Written by one of the said Captaines, and sent to Sir Walter Raleigh, knight, at whose charge, and direction, the said voyage was set foorth. (*VV*, 1)

To stress the ideological force of the travel narrative, or narrative of conquest, is not to deny its ethnographical "accuracy" in certain respects, though as the Quinn footnotes to the Barlowe narrative suggest, *accuracy* itself is inevitably inflected with expectation. So the Barlowe narrative develops a partial portrait of the Indians encountered, through accounts of their material culture (habitation, agriculture, tools, weapons, clothing, personal ornamentation) and their environment (flora and fauna). Physique is mentioned but is generally part of an assemblage of cultural differences rather than the primary marker of "racial" difference (*VV*, 5). The "Inhabitants of Sequotan," Barlowe relates, "wondred marvelously when we were amongst them, at the whitenes of our skinnes," but that was because "sixe and twentie yeeres past, there was a shippe cast away, whereof some of the people were saved, and those were white people, whom the Countrey people preserved" (*VV*, 9). Hariot's narrative makes no mention of physical characteristics as a mark of difference. And while De Bry's faithfulness to White's representation of the Indians' physiques allows for considerable slippage in the direction of European types, his representation of clothing as a cultural marker does not.

The Western concept of *race* in the sixteenth century was primarily a matter of cultural difference—particularly of language and clothing—not of physical or biological difference. Between the sixteenth century and the nineteenth century, when the term *biology* is coined and the discipline itself emerges, the Western concept of race undergoes a rigidification in which its denotation becomes natural rather than cultural. In Native American cultures, where nature was never conceptualized as an absolutely alien domain (the condition of both its economic and scientific exploitation in the West) but remained conceptually within the social or cultural sphere (the condition of its reciprocal relation to the human in Native cultures), the idea of human affinity took a different trajectory. The community, as linguistic group, not some transsocial concept of nature, was the frontier between "them" and "us." Hence, as the history of European captivity among the Indians suggests, "white" people, through both rigorous ceremonial procedure and length of tenure with the group, could be adopted fully as Indians.[19] The Native concept of affinity, coupled with the absolute importance (economically and socially) of every person in the group to the group in these kinship-based cultures, allowed for a much more permeable "racial" frontier than the one that developed in European cultures, where hierarchical notions of human worth (class and gender) were coupled with rigidifying racial norms to fracture actual and potential social bonds.

At the point of contact, then, Native cultures presented alternative modes of living to European invaders, who were driven to America in the first place by the radically changing social, political, and economic conditions in their own countries, conditions brought about by the concurrent emergence of capitalism and nationalism. In these cultures based in the community of extended kinship, the alternative modes were relatively nonhierarchical and noncompetitive, particularly in the economic sphere, where the basis of wealth, the land and its fruits, was shared by all and owned by no one. In Native cultures land was not a commodity. That is, it could not be alienated in the form of *property*, that form in which an individual or a group acting as an individual has the legal right to *market* land, to put land into what Marx calls "the circulation of commodities":

> The circulation of commodities is the starting-point of capital. The production of commodities and their circulation in its developed form, namely trade, form the historic presuppositions under which capital arises. World trade and the world market date from the sixteenth century, and from then on the modern history of capital starts to unfold.[20]

On a number of fronts, from the English crisis of enclosure to the Indian crisis of the fur trade, the institution of the market witnesses the translation of culturally diverse use values into the universal exchange value of money, "the universal commodity" (K. Marx, 235). Within this context, where surplus value is emerging as the dominant value of invasive Western economies, *The Poetics of Imperialism* is a history of the term *property,* in both its imbricated physical and metaphysical senses, and of its absolute untranslatability into the terms of traditional Native American cultures. I use the term "traditional" here both to imagine a pre-contact Native world and to imagine the central, ongoing form of Native resistance to these invasive economies. In both senses of the word, *tradition* is a dynamic not a static force, and it is certainly subject to forms of fragmentation.

The contradictions that structure the travel narrative are a reaction to the resistance presented by these alternative Native American economies. Indeed, one way of understanding the travel narrative is as a representation of this present resistance in ideological, or unconscious, terms. In this sense the travel narrative is a dream of resistance. Or as Louis Althusser defines "ideology," we might say that the travel narrative is "the imaginary relation [of the travelers] to the real relations [of travel] in which they live." [21] In the Barlowe narrative, and this is typical of European ideology from contact to the present, this dream of resistance is articulated in the simultaneous sacralization and demonization of the Indians. We can read this contradictory structure quite clearly in a scene where the English are visiting the "village" of "Grangyno," "the Kings brother":

> We were entertained with all love, and kindnes, and with as much bountie, after their manner, as they could possibly devise. Wee found the people most gentle, loving, and faithfull, void of all guile, and treason, and such as lived after the manner of the golden age. . . . While we were at meate, there came in at the gates, two or three men with their bowes, and arrowes, from hunting, whom when we espied, we beganne to looke one towardes another, and offered to reach our weapons: but assoone as she [Granganimeo's wife, who has been entertaining the English in the absence of her husband] espied our mistrust, she was very much mooved, and caused some of her men to runne out, and take away their bowes, and arrowes, and breake them, and withall beate the poore fellowes out of the gate againe. When we departed in the evening, and would not tarry all night, she was very sorie, and gave us into our boate our supper halfe dressed, pots, and all, and brought us to our boates side, in which wee laye all night, remoov-

ing the same a pretie distance from the shoare: shee perceiving our jeal-
ousie, was much grieved, and sent divers men, and thirtie women, to sitte
all night on the bankes side by us, and sent us into our boates five mattes
to cover us from the rayne, using very many wordes to intreate us to rest in
their houses: but because wee were fewe men, and if wee had miscarried,
the voyage had beene in very great daunger, wee durst not adventure any
thing, although there was no cause of doubt: for a more kinde, and loving
people, there can not be found in the world, as farre as we have hitherto
had triall. (*VV,* 8–9)

There is "no cause" to "doubt" these Edenic Indians, and yet there is
nothing but doubt on the part of the English. The narrator tries to rationalize this contradiction with his appeal to his group's primary responsibility, "the voyage," but the rationalization only serves to heighten the
contradiction. If the Indians are so utterly innocent that they live "after
the manner of the golden age. . . . [in a land that] bringeth foorth all
things in aboundance, as in the first creation, without toile or labour"
(*VV,* 8), then why is there any need to doubt them? Earlier in the narrative, the narrator tell his readers that these "people maintaine a deadlie
and terrible warre, with the people and King adjoyning" (*VV,* 5), so
that the English would seem to know that these innocent Indians know
bloodshed, that Eden is Eden after the Fall, paradoxically enough. But
this knowledge of this knowledge doesn't explain the contradictory form
of the narrative; it only heightens it.

One response to this contradictory scenario, where the narrative nego-
tiates the chasm from innocence to experience without a bridge, is to say
that the notion of America as Eden (the brand-New World) and of its
inhabitants as therefore absolutely innocent is simply a set piece of the
genre of the travel narrative. Thus, this scenario is not meant to be taken
literally by Renaissance readers, who, after all, had a sophisticated grasp
of rhetoric and rhetorical theories of metaphor. *The Poetics of Imperialism* explores this rhetorical sophistication in undertaking to articulate
what I would call *an imperial history of metaphor,* a history that, as I argue, is also a history of *property.* The *Poetics* is, therefore, a *Politics* and
an *Economics.* However, to say that something is not to be taken literally but metaphorically is to deny the significant, indeed, the unbreak-
able link between the *metaphoric* and the *proper* (the typical Renaissance
term, with all its packed meanings from *decorum* to *property,* for what
the English language terms today the *literal*). To say that something is a

set piece, a cultural cliché, used, for example, by Shakespeare and Montaigne in ways that *The Poetics of Imperialism* analyzes, is not to deny its power to compel belief. For belief is itself a movement that hovers ambiguously between the literal and the metaphoric. So what we are left with in this scenario is the contradiction, and most particularly the fact that the narrative does not comment on it, does not appear to notice it.

As I noted, this *unconscious* contradictory movement marks the space of *ideology*, which like the dream represents "the imaginary relation" of dreamers to "the real relations in which they live." In the Barlowe narrative these imaginary relations are constituted by the contradiction that exists between the extremes of innocence and experience, or more particularly, in the scene under consideration, between *peace* and *treachery*. This same contradiction exists in the relation between the Lane and the Hariot narratives, where, as noted, Hariot represents Wingina as a figure of peace; Lane, as a figure of treachery.

Modern scholarship that is not prepared to come to terms with this dynamic of contradictions will inevitably repeat it through constructing its own fiction of translation about these early fictions of translation. This is in effect what Quinn does in order to assert the coherency of the Barlowe narrative. That is, he moves from acknowledging the impossibility or improbability of accurate or adequate translation under the time constraints and radical cultural differences of the contact situation to asserting the probability of such translation: the "sufficien[cy]" of the Indians' English and the "adequa[cy]" of Hariot's Algonquian, with a particular emphasis placed on the linguistic expertise of Hariot. This transformation takes place under the auspices of a fiction, which Quinn acknowledges is a fiction—the fiction of Hariot's presence on the 1584 voyage, a fiction that even if it were true would not obviate the conditions of translation that made for the improbability of adequate translation in the first place.

But at this point the readers of Quinn's narrative, if they are not following both the narrative's contradictions and the way the narrative can live with these contradictions without acknowledging them as such, are "living in oblivion," to borrow the title of Tom DiCillo's recent film, which explores with comic brilliance the radical breakdown of the frontier between fantasy and reality that occurs in the process of making a film. The structure of narrative contradiction here, particularly the way contradictions go unacknowledged in the narrative, is also the structure of what Freud terms the *unconscious*. In his narrative, Barlowe acknowledges on his company's first meeting with a local inhabitant that he spoke "of many things not understoode by us" (*VV*, 3). But as the narrative proceeds this problem of translation is never mentioned again, and it is assumed throughout that the English and the Indians can communicate without problems.

The contradiction *peace/treachery* is repeated in the contradiction *I understand/I do not understand.* In actuality this pair of contradictions represents not an intercultural relationship but an intracultural one that has been projected as intercultural: a relationship between the English themselves that has been projected as a relationship between the English and the Indians. This intracultural relationship that is in contradiction is one between the commonable, or communal, and the individual, to put it in its starkest, even its most reductive terms. The relationship played in a number of significant social, cultural, economic, and political transformations that were taking place in sixteenth-century England in response to the development of the world market, from the privatization of common lands, known as *enclosure,* which was seen as a crisis for the *commonwealth,* to the centralization of power in the Tudor state, which included the forging of a national language by the court. Within the dynamic of these transformations, the value of the commonable and the individual could change radically. That is, the value of value was no longer stable or, more precisely, was perceived as radically unstable, since the question of stability is a relative matter. So, for example, in the crisis of enclosure a certain kind of emergent individuation was understood as threatening the stable value of communality, whereas in the consolidation of the Tudor state an emergent form of commonality could be understood as threatening, indeed repressing, a stable form of regional individuation, articulated through regional dialects of English. But what was perceived as fractious individuation (regionalism) from the perspective of the emergent nation-state could be perceived as a traditional form of commonality from the perspective of the region. For in sixteenth-century England, every region considered itself a "country," even as the court acted to translate these countries, politically and culturally, into its own terms.

The contradiction *peace/treachery, I understand/I do not understand* figures this radical destabilization of the value of value: the colonist sailing from a home that, in terms of its *internal* changes, is poised precariously between the domestic and the foreign, the familiar and the alienated, which is the state of translation. In Raleigh's Virginia and later at Jamestown, the English confronted communities that had a wholly different conception of the value of value. Their conceptions of person-hood did not include a notion of the *individual,* as it was emerging in England in an inseparable relationship with the institution of *property.* And their commitments to the *communal,* based as they were in the dy-namic of extended kinship, were in practice radically egalitarian when compared to the class structure within which the European notion of the communal had developed. Europeans, of course, had mythologies, ex-tending back to classical times, of a Golden Age characterized by a pleni-tude of natural abundance and the absence of any government: the ab-sence of class and property. In *The Tempest* Gonzalo voices one version of this mythology, which Shakespeare based on the Florio translation of Montaigne's "Des cannibales" (II.i.143–52). But those consummate ironists Antonio and Sebastian are quick to perceive that this mythology of Edenic egalitarianism merely masks the European class system from which it springs and for which it is an alibi.

As we have read in the Barlowe narrative, the colonists were quick to translate the Indians into this nostalgic mythology and simultaneously into its opposite. Columbus had inaugurated this process of translation in his journal through the opposition he hallucinated between the peaceful Arawaks and the treacherous Caribs, who quickly became the Western prototype of the *cannibal,* a word Columbus coined. This kind of trans-lation process no doubt helped these adventurers and colonists allay the anxieties they must have felt venturing from a home that was estranged in powerful ways and encountering these radically estranged communi-ties and languages, communities they were dependent on for sustenance in a world where the technologies the Europeans reported as inspiring awe in the Indians could not even produce food. Arriving in the name of imperial power to claim the New World for their own, the early invaders must have felt the contradiction of their powerlessness keenly.

Even before they could begin to understand any of the languages en-countered or make themselves understood in English, the Roanoke voy-agers, and the Jamestown voyagers seventeen years later, must have felt as *resistance,* in both overt hostility and sheer cultural alienation, the radically different value of value they encountered in Virginia as a fur-ther threat to their already destabilized values. But because of the prob-lems of translation that I have rehearsed in this Afterword and which *The*

Poetics of Imperialism elaborates, this resistance could only articulate itself in these narratives as a dynamic of contradictions incorporated as ideology. The colonizer lives the contradictions of his own culture as if they were the contradictions of the colonized, not as contradictions but as ideology. In turn, ideology represents the resistance of the colonized not as resistance but as contradiction.

Even as the technical conditions of translation have improved because of increased cultural contact over the last four centuries, this dynamic of contradiction has persisted, not as a transcendent paradigm but as a political reality of the Americas. Here, within a historical context that since 1492 has seen the radical revaluing of values throughout the world's cultures, various Native forms of communality, from the Zapatista revolt in Mexico to the diverse actions in North America to maintain the integrity of reservation lands under what remains a colonial system, continue to resist, though not without their own forms of contradiction, a "free" market individualism that is increasingly and dangerously alienated from any concept of the communal. I wrote *The Poetics of Imperialism* inspired by this resistance. I write this Afterword similarly inspired.

Notes

After a source has been cited once, subsequent citations of it appear in the text proper.

Introduction

1. Frantz Fanon, *Black Skins, White Masks* (New York: Grove Press, 1967), 115–16, 118–19, 122.

2. Shakespeare, *The Tempest*, II.ii.39. I am using the Arden edition, edited by Frank Kermode (1954; New York: Methuen, 1983).

3. Vine Deloria, Jr., *We Talk, You Listen: New Tribes, New Turf* (New York: Macmillan, 1970), 37, 89, 120–21. See Deloria's comments on Israel on p. 131 as well.

4. Keith H. Basso, *Portraits of "The Whiteman": Linguistic Play and Cultural Symbols Among the Western Apache* (1979; New York: Cambridge University Press, 1980).

5. In *The Names: A Memoir* (Tucson: University of Arizona Press, 1976), Momaday writes of his felt closeness to and his simultaneous alienation from the Native American languages he grew up with:

> When I was three years old my head must have been full of Indian as well as English words. The sounds of both Kiowa and Navajo are quite natural and familiar to me, and even now I can make these sounds easily and accurately with my voice, so well established are they in my ear. I lived very close to these "foreign" languages, poised at a crucial time in the learning process to enter either or both of them wholly. But my mother was concerned that I should learn English as my "native" language, and so English is first and foremost in my possession. (59–60)

My information on Silko's relationship to Laguna is second-hand, but seems reliable. I have not been able to locate at this time any statements by Silko herself on this matter.

6. Richard Beale Davis, *Intellectual Life in the Colonial South, 1585–1763* (Knoxville: University of Tennessee Press, 1978), vol. 1, 428.

7. Leslie Marmon Silko, *Ceremony* (New York: Penguin Books, 1977):

Frederick Douglass, *Narrative of the Life of Frederick Douglass, an American Slave* (1845; New York: Penguin, 1982); Stephen J. Greenblatt, "Learning to Curse," in *First Images of America: The Impact of the New World on the Old*, ed. Fredi Chiappelli (Berkeley: University of California Press, 1976), vol. 2, 561–80; Tzvetan Todorov, *The Conquest of America: The Question of the Other*, trans. Richard Howard (New York: Harper & Row, 1984).

8. Eric R. Wolf, *Europe and the People without History* (Berkeley: University of California Press, 1982).

9. For a discussion of anthropology as allegory, see James Clifford, "On Ethnographic Allegory," in *Writing Culture: The Poetics and Politics of Ethnography*, eds. James Clifford and George E. Marcus (Berkeley: University of California Press, 1986). For a particularly powerful example of how Western imperialism uses allegory as a mechanism of domination, see Haunani-Kay Trask, "From a Native Daughter," in *The American Indian and the Problem of History*, ed. Calvin Martin (New York: Oxford University Press, 1987).

10. Edgar Rice Burroughs, *Tarzan of the Apes* (1912; New York: Ballantine Books, 1983).

1. U.S. Foreign Policy in the Twentieth Century

1. John Higham, *Send These to Me: Immigrants in Urban America* (Baltimore: Johns Hopkins University Press, 1984), 21, 46.

2. Howard K. Beale, *Theodore Roosevelt and the Rise of America to World Power* (Baltimore: Johns Hopkins Univeristy Press, 1956), 32, 34.

3. E. G. R. Taylor, ed., *Discourse of Western Planting*, in *The Original Writings & Correspondence of the Two Richard Hakluyts* (London: The Hakluyt Society, 1935), vol. 2, 214, 215. I have preserved the Renaissance spellings to the extent allowed by the typography I am using and the editions I am employing.

4. *Instructions to Sir Thomas Gates* (1609), quoted in Alden T. Vaughan, *American Genesis: Captain John Smith and the Founding of Virginia* (Boston: Little, Brown and Co., 1975), 59; and in Philip L. Barbour, ed., *The Jamestown Voyages under the First Charter 1606–1609* (London: The Hakluyt Society, 1969), vol. 2, 266.

5. *A True Declaration of the Estate of the Colonie in Virginia*, in Peter Force, ed., *Tracts and Other Papers Relating Principally to the Origin, Settlement, and Progress of the Colonies in North America. From the Discovery of the Country to the Year 1776* (Washington: William Q. Force, 1844), vol. 3, 6. In considering translation as a form of imperialism, it is worth noting, in Karen Kupperman's words, that "Powhatan's real name was Wahunsonacock. The English extended the name Powhatan, which meant 'falls in a current of water,' to him and to all the tribes under his dominion. The actual Powhatans were a small tribe living at the falls in the James River at the present-day site of Richmond, Virginia." Karen

Ordahl Kupperman, *Settling with the Indians: The Meeting of English and Indian Cultures in America, 1580–1640* (Totowa: Rowman and Littlefield, 1980), 7. Powhatan himself was not a Powhatan, but a Pamunkey. See note 9 for my comments on Kupperman's use of the word ''dominion'' in relation to Powhatan.

6. Wolf's tripartite analytic scheme, which is admirable insofar as it takes us away from thinking in evolutionary or ''progressive'' paradigms about the West's relation to the rest of the world, implies the long-standing debate about precisely what constitutes the capitalist mode of production and when historically it arises. It does not serve my purpose to rehearse that debate here, but only to note that in Western history, whether one talks of tributary or capitalist modes of production, the land is always potentially or actually alienable; that is, it is inscribed within a legal system of *property,* whereas in kin-ordered societies of the kind found in the Americas it is not.

7. For Wolf in the tributary mode of production labor, because it has certain rights to the means of production (the land), is not alienated from it, in the strict Marxist sense. My sense of alienation, then, differs from Wolf's. For although labor may have certain customary rights to the means of production in this case, it controls, finally, neither the means nor the product. Both Marx and Wolf are well aware of this, as Wolf's quote from Marx on the form of the tributary mode makes clear (Wolf, 80).

8. Jimmie Durham, ''Those Dead Guys for a Hundred Years,'' in *I Tell You Now: Autobiographical Essays by Native American Writers,* eds. Brian Swann and Arnold Krupat (Lincoln: University of Nebraska Press, 1987), 161. In their introduction Krupat and Swann comment on the problem of *meum et tuum* and the anomalous form of American Indian autobiography: ''The form of writing generally known to the West as *autobiography* had no equivalent among the oral cultures of the indigenous inhabitants of the Americas. Although the tribes, like people the world over, kept material as well as mental records of collective and personal experience, the notion of telling the whole of any one individual's life or taking merely personal experience as of particular significance was, in the most literal way, foreign to them, if not also repugnant'' (ix). The Western, or property-owning, self (the self that can own itself as property, and have this self alienated as property as well), this suggests, is radically different from the concept of personhood in kin-ordered cultures.

9. My critique of the English translation of *weroance* into *king* or *emperor* differs substantially from the notions of certain contemporary scholars, whose work has been important to me in other ways. Nancy Lurie, for example, remarks: ''If the exploring parties overstated the case when they translated *weroance* as 'king' and likened tribal territories to European kingdoms, they at least had a truer understanding of the nature of things than did the democratic Jefferson, who first designated the Virginia tribes as the 'Powhatan Confederacy'. . . . Powhatan was in the process of building something that approxi-

mated an empire." Nancy Lurie, "Indian Cultural Adjustment to European Civilization," in *Seventeenth-Century America: Essays in Colonial History,* ed. James Morton Smith (Chapel Hill: University of North Carolina Press, 1959), 39–40. And, more recently, Karen Kupperman has repeated Lurie's assessment. Both Lurie and Kupperman are interested in emphasizing the similarities rather than the differences between seventeenth-century English culture and the Algonquian cultures that the English encountered, and they are interested in doing this in order to criticize the European ethnocentrism that projects the polar terminology of the "savage" and the "civilized." While it is absolutely necessary that such criticism be rigorously pursued, and while both Kupperman and Lurie make important contributions in giving us a more complex figure of seventeenth-century culture contact, it seems to me that both scholars are, unconsciously, employing Western models of complexity as a universal model, which results in an ironic repetition of the translation process that I am criticizing in the documents under scrutiny. Wolf's conceptual scheme helps avoid this kind of translation, which is ultimately monologic, by providing a dialogic model that, while operating within a common set of economic terms (those of *labor* and *modes of production*) embeds these terms within specific cultural formations that suggest how profoundly divided within, or foreign to themselves, these terms can be. With Wolf in mind, then, we cannot make a statement asserting that "Powhatan was in the process of building something like an empire" (a vague enough statement in and of itself) without querying how we are to translate the language of empire (the language, for example, of the economic exploitation of one *class* by another) into the language of kin-ordered societies, which, as Wolf articulates this language, possesses a terminology of *rank* but not of *class*. Wolf's discussion of "chiefdoms" (96–100) suggests how a kin-ordered society might be translated into an "empire" or, more precisely, into a tributary mode of production. But it remains to be seen whether or not the so-called "Powhatan Confederacy" was in such a state of translation. I have seen no evidence to suggest that it was. More to the point, the mode of production that structured North American cultures at the time, the kin-ordered mode, suggests that it was not.

10. Ronald Reagan, "Freedom, Regional Security, and Global Peace," Congress of the United States, 14 March 1986, Special Report No. 143, United States Department of State, *Bureau of Public Affairs,* Washington, D.C., 2, 3. Since the recent signing of the nuclear-arms treaty with the Soviet Union, Reagan has abandoned the rhetoric of the "evil empire." If, however, we read the speech he made in England shortly after the signing, we will see that the ideology of translation that projects that rhetoric is still very much intact. For in his speech, Reagan reads the signing as a sign that the Soviets are becoming more like us, that is, "civilized." In keeping with this pattern of interpretation, the official U.S. reading of the recent trend toward democratization in the Soviet Union and

Eastern Europe is that this part of the world is finally translating itself into capitalism. I want to thank Dan Seligson for calling Reagan's foreign-policy speech before Congress to my attention.

11. *Cases Argued and Decided in the Supreme Court of the United States,* Book 5, The Lawyer's Edition (Rochester: The Lawyer's Cooperative Publishing Co., 1882), 688–89, 692.

12. The 1831 decision is cited in Vine Deloria, Jr., and Clifford Lytle, *The Nations Within: The Past and Future of American Indian Sovereignty* (New York: Pantheon Books, 1984), 16–17.

13. For a reading of Cooper's *The Pioneers* in relation to the ideology of the literal and the metaphoric and the relation of this ideology to translation, see my essay, "Literally White, Figuratively Red: The Frontier of Translation in *The Pioneers,*" *James Fenimore Cooper: New Critical Essays,* ed. Robert Clark (Totowa: Barnes & Noble, 1985), 55–95.

14. Leo Marx, of course, in *The Machine in the Garden* (New York: Oxford University Press, 1964), has read *The Tempest* "as a prologue to American literature" (72). But Marx's reading, which reduces Caliban to a figure of wilderness rather than analyzing this figure as an ideological projection that conflates European ideas of Native Americans, Africans, and Europe's own lower classes, remains within the phallo-/ethnocentric tradition of reading the American frontier that I refer to in this essay. I will have more to say about Marx's reading of *The Tempest* in Chapter 2.

15. James Fenimore Cooper, *The Prairie: A Tale* (1827; New York: New American Library, 1964), 293.

2. The Foreign Policy of Metaphor

1. Hanna H. Gray, "Renaissance Humanism: The Pursuit of Eloquence," *Journal of the History of Ideas,* 24 (Oct.–Dec. 1963), 503.

2. Harry Berger, Jr., "Miraculous Harp: A Reading of Shakespeare's Tempest," *Shakespeare Studies,* 5 (1969), 256.

3. Stephen Orgel, *The Illusion of Power: Political Theatre in the English Renaissance* (Berkeley: University of California Press, 1975), 16–17, 19.

4. Margreta De Grazia has argued that between the sixteenth and the seventeenth century, language lost its divine associations, so that in the scholarly view mathematics rather than ordinary language became the proper language for understanding the Book of Nature. In this reading, traditional eloquence, associated with the divine through the sixteenth century, loses some of its charisma. Even if we accept this interpretation, we should note that the metaphor of the Book, of language, persists in organizing the field. We might, then, read mathematics as an emerging form of eloquence, rather than read the figure of

eloquence as in decline. See Margreta De Grazia, "The Secularization of Language in the Seventeenth Century," *Journal of the History of Ideas,* 41 (April–June 1980), 319–29.

5. Henry Peacham, *The Garden of Eloquence* (1577). English Linguistics 1500–1800 (A Collection of Facsimile Reprints), no. 267 (Menston, England: Scolar Press Limited, 1971), A.iii.

6. Ralph Waldo Emerson, *Nature, Selected Essays: Ralph Waldo Emerson,* ed. Larzer Ziff (1836; New York: Penguin Books, 1982), 58.

7. See Eric Cheyfitz, *The Trans-Parent: Sexual Politics in the Language of Emerson* (Baltimore: Johns Hopkins University Press, 1981).

8. I have not sought to determine whether this is a fault in Emerson's text of Shakespeare or in Emerson, because such a distinction is of no moment to my argument.

9. David Noble, *America by Design: Science, Technology, and the Rise of Corporate Capitalism* (New York: Oxford University Press, 1977), 20, 24.

10. Myra Jehlen, "The Novel and the Middle Class in America," in *Ideology and Classic American Literature,* eds. Sacvan Bercovitch and Myra Jehlen (New York: Cambridge University Press, 1986), 126.

11. Mark Twain, *A Connecticut Yankee in King Arthur's Court* (1889; New York: Penguin Books, 1986), 53.

12. Henry Peacham, *The Garden of Eloquence,* 1593 ed. (London, 1593), 1–2.

13. Aristotle, *Poetics,* trans. S. H. Butcher (New York: Hill and Wang, 1961). I am grateful to Professor Victoria Pedrick of the Georgetown University Classics Department for helping me find my way through the Greek, while at the same time I accept all responsibility for the variant translations and the interpretations based on them.

14. Roland Barthes, "l'ancienne rhetorique: aide-mémoire," *Communications,* 16 (1970), 220, 221.

15. George Puttenham, *The Arte of English Poesie,* eds. Gladys Doidge Willcock and Alice Walker (1589; Cambridge: Cambridge University Press, 1936), 178.

16. Abraham Fraunce, *The Arcadian Rhetoric.* English Linguistics 1500–1800 (A Collection of Facsimile Reprints), no. 176 (Menston, England: Scolar Press Limited, 1969), A2.

17. Cicero, *De Oratore,* trans. E. W. Sutton, The Loeb Classical Library (1942; Cambridge: Harvard University Press, 1967).

3. *Translating Property*

1. *The Journal of Christopher Columbus,* trans. Cecil Jane (London: Anthony Blond, 1968), 68–69.

2. Roberto Fernandez Retamar, "Caliban: Notes Toward a Discussion of Culture in Our America," trans. Lynn Garafola, David Arthur MacMurray, and Robert Marquez, *The Massachusetts Review*, 15 (Winter–Spring 1974), 12. Peter Hulme, *Colonial Encounters: Europe and the Native Caribbean 1492–1797* (London: Methuen, 1986), 63. The notion of dialectical variants comes from the OED's definition of *cannibal*. In the same entry, which also lists *l* as a possible dialectical variant, we find the speculation that *Caliban* is a variant of *Cariban*. Of course, Shakespeare could have known nothing of such dialectical variations, even if they were linguistic facts. I am particularly indebted to Hulme's fine book for its discussion of the translation of that missing Arawakan/Cariban term.

3. See Columbus's journal entries for Monday, Dec. 17 (102) for his doubts about cannibalism, and Tuesday, Dec. 18 (107) for his dependence on a language of gesture.

4. When I refer to a "significant part of the population," I am referring to the qualitative impact of enclosures, not the actual number of people put off the land, a figure that I have not found in my research. Summing up in her essay "Tudor Enclosures," Joan Thirsk writes:

> When Edwin Gay examined the enclosure evidence collected by the commissions of enquiry in the Tudor and early Stuart period, he suggested that the complaints against depopulating enclosure were somewhat exaggerated. If one measures the importance of the problem from a national standpoint, this may be a fair judgment. . . . But this was cold comfort to the husbandman of the sixteenth century watching the progress of enclosure in and around his own village.

So, though "[e]nclosure has first to be recognized as a social problem concentrated in the Midlands," its impact was national, as is attested by the official concern of the Crown in the form of commissions and by the visible body of literature of the period that read enclosure, which entailed the privatization of traditionally common land, as the end of a particular "common" way of life. "To enclose land," Thirsk notes, "was to extinguish common rights over it. . . . To effect this, it was usual for the encloser to hedge or fence the land. Thus in contemporary controversy anger was directed mainly at the hedges and fences— the outward and visible signs of enclosure." When later in this chapter I discuss the fence as an important sign of "civilization" for the English who invaded America, it will be worth remembering that at a certain moment in English history, a moment virtually contemporaneous with this invasion, a significant part of public opinion in England saw the fence as the sign of a savage attack on the commonwealth. See Joan Thirsk, *The Rural Economy of England: Collected Essays* (London: Hambledon Press, 1984), 81; and Joan Thirsk, ed., *The Agrarian History of England and Wales*, vol. 4, 1500–1640 (Cambridge: Cambridge University Press, 1967), 200.

5. Claude Lévi-Strauss, *The Savage Mind*, no translator named (London: Weidenfeld and Nicolson, 1966), 10.

6. William Cronon, *Changes in the Land: Indians, Colonists, and the Ecology of New England* (New York: Hill and Wang, 1983), 69.

7. J. W. Erlich, ed., *Erlich's Blackstone* (San Carlos, Calif.: Nourse, 1959), 240, 243, 300.

8. Alan Macfarlane, *The Origin of English Individualism: The Family, Property and Social Transition* (New York: Cambridge University Press, 1978), 39, 100, 163. See pp. 103 and 106 in particular for Macfarlane's argument about the early individualization of landholdings in the case of both freehold and copyhold.

9. Aristotle, *Topics*, trans. W. A. Pickard-Cambridge, in *The Basic Works of Aristotle*, ed. Richard McKeon (New York: Random House, 1941).

10. Jean-Pierre Vernant, "Greek Tragedy: Problems of Interpretation," in *The Structuralist Controversy: The Languages of Criticism and the Sciences of Man*, ed. Richard Macksey and Eugenio Donato (Baltimore: Johns Hopkins University Press, 1972), 273–95. My ideas about the history of the self in the West come from my interpretation of Vernant. For the notion of a "social history" of the "self," see Marcel Mauss, "A Category of the Human Mind: The Notion of Person; the Notion of Self" (1938), trans. W. D. Halls, in *The Category of the Person: Anthropology, Philosophy, History*, eds. Michael Carrithers, Steven Collins, and Steven Lukes (1985; Cambridge: Cambridge University Press, 1987), 1–25.

11. Raymond Williams, *The Country and the City* (New York: Oxford University Press, 1973), see especially 35–39, 50.

12. Claude Lévi-Strauss, *Tristes Tropiques*, trans. John and Doreen Weightman (New York: Atheneum, 1974), 392.

13. In his introduction to *The American Indian and the Problem of History* (New York: Oxford University Press, 1987). Calvin Martin criticizes Cronon and Wolf for their translation of Native American cultures into Western paradigms. Clearly, I am criticizing Cronon as well. Wolf, on the other hand, as I point out in the body of my text, appears to have been careful to note the figurative force of his model; that is, he does not take his conception of kinship cultures as simple fact. While I agree with Martin that "the two core philosophies" represented by Western and Native American cultures "are fundamentally antagonistic and irreconcilable, at least as presently practiced" (9), I disagree about how this antagonism is figured. Martin's figure of the "biological" (Indian) vs. the "anthropological" (white) risks naturalizing the Indians, that is, identifying them with nature in a way that Western ideology has always done in its retrogressive evolutionary model. William Bevis has an appropriate response to this model, which I cite in Chapter 7, telling us that for Native American cultures nature is urban. Martin's biological paradigm bothers me as well because it does

not consider its own figurative force, which necessarily includes the history of the term *biology* in the West. At the end of Chapter 6, I discuss the "fundamentally antagonistic and irreconcilable" cultures of Native and Anglo-America in terms of the terms of kinship and capitalist economies.

14. Francis Jennings, *The Ambiguous Iroquois Empire: The Convenant Chain Confederation of Indian Tribes with English Colonies from Its Beginnings to the Lancaster Treaty of 1744* (New York: W. W. Norton, 1984), 44–45.

15. John Locke, *The Second Treatise of Government*, ed. Thomas P. Peardon (1690; New York: Bobbs-Merrill, 1952).

4. *Translation, Transportation, Usurpation*

1. *A Good Speed to Virginia,* quoted in W. Stitt Robinson, Jr., *Mother Earth: Land Grants in Virginia* (Williamsburg: Virginia 350th Anniversary Celebration Corporation, 1957), 3.

2. Edmond Malone, "An Account of the Incidents from Which the Title and Part of the Story of Shakespeare's Tempest Were Derived; And Its True Date Ascertained," in *The Plays and Poems of William Shakespeare*, vol. 15 (London, 1821).

3. James Fenimore Cooper, *The Last of the Mohicans: A Narrative of 1757* (1826; New York: New American Library, 1962), 247.

4. See Hulme, *Colonial Encounters*, 94–101, for a discussion of the significance of *tempest/hurricane*.

5. William Strachey's letter of 1610 and Sylvester Jourdain's *A Discovery of the Bermudas* (1610) are reprinted in Louis B. Wright, ed., *A Voyage to Virginia in 1609: Two Narratives* (Charlottesville: The University Press of Virginia, 1964). *A True Declaration* is in Force's collection, *Tracts and Other Papers.* The dates I am using correspond to those given in both Strachey's letter and *A True Declaration.* Jourdain's text gives dates of a day later in each case.

6. Morton Luce, ed., *The Tempest* (London: Methuen, 1901).

7. John Florio, trans., *The Essayes of Montaigne* (1603; New York: The Modern Library, 1933), xxi.

8. See Taylor, ed., *The Original Writings and Correspondence of the Two Richard Hakluyts*, vol. 2, 216.

9. See Bernard Sheehan's recounting of these events in *Savagism and Civility: Indians and Englishmen in Colonial Virginia* (New York: Cambridge University Press, 1988), 112.

5. *The Frontier of Decorum*

1. See, for example, Barbour, 1, 103, and Kupperman's discussion of the cultural basis of skin color (36–37).

2. Leslie Fiedler, *The Stranger in Shakespeare* (New York: Stein and Day, 1972), 199–253; Jan Kott, "La Tempête, Ou La Répétition," *Tel Quel* 71–73 (Autumne 1977), 136–162.

3. D. D. Carnicelli, "The Widow and the Phoenix: Dido, Carthage, and Tunis in *The Tempest*," *Harvard Library Bulletin* 27 (1979), 414.

4. H. D. F. Kitto, *The Greeks* (1951; Baltimore: Penguin Books, 1963), 7.

5. Cicero, *De Optimo Genere Oratorum*, trans. H. M. Hubbell. The Loeb Classical Library (1949; Cambridge: Harvard University Press, 1976).

6. Quintillian, *Institutio Oratoria*, trans. H. E. Butler. The Loeb Classical Library (New York: G. P. Putnam's Sons, 1921).

7. Cited in Richard Foster Jones, *The Triumph of the English Language: A Survey of Opinions Concerning the Vernacular from the Introduction of Printing to the Restoration* (1953; Stanford: Stanford University Press, 1966), 5.

8. In 1553, for example, a land survey of a particular manor read: "No tenant or other person, or inhabitant, shall graunt a lyen, or demyse his said common to any forener, but to suche as inhabyte within the lordshipp of Y. . . ." See R. H. Tawney and Eileen Power, eds., *Tudor Economic Documents*, vol. 1 (London, 1924), 60.

9. My information on the causes of the rebellions comes from Roger Lockyear, *Tudor and Stuart Britain, 1471–1714* (London: Longmans, 1964).

10. F. O. Matthiessen, *Translation, an Elizabethan Art* (Cambridge, Mass.: Harvard University Press, 1931), 3.

11. Julia G. Ebel, "Translation and Cultural Nationalism in the Reign of Elizabeth," *Journal of the History of Ideas*, 30 (Oct.–Dec. 1969), 595.

12. *The Historie of the World, Commonly Called, the Natural Historie of C. Plinus Secundus, Translated into English by Philemon Holland, Doctor in Physicke* (London, 1601).

13. John Cheek, "A LETTER OF SYR J. CHEEKES to his Loving frind Mayster THOMAS HOBY," in *The Book of the Courtier from the Italian of Count Baldassare Castiglione: Done into English by Sir Thomas Hoby* (1561; New York: AMS Press, Inc., 1967), 12.

6. *The Empire of Poetics*

1. Wilcomb Washburn, *Red Man's Land/White Man's Law: A Study of the Past and Present Status of the American Indian* (New York: Scribner's, 1971), 6.

2. See Hulme, *Colonial Encounters*, 17.

3. Ernst Robert Curtius, *European Literature and the Latin Middle Ages* (Princeton: Princeton University Press, 1953), 28–29.

4. Robert Folz, *The Concept of Empire in Western Europe from the Fifth to the Fourteenth Century*, trans. Sheila Ann Ogilvie (London: Edward Arnold, 1969), 4.

5. Wilbur Samuel Howell, trans., *The Rhetoric of Alcuin and Charlemagne* (Princeton: Princeton University Press, 1941), 3, 30.

6. Cicero, *De Inventione*, trans. H. M. Hubbell. The Loeb Classical Library (1949; Cambridge: Harvard University Press, 1976).

7. W. H. D. Rouse, ed., *Scenes of School and College Life in Latin Dialogues* (Oxford: Clarendon Press, 1931), 11.

8. Cicero, *Topica*, trans. H. M. Hubbell. The Loeb Classical Library (1949; Cambridge: Harvard University Press, 1976).

9. John Crook, *Law and Life of Rome* (Ithaca: Cornell University Press, 1967), 147.

10. Walter J. Ong, S.J., *Ramus, Method, and the Decay of Dialogue: From the Art of Discourse to the Art of Reason* (1958; New York: Octagon Books, 1974), 104.

11. Sacvan Bercovitch, *The American Jeremiad* (Madison: University of Wisconsin Press, 1978); Hans Baron, "The Querelle of the Ancients and the Moderns as a Problem for Renaissance Scholarship," *Journal of the History of Ideas*, 20 (January 1959), 3–22.

12. Cited in Reginald Horsman, *Race and Manifest Destiny: The Origins of American Racial Anglo-Saxonism* (Cambridge: Harvard University Press, 1981), 86, 92–93.

13. Thomas R Hietala, *Manifest Design: Anxious Aggrandizement in Late Jacksonian America* (Ithaca: Cornell University Press, 1985), 177, 192.

14. Walter Benjamin, "The Task of the Translator," *Illuminations,* ed. Hannah Arendt, trans. Harry Zohn (New York: Schocken Books, 1973), 72, 73–74, 74. The translation of *das Gemeine* as "object" can be misleading. "Common (basic or crudest) meaning" would be closer to a literal translation.

15. Don Cameron Allen, *Image and Meaning: Metaphoric Traditions in Renaissance Poetry* (Baltimore: Johns Hopkins University Press, 1960), 65.

16. Vine Deloria, Jr., *Behind the Trail of Broken Treaties: An Indian Declaration of Independence* (Austin: University of Texas Press, 1985), 2.

17. William Bevis, "Native American Novels: Homing In," in *Recovering the Word: Essays on Native American Literature,* eds. Brian Swann and Arnold Krupat (Berkeley: University of California Press, 1987), 593.

18. Leslie Marmon Silko, *Ceremony* (New York: Penguin Books, 1977), 68–69.

19. N. Scott Momaday, "Personal Reflections," in *The American Indian and the Problem of History,* ed. Calvin Martin (New York: Oxford University Press, 1987), 160.

20. John Winthrop, *A Model of Christian Charity* (1630), in *The Norton Anthology of American Literature,* eds. Ronald Gottesman, et al. (New York: W. W. Norton & Company, 1979), vol. 1, 11–12.

21. James Madison, *The Federalist* (1787), No. 10, in *The Norton Anthology*

of American Literature, eds. Ronald Gottesman, et al. (New York: W. W. Norton & Company, 1979), vol. 1, 532.

7. *Eloquent Cannibals*

1. W. Arens, *The Man-Eating Myth: Anthropology and Anthropophagy* (New York: Oxford University Press, 1979), 49.

2. Claude Lévi-Strauss, *The Elementary Structures of Kinship,* trans. James Harle Bell, John Richard von Sturmer, and Rodney Needham (Boston: Beacon Press, 1969), 29.

3. Richard Hakluyt, *The Principal Navigations, Voyages, Traffiques, and Discoveries of the English Nation . . .* ed. Edmund Goldsmid (1598; Edinburgh, 1885–1890), vol. 12, 365.

4. Frantz Fanon, *The Wretched of the Earth,* trans. Constance Farrington (New York: Grove Press, 1968), 39.

5. Dean Ebner, *"The Tempest:* Rebellion and the Ideal State," *Shakespeare Quarterly,* 16 (1965), 168. Ebner refers to Miranda as a "virtuous primitive."

Afterword

1. Paul Hulton and David Beers Quinn, *The American Drawings of John White, 1577–1590,* 2 vols. (London and Chapel Hill: The Trustees of the British Museum and University of North Carolina Press, 1964), vol. 1, 2. Subsequent material quoted from this two-volume set will be cited in the body of my text as *ADJW.*

2. Section 3, which does not concern me in this essay, consists of five engravings after White of Picts and ancient Britons. Accompanying text tells us that the purpose of this section is "to showe how that the Inhabitants of the great Bretannie haue bin in times past as sauvage as those of Virginia." See *Discovering the New World: Based on the Works of Theodore de Bry,* ed. Michael Alexander (New York: Harper & Row, 1976), 89.

3. David Beers Quinn, ed. *The Roanoke Voyages, 1584–1590: Documents to Illustrate the English Voyages to North America under the Patent Granted to Walter Raleigh in 1584,* 2 vols. (London: The Hakluyt Society, 1955), vol. 1, 81. I will cite subsequent material from this source in the body of my text as *RV.*

4. Questions remain about the identity of John White the artist and John White the governor of the 1587 colony (*ADJW,* vol. 1, 6). Following the weight of scholarly opinion here, I am acting as if they are one and the same person. It would also seem to me that the linking of the name of White the artist with the voyage of 1588 in the second title page to *America* (see my discussion in what follows) suggests the identity of governor and artist.

5. David B. Quinn and Alison M. Quinn, eds. *Virginia Voyages from Hakluyt* (London: Oxford University Press, 1973), 109. Subsequent material from this edition will be cited in the body of my text as *VV.*

6. In his narrative of the 1585–1586 expedition, Ralph Lane accuses Wingina/ Pemisapan (see my discussion in what follows of the change in Wingina's name) of forging a conspiracy with other Indian communities to destroy the English (*VV,* 37–38). For a critique of this conspiracy theory, see Michael L. Oberg, "Indians and Englishmen at the First Roanoke Colony: A Note on Pemisapan's Conspiracy, 1585–86," *American Indian Culture and Research Journal* 18:2 (1994), 75–89. Oberg is rightly critical of how historians have uncritically accepted Lane's version of events; yet in constructing his own version, which presupposes sophisticated dialogue between Lane and the Indians, he never mentions the problem of translation.

7. For a speculative analysis, which makes sense, of Manteo's position between the English and the Indians, see Karen Ordahl Kupperman, *Roanoke: The Abandoned Colony* (Totowa, N.J.: Rowman & Allanheld, 1984), 117–18.

8. The narratives of 1587 and 1588 are written in the first person plural, referring to White in the third person, as the governor. The narrative of 1590 is written in the first person singular in the voice of White himself. Whether or not the first two narratives were written by someone else remains an open question. I attribute all three to White, following convention.

9. *Handbook of North American Indians,* vol. 15, Bruce G. Trigger, ed., William C. Sturtevant, gen. ed. (Washington, D.C.: Smithsonian Institution, 1978), 279, 280. The *Handbook* will hereafter be cited in the body of my text as *HNAI.*

10. David Beers Quinn notes that this dedication to Raleigh is the "general epistle dedicatory to all three sections of the volume and is followed immediately by his [De Bry's] reprint of the 1588 edition of Hariot." Thus the title from Hariot that precedes the dedication might logically be taken as the general title of the volume. *RV,* vol. 1, 401.

11. Paul Hulton, *America 1585: The Complete Drawings of John White* (Chapel Hill and London: University of North Carolina Press and British Museum Publications, 1984), figure 1, 103. Subsequent references to the Hulton will appear in the body of my essay as *America 1585.* The number following the figure or plate number is the page number in *America 1585.* I am using *America 1585* rather than *The American Drawings of John White* as the reference for the title pages and the specific White drawings and De Bry engravings that I describe and/or reproduce because of the wider availability of the former.

12. David B. Quinn, *Explorers and Colonies: America, 1500–1625* (London: Hambledon Press, 1990), 251. Cited hereafter in my text as *EC.* The introduc-

tory material to *ADJW* is not pejorative, stating simply that "the version [of the notes] as published owes much to De Bry and his printers" (vol. 1, 26).

13. For a history of the reemergence of the White watercolors, see the preface to *ADJW*, vol. 1, ix–xiv.

14. In her essay " 'To Know, To Fly, To Conjure': Situating Baconian Science at the Juncture of Early Modern Modes of Reading," *Renaissance Quarterly* (Autumn 1991), 513–58, Julie Robin Solomon in her reading of White's "The flyer" and De Bry's "The Coniuerer" articulates a dialectic that is similar to the dialectic between the *regressive* and the *progressive* that I am suggesting here. I will have occasion to refer to Solomon again when I read "The flyer" and "The Coniuerer."

15. I am indebted to the work of Pauline Turner Strong on the captivity narrative of Mary Rowlandson for calling my attention to the presence of female sachems among Algonquian-speaking communities of New England. Robert Steven Grumet has called our attention in seventeenth- and eighteenth-century Middle Atlantic Coastal Algonquian communities to the power women held in the areas of politics, religion, and economics (to use Western categories for the moment). However, Grumet differentiates these "egalitarian" communities from those in "the Chesapeake Bay area," which, like the scholars I am discussing, he finds "stratified," though he marshals no evidence for this latter conclusion. Curiously, one of his prime examples of Native female political equality is in the so-called "Powhatan confederacy," which Grumet places, contradictorily, in both the Middle Atlantic area and the Chesapeake. What we have then, if we follow Grumet's geopolitical logic, is an anomaly: a case of gender egalitarianism in what should be a stratified society. What this anomaly suggests—and Grumet's ambiguous geographical placement of Powhatan (at once Middle Atlantic and Chesapeake) only intensifies the contradiction—is what my argument insists: the ideological motives of this kind of geopolitical frontier that suddenly translates egalitarian Native kinship communities into hierarchical state structures. See Robert Steven Grumet, "Sunksquaws, Shamans, and Tradeswomen: Middle Atlantic Coastal Algonkian Women During the 17th and 18th Centuries," in *Women and Colonization: Anthropological Perspectives,* ed. Mona Etienne and Eleanor Burke Leacock (New York: Praeger, 1980), 43–62. The pioneering work of Eleanor Burke Leacock supports my argument here, which is that class-based or stratified societies are antithetical to gender equality; or to put it another way: gender inequality is a distinct component of class-based societies, while gender equality is a distinct feature of kinship-based, or communal, cultures, though once again we must be careful in using Western political terminology in

translating Native American social arrangements. See Leacock's introduction to Frederick Engels, *The Origin of the Family, Private Property and the State* (1972, rpt. New York: International Publishers, 1993). In light of my argument with Kupperman in this afterword, it is worth quoting Leacock from her introduction, in which she defines the "state": "there is widespread recognition among contemporary anthropologists that the state emerged as a qualitatively new institution associated with marked economic inequalities, a well developed division of labor, and sizable urban centers. Furthermore, the use of coercive force to control a territorially based citizenry is generally accepted by anthropologists as a central feature of state organization" (48). Reading the historical record, as I am trying to do, with attention to its contradictions, I find it difficult, to say the least, to place Carolina Algonquian-speaking communities or those in the area of Jamestown within this definition.

16. Kupperman (*Roanoke*, 44), extrapolating from Quinn, assumes that there are a lost set of watercolors with backgrounds matching those of the De Bry engravings. In such a reading, of course, the variation is not De Bry's but White's.

17. Robert Beverley, *The History and Present State of Virginia*, ed. Louis B. Wright (Chapel Hill: University of North Carolina Press, 1947), 195.

18. Kupperman claims: "The name implied a watchful, wary attitude in the Algonquian language" (*Roanoke*, 76). But she gives no linguistic evidence whatsoever for this claim.

19. See James Axtell, "The White Indians of Colonial America," in his *The European and the Indian: Essays in the Ethnohistory of Colonial North America* (New York: Oxford University Press, 1981).

20. Karl Marx, *Capital*, vol. 1, trans. Ben Fowkes (London: Penguin Books, 1990), 247.

21. Louis Althusser, "Ideology and Ideological State Apparatuses (Notes towards an Investigation)," in *Essays on Ideology* (London: Verso, 1984), 39. The essay was first published in French in 1970; no translator is given.

Bibliography

Alexander, Michael, ed. *Discovering the New World: Based on the Works of Theodore de Bry.* New York: Harper & Row, 1976.

Allen, Don Cameron. *Image and Meaning: Metaphoric Traditions in Renaissance Poetry.* Baltimore: Johns Hopkins University Press, 1960.

Allen, Paula Gunn. "I Climb the Mesas in My Dreams." In *Survival This Way: Interviews with American Indian Poets,* edited by Joseph Bruchac. Tucson: University of Arizona Press, 1987.

Althusser, Louis. "Ideology and Ideological State Apparatuses (Notes towards an Investigation)." In *Essays on Ideology* (no translator named). 1970. Reprint. London: Verso, 1984.

Arens, W. *The Man-Eating Myth: Anthropology and Anthropophagy.* New York: Oxford University Press, 1979.

Aristotle. *Poetics,* translated by S. H. Butcher. New York: Hill and Wang, 1961.

———. *Topica,* translated by W. A. Pickard-Cambridge. In *The Basic Works of Aristotle,* edited by Richard McKeon. New York: Random House, 1941.

Axtell, James. "The White Indians of Colonial America." In *The European and the Indian: Essays in the Ethnohistory of Colonial North America.* New York: Oxford University Press, 1981.

Barbour, Philip L., ed. *The Jamestown Voyages Under the First Charter 1606–1609,* 2nd ser., 2 vols. London: The Hakluyt Society, 1969.

Baron, Hans. "The Querelle of the Ancients and the Moderns as a Problem for Renaissance Scholarship." *Journal of the History of Ideas* 20 (January 1959), 3–22.

Barthes, Roland. "L'ancienne rhetorique: aide-memoire." *Communications* 16 (1970), 172–223.

Basso, Keith H. *Portraits of "The Whiteman": Linguistic Play and Cultural Symbols Among the Western Apache.* 1979. Reprint. New York: Cambridge University Press, 1980.

Beale, Howard K. *Theodore Roosevelt and the Rise of America to World Power.* Baltimore: Johns Hopkins University Press, 1956.

Benjamin, Walter. "The Task of the Translator." In *Illuminations,* edited by Hannah Arendt; translated by Harry Zohn. New York: Schocken Books, 1973.

Bercovitch, Sacvan. *The American Jeremiad.* Madison: University of Wisconsin Press, 1978.

232 *Bibliography*

Berger, Harry, Jr. "Miraculous Harp: A Reading of Shakespeare's Tempest." *Shakespeare Studies* 5 (1969), 253–83.

Beverley, Robert. *The History and Present State of Virginia*, edited by Louis B. Wright. Chapel Hill: University of North Carolina Press, 1947.

Bevis, William. "Native American Novels: Homing In." In *Recovering the Word: Essays on Native American Literature*, edited by Brian Swann and Arnold Krupat. Berkeley: University of California Press, 1987.

Burroughs, Edgar Rice. *Tarzan of the Apes* (1912). New York: Ballantine Books, 1984.

Carnicelli, D. D. "The Widow and the Phoenix: Dido, Carthage, and Tunis in *The Tempest*." In *Harvard Library Bulletin* 27 (1979), 389–433.

Cheek, John. "A LETTER OF SYR J. CHEEKES to his Loving frind Mayster THOMAS HOBY." In *The Book of the Courtier from the Italian of Count Baldassare Castiglione: Done into English by Sir Thomas Hoby*. 1561. Reprint. New York: AMS Press, 1967.

Cheyfitz, Eric. "Literally White, Figuratively Red: The Frontier of Translation in *The Pioneers*." In *James Fenimore Cooper: New Critical Essays*, edited by Robert Clark. Totowa: Barnes & Noble, 1985.

———. "Savage Law: The Plot Against American Indians in *Johnson and Graham's Lessee v. M'Intosh* and *The Pioneers*." In *The Cultures of United States Imperialism*, edited by Amy Kaplan and Donald E. Pease. Durham, N.C.: Duke University Press, 1993.

Churchill, Ward. *Struggle for the Land: Indigenous Resistance to Genocide, Ecocide and Expropriation in Contemporary North America*. Monroe, Maine: Common Courage Press, 1993.

Cicero. *De Inventione*, translated by H. M. Hubbell. The Loeb Classical Library. 1949. Reprint. Cambridge: Harvard University Press, 1976.

———. *De Optimo Genere Oratorum*, translated by H. M. Hubbell. The Loeb Classical Library. 1949. Reprint. Cambridge: Harvard University Press, 1976.

———. *De Oratore*, translated by E. W. Sutton. The Loeb Classical Library. 1942. Reprint. Cambridge: Harvard University Press, 1967.

———. *Topica*, translated by H. M. Hubbell. The Loeb Classical Library. 1949. Reprint. Cambridge: Harvard University Press, 1976.

Clifford, James. "On Ethnographic Allegory." In *Writing Culture: The Poetics and Politics of Ethnography*, edited by James Clifford and George E. Marcus. Berkeley: University of California Press, 1986.

Columbus, Christopher. *The Journal of Christopher Columbus* (1492–93), translated by Cecil Jane. London: Anthony Blond, 1968.

Cooper, James Fenimore. *The Last of the Mohicans: A Narrative of 1757* (1826). New York: New American Library, 1962.

———. *The Prairie: A Tale* (1827). New York: New American Library, 1964.

Cronon, William. *Changes in the Land: Indians, Colonists, and the Ecology of New England*. New York: Hill and Wang, 1983.

Crook, John. *Law and Life of Rome*. Ithaca: Cornell University Press, 1967.

Curtius, Ernst Robert. *European Literature and the Latin Middle Ages*. Princeton: Princeton University Press, 1953.

Davis, Richard Beale. *Intellectual Life in the Colonial South, 1585–1763*, vol. 1. Knoxville: University of Tennessee Press, 1978.

De Grazia, Margreta. "The Secularization of Language in the Seventeenth Century." *Journal of the History of Ideas* 41 (April–June 1980), 319–29.

Deloria, Vine, Jr. *Behind the Trail of Broken Treaties: An Indian Declaration of Independence.* Austin: University of Texas Press, 1985.

———. *We Talk, You Listen: New Tribes, New Turf.* New York: Macmillan, 1970.

Deloria, Vine, Jr., and Clifford Lytle. *The Nations Within: The Past and Future of American Indian Sovereignty.* New York: Pantheon Books, 1984.

Douglass, Frederick. *Narrative of the Life of Frederick Douglass, an American Slave* (1845), edited by Houston A. Baker, Jr. 1982. Reprint. New York: Penguin, 1983.

Durham, Jimmie. "Those Dead Guys for a Hundred Years." In *I Tell You Now: Autobiographical Essays by Native American Writers*, edited by Brian Swann and Arnold Krupat. Lincoln: University of Nebraska Press, 1987.

Ebel, Julia G. "Translation and Cultural Nationalism in the Reign of Elizabeth." *Journal of the History of Ideas* 30 (Oct.–Dec. 1969), 593–602.

Ebner, Dean. "*The Tempest:* Rebellion and the Ideal State." *Shakespeare Quarterly* 16 (1965), 161–73.

Emerson, Ralph Waldo. *Nature* (1836). In *Selected Essays: Ralph Waldo Emerson*, edited by Larzer Ziff. New York: Penguin Books, 1982.

Erlich, J. W., ed. *Erlich's Blackstone.* San Carlos: Nourse, 1959.

Fanon, Frantz. *Black Skins, White Masks*, translated by Charles Lam Markmann. New York: Grove Press, 1967.

———. *The Wretched of the Earth*, translated by Constance Farrington. New York: Grove Press, 1968.

Fiedler, Leslie. *The Stranger in Shakespeare.* New York: Stein and Day, 1972.

Florio, John, trans. *The Essayes of Montaigne* (1603). New York: The Modern Library, 1933.

Folz, Robert. *The Concept of Empire in Western Europe from the Fifth to the Fourteenth Century*, translated by Sheila Ann Ogilvie. London: Edward Arnold, 1969.

Force, Peter, ed. *Tracts and Other Papers Relating Principally to the Origin, Settlement, and Progress of the Colonies in North America, from the Discovery of the Country to the Year 1776*, vol. 3. Washington: William Q. Force, 1844.

Fraunce, Abraham. *The Arcadian Rhetoric* (1588). English Linguistics 1500–1800 (A Collection of Facsimile Reprints), no. 176. Menston, England: Scolar Press Limited, 1969.

Gray, Hanna H. "Renaissance Humanism: The Pursuit of Eloquence." *Journal of the History of Ideas* 24 (Oct.–Dec. 1963), 497–514.

Greenblatt, Stephen J. "Learning to Curse: Aspects of Linguistic Colonialism in the Sixteenth Century." In *First Images of America: The Impact of the New World on the Old*, edited by Fredi Chiappelli, vol. 2. Berkeley: University of California Press, 1976.

Grumet, Robert Steven. "Sunksquaws, Shamans, and Tradeswomen: Middle Atlantic Coastal Algonkian Women During the 17th and 18th Centuries."

In *Women and Colonization: Anthropological Perspectives,* edited by Mona Etienne and Eleanor Burke Leacock. New York: Praeger, 1980.

Hakluyt, Richard. *The Principal Navigations, Voyages, Traffiques, and Discoveries of the English Nation . . .* (1598), edited by Edmond Goldsmid, vol. 12. Edinburgh, 1885–1890.

Hietala, Thomas R. *Manifest Design: Anxious Aggrandizement in Late Jacksonian America.* Ithaca: Cornell University Press, 1985.

Higham, John. *Send These to Me: Immigrants in Urban America,* rev. ed. Baltimore: Johns Hopkins University Press, 1984.

Holland, Philemon. *The Historie of the World, Commonly Called, the Natural Historie of C. Plinus Secundus, Translated into English by Philemon Holland, Doctor in Physicke.* London, 1601.

Horsman, Reginald. *Race and Manifest Destiny: The Origins of American Racial Anglo-Saxonism.* Cambridge: Harvard University Press, 1981.

Howell, Wilbur Samuel, trans. *The Rhetoric of Alcuin and Charlemagne.* Princeton: Princeton University Press, 1941.

Hulme, Peter. *Colonial Encounters: Europe and the Native Caribbean 1492–1797.* London: Methuen, 1986.

Hulton, Paul. *America 1585: The Complete Drawings of John White.* Chapel Hill and London: University of North Carolina Press and British Museum Publications, 1984.

Hulton, Paul, and David Beers Quinn. *The American Drawings of John White, 1577–1590.* 2 vols. London and Chapel Hill: The Trustees of the British Museum and University of North Carolina Press, 1964.

Jehlen, Myra. "The Novel and the Middle Class in America." In *Ideology and Classic American Literature,* edited by Sacvan Bercovitch and Myra Jehlen. New York: Cambridge University Press, 1986.

Jennings, Francis. *The Ambiguous Iroquois Empire: The Covenant Chain Confederation of Indian Tribes with English Colonies from Its Beginnings to the Lancaster Treaty of 1744.* New York: W. W. Norton, 1984.

Johnson, E. Pauline. "As It Was in the Beginning." In *Spider Woman's Granddaughters: Traditional Tales and Contemporary Writing by Native American Women,* edited by Paula Gunn Allen. Boston: Beacon Press, 1989.

Jones, Richard Foster. *The Triumph of the English Language: A Survey of Opinions Concerning the Vernacular from the Introduction of Printing to the Restoration.* 1953. Reprint. Stanford: Stanford University Press, 1966.

Kermode, Frank, ed. Shakespeare's *The Tempest.* 1954. Reprint. New York: Methuen, 1983.

Kitto, H. D. F. *The Greeks.* 1951. Reprint. Baltimore: Penguin Books, 1963.

Kott, Jan. "La Tempete, Ou La Repetition." *Tel Quel* 71–73 (Automne 1977), 136–62.

Kupperman, Karen Ordahl. *Roanoke: The Abandoned Colony.* Totowa, N.J.: Rowman & Allanheld, 1984.

———. *Settling with the Indians: The Meeting of English and Indian Cultures in America, 1580–1640.* Totowa: Rowman and Littlefield, 1980.

Leacock, Eleanor Burke. Introduction to Frederick Engels, *The Origin of the*

Family, Private Property and the State. 1972. Reprint. New York: International Publishers, 1993.

Lévi-Strauss, Claude. *The Elementary Structures of Kinship,* translated by James Harle Bell, John Richard von Sturmer, and Rodney Needham. Boston: Beacon Press, 1969.

———. *The Savage Mind* (no translator named). London: Weidenfeld and Nicolson, 1966.

———. *Tristes Tropiques,* translated by John and Doreen Weightman. New York: Atheneum, 1981.

Locke, John. *The Second Treatise of Government* (1690), edited by Thomas P. Peardon. New York: Bobbs-Merrill, 1952.

Lockyear, Roger. *Tudor and Stuart Britain, 1471–1714.* London: Longmans, 1964.

Luce, Morton, ed. *The Tempest.* London: Methuen, 1901.

Lurie, Nancy Oestreich. "Indian Cultural Adjustment to European Civilization." In *Seventeenth-Century America: Essays in Colonial History,* edited by James Morton Smith. Chapel Hill: University of North Carolina Press, 1959.

Macfarlane, Alan. *The Origin of English Individualism: The Family, Property and Social Transition.* New York: Cambridge University Press, 1978.

Madison, James. *The Federalist,* no. 10. In *The Norton Anthology of American Literature,* edited by Ronald Gottesman, et al., vol. 1. New York: W. W. Norton & Company, 1979.

Malone, Edmond. "An Account of the Incidents from Which the Title and Part of the Story of Shakespeare's Tempest Were Derived; and Its True Date Ascertained." In *The Plays and Poems of William Shakespeare,* edited by Edmond Malone, vol. 15. London, 1821.

Marshall, John. *Johnson and Graham's Lessee v. M'Intosh.* In *Cases Argued and Decided in the Supreme Court of the United States,* lawyer's ed., book 5. Rochester: Lawyer's Co-operative Publishing Company, 1882.

Martin, Calvin. "An Introduction Aboard the *Fidele.*" In *The American Indian and the Problem of History,* edited by Calvin Martin. New York: Oxford University Press, 1987.

Marx, Karl. *Capital,* vol. 1, translated by Ben Fowkes. London: Penguin Books, 1990.

Marx, Leo. *The Machine in the Garden: Technology and the Pastoral Ideal in America.* 1964. Reprint. New York: Oxford University Press, 1967.

Matthiessen, F. O. *Translation, an Elizabethan Art.* Cambridge: Harvard University Press, 1931.

Mauss, Marcel. "A Category of the Human Mind: the Notion of Person; the Notion of Self" (1938), translated by W. D. Halls. In *The Category of the Person: Anthropology, Philosophy, History,* edited by Michael Carrithers, Steven Collins, and Steven Lukes. 1985. Reprint. Cambridge: Cambridge University Press, 1987.

Momaday, N. Scott. "Personal Reflections." In *The American Indian and the Problem of History,* edited by Calvin Martin. New York: Oxford University Press, 1987.

———. *The Names: A Memoir.* Tucson: University of Arizona Press, 1976.

Noble, David. *America by Design: Science, Technology, and the Rise of Corporate Capitalism.* 1977. Reprint. New York: Oxford University Press, 1979.

Oberg, Michael L. "Indians and Englishmen at the First Roanoke Colony: A Note on Pemisapan's Conspiracy, 1585–86." *American Indian Culture and Research Journal* 18:2 (1994), 75–89.

Ong, Walter J., S. J. *Ramus, Method, and the Decay of Dialogue: From the Art of Discourse to the Art of Reason.* 1958. Reprint. New York: Octagon Books, 1974.

Orgel, Stephen. *The Illusion of Power: Political Theatre in the English Renaissance.* Berkeley: University of California Press, 1975.

Peacham, Henry. *The Garden of Eloquence* (1577). English Linguistics 1500–1800 (A Collection of Facsimile Reprints), no. 267. Menston, England: Scolar Press Limited, 1971.

———. *The Garden of Eloquence.* London, 1593.

Puttenham, George. *The Arte of English Poesie* (1589), edited by Gladys Doidge Willcock and Alice Walker. Cambridge: Cambridge University Press, 1936.

Quinn, David Beers. *Explorers and Colonies: America, 1500–1625.* London: Hambledon Press, 1990.

———, ed. *The Roanoke Voyages, 1584–1590: Documents to Illustrate the English Voyages to North America under the Patent Granted to Walter Raleigh in 1584.* 2 vols. London: The Hakluyt Society, 1955.

———, and Alison M. Quinn, eds. *Virginia Voyages from Hakluyt.* London: Oxford University Press, 1973.

Quintillian. *Institutio Oratoria,* translated by H. E. Butler. The Loeb Classical Library. New York: G. P. Putnam's Sons, 1921.

Reagan, Ronald. "Freedom, Regional Security, and Global Peace." Congress of the United States. Special Report No. 143. United States Department of State. *Bureau of Public Affairs.* Washington, D.C., 14 March 1986.

Retamar, Roberto Fernandez. "Caliban: Notes Toward a Discussion of Culture in Our America," translated by Lynn Garafola, David Arthur MacMurray, and Robert Marquez. *The Massachusetts Review* 15 (Winter–Spring 1974), 7–72.

Robinson, W. Stitt, Jr. *Mother Earth: Land Grants in Virginia.* Williamsburg: Virginia 350th Anniversary Celebration Corporation, 1957.

Rouse, W. H. D., ed. *Scenes of School and College Life in Latin Dialogues.* Oxford: Clarendon Press, 1931.

Sheehan, Bernard. *Savagism and Civility: Indians and Englishmen in Colonial Virginia.* New York: Cambridge University Press, 1988.

Silko, Leslie Marmon. *Ceremony.* New York: Penguin Books, 1977.

Solomon, Julie Robinson. " 'To Know, To Fly, To Conjure': Situating Baconian Science at the Juncture of Early Modern Modes of Reading." *Renaissance Quarterly* (Autumn 1991), 513–58.

Tawney, R. H., and Eileen Power, eds. *Tudor Economic Documents,* vol. 1. London, 1924.

Taylor, E. G. R., ed. *The Original Writings & Correspondence of the Two Richard Hakluyts,* 2nd ser., vol. 2. London: The Hakluyt Society, 1935.

Thirsk, Joan. *The Rural Economy of England: Collected Essays.* London: Hambledon Press, 1984.

———, ed. *The Agrarian History of England and Wales,* vol. 4, 1500–1640. Cambridge: Cambridge University Press, 1967.

Todorov, Tzvetan. *The Conquest of America: The Question of the Other,* translated by Richard Howard. New York: Harper & Row, 1984.

Trask, Haunani-Kay. "From a Native Daughter." In *The American Indian and the Problem of History,* edited by Calvin Martin. New York: Oxford University Press, 1987.

Trigger, Bruce G., ed. *Handbook of North American Indians,* vol. 15. Gen. ed. William C. Sturtevant. Washington, D.C.: Smithsonian Institution, 1978.

Twain, Mark. *A Connecticut Yankee in King Arthur's Court* (1889). New York: Penguin Books, 1986.

Vaughan, Alden T. *American Genesis: Captain John Smith and the Founding of Virginia.* Boston: Little, Brown and Co., 1975.

Vernant, Jean-Pierre. "Greek Tragedy: Problems of Interpretation." In *The Structuralist Controversy: The Languages of Criticism and the Sciences of Man,* edited by Richard Macksey and Eugenio Donato. 1970. Reprint. Baltimore: Johns Hopkins University Press, 1972.

Vizenor, Gerald. "Socioacupuncture: Mythic Reversals and the Striptease in Four Scenes." In *The American Indian and the Problem of History,* edited by Calvin Martin. New York: Oxford University Press, 1987.

Washburn, Wilcomb. *Red Man's Land/White Man's Law: A Study of the Past and Present Status of the American Indian.* New York: Scribner's, 1971.

Williams, Raymond. *The Country and the City.* New York: Oxford University Press, 1973.

Winthrop, John. *A Model of Christian Charity* (1630). In *The Norton Anthology of American Literature,* edited by Ronald Gottesman, et al., vol. 1. New York: W. W. Norton & Co., 1979.

Wolf, Eric R. *Europe and the People without History.* Berkeley: University of California Press, 1982.

Wright, Louis B., ed. *A Voyage to Virginia in 1609: Two Narratives.* Charlottesville: University Press of Virginia, 1964.

Index

239